Building German Airpower, 1909–1914

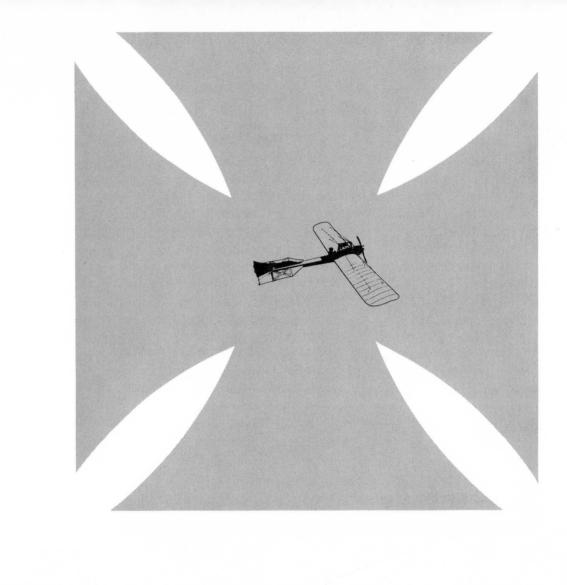

JOHN HOWARD MORROW, JR.

# Building German Airpower, 1909–1914

THE UNIVERSITY OF TENNESSEE PRESS : KNOXVILLE

*Library of Congress Cataloging in Publication Data*

Morrow, John Howard, 1944–
  Building German airpower, 1909–1914.

  Bibliography: p.
  Includes index.
    1.  Aeronautics, Military—Germany—History.
2.  Aircraft industry—Germany—History. I.  Title.
UG635.G3M67      358.4'12'60943      76–15287
ISBN 0–87049–196–2

*In memory of* John L. Snell, *mentor and friend*

During the twentieth century, man's existence has been profoundly affected by the invention and development of the airship, the airplane, and the rocket. Yet, with a few exceptions, aeronautical studies have remained the province of popular, technical, and military writers. The excitement of air warfare, famous aircraft, and heroic pilots, and the technical aspects of aircraft construction and development have been treated in detail. Histories of military aviation have devoted much space to the minutiae of combat strategy and tactics, the organization of air forces, the recruitment and training of manpower, and the performance of aircraft, but relatively little to an essential topic—the link between the armed forces and the creators of the airplane, the aircraft industry.

Although military-industrial relations in general have been a subject of much debate, they have been the subject of very little research. Most studies that attempt to analyze the so-called "military-industrial complex" have concentrated on the connections between the civilian government, the armed forces, and "big business," condemning these bonds along with the capitalist system for conspiring against the people and leading nations into war. In the case of imperial Germany, such studies have focused upon the affairs of the Friedrich Krupp Steel Works and the other large manufacturers of armaments. But the fledgling aircraft industry, discussed here, provides a marked contrast in military-industrial relations to the domination that Krupp exercised.

In studying the growth of aviation, the historian has a unique opportunity to observe the military-industrial relationship as it quickly evolved within a few decades from its rudimentary form to an advanced stage. Since its beginnings, the aircraft industry and its fortunes have been inextricably linked with the armed forces, and both are of great importance in the modern industrialized, highly armed nation.

The European states, because of their proximity to one another, had long felt the need of strong armed forces. In imperial Germany, the Prussian Army was highly esteemed for its successes in the wars of German unification from 1864 to 1871, which it won with the weaponry developed by a progressive German armaments industry. The army and heavy industry were extremely powerful in Germany, and most Germans, with the exception of the Marxists, probably regarded their interconnection not as sinister but as necessary for survival in a world of hostile states. By 1909, close connections between the armed forces and powerful armaments firms had been well established in both Germany and Austria-Hungary for more than half a century.

The relationship upon which I have focused—that of the armed forces and the aircraft industry among the Central Powers from the origins of the industry in 1909 until the opening of the First World War in August 1914—illuminates the nature of industrial-military relations more broadly, but especially at that time and place. This relationship was reflected in the organization, roles, motives, attitudes, and policies of the aircraft industry and the armed forces; it was influenced by the civilian government, public opinion, and other interested groups; and, finally, it had its effect on both the military establishment and the aircraft industry, particularly as war approached.

The Prussian Army and the north German airplane industry overwhelmingly dominated military aviation among the Central Powers. Bavarian and Austro-Hungarian military aviation was much smaller in scope, and naval aviation in the two states was in an experimental and embryonic state prior to World War I. Nevertheless, treating these "side shows" along with the Prussian Army and the northern German aircraft industry has two major advantages: it emphasizes the joint nature of military aviation in Germany and Austria-Hungary, and it broadens the validity of my observations.

One might at first dismiss the implications for the present of a study of two central European empires long since deceased, aristocratically led armies of powerful political and social influence long since crushed, and an embryonic industry that has now reached tremendous proportions. Yet I believe such implications do exist.

The experience of the Central Powers confirms that successful procurement of armaments depends upon industrial competition enforced and controlled by the military. In Germany and Austria-Hungary before 1914, the Prussian Army resisted a tendency to rely on one superior aircraft firm, but the Bavarian and Austro-Hungarian armies did not. As a result, several expensive fiascoes severely damaged Bavarian and Austro-Hungarian military aviation before the war. The sophisticated military airplanes of today have supposedly rendered obsolete a procurement system based on competition between firms and observation of an aircraft's performance prior to its acceptance. Yet an uncritical and uncompetitive reliance on one or two firms has led to expensive debacles in contemporary American aircraft production, as A. Ernest Fitzgerald's book *The High Priests of Waste* (New York: W. W. Norton & Company, 1972) amply indicates. The complexity of modern weaponry and the ever-present necessity of military readiness do not excuse favoritism or monopoly. Enforcing competition among arms producers does not render the military immune to error, as this book will illustrate; but by judiciously promoting competition and by exercising stringent technical and economic control over its manufacturers, the military can obtain good results more cheaply and avoid the dangers of excessive reliance on too few firms. Military-industrial relationships can be reduced basically to a question of leverage. If a firm or industry has the power implicit in monopoly or near-monopoly, it can virtually dictate terms to the armed forces. The cause of national defense is better served when the armed forces control the relationship by maintaining competition among their producers.

For their help, I am grateful to a number of organizations and individuals. The Germanistic Society of America, the University of Pennsylvania, and the German Academic Exchange Service provided grants that enabled me to spend the year 1969–1970 in

Germany; and a summer stipend from the National Endowment for the Humanities allowed me to complete the research in Vienna in 1972. Drs. Sandhofer and Fleischer of the Military Archive in Freiburg, Dr. Harald Jaeger of the Bavarian War Archive in Munich, and the staffs of the Military History Research Office and its library in Freiburg and of the Federal Archive in Koblenz generously made the necessary documents on imperial German aviation available to me, as did the archivists of the Austrian War Archive in Vienna, in particular Robert Feinfurter, with documents on Austro-Hungarian aviation. Peter Grosz most hospitably opened his private collection of documents and pictures to me, and deserves credit for most of the pictures in the book. Professors Charles E. McClelland, the late John L. Snell, and Robin Higham gave much helpful advice and criticism. I am especially grateful to Professor Snell, who, as my first adviser at Pennsylvania, gave me the rigorous training necessary to research and write this book and later, as friend and correspondent, was instrumental in helping me get my start in the historical profession. Finally, my wife, Diane, and my parents, Ann Rowena and John Sr., have always been ready with support and inspiration when I have needed it. My wife has helped me unswervingly in my research, has borne much of the difficult burden of proofreading, editing, and general advice, and knows the topic almost as well as I do. Without her this book would not have been possible.

JOHN HOWARD MORROW, JR.

*Knoxville, Tennessee*
*1976*

# CONTENTS

| | | | |
|---|---|---:|---:|
| | Preface | *page* | vii |
| I | Introduction | | 3 |
| II | The Prussian Army and the North German Aircraft Industry, 1908–1911 | | 14 |
| III | The Growth and Mobilization of North German Military Aviation, 1912–1914 | | 48 |
| IV | German Naval and Bavarian and Austro-Hungarian Military Aviation, 1909–1914 | | 88 |
| V | Conclusion | | 115 |
| | Abbreviations | | 124 |
| | Notes | | 126 |
| | Bibliography | | 140 |
| | Index | | 147 |

# ILLUSTRATIONS

Naval Captain (ret.) Paul Englehard in a Wright biplane, 12 August 1910     *page* 4

Prince Heinrich of Prussia, August Euler, and others, November 1910     10

Germany's first aircraft factory, the Euler Works, Frankfort on the Main     12

An Aviatik monoplane, 1911     18

An Aviatik monoplane on display at the *Salon d'aéronautique*, Paris, 1911/1912     20

Wing of a Gotha Taube under construction, 1912/1913     22

A Taube nears completion, 1912/1913     24

A Gotha biplane under construction     28

"The Flying Dutchman," Anthony Fokker, conferring with the pilot of a Fokker Spinne, 1913     32

Fokker Spinnes at Anthony Fokker's flying school, 1913     38

A Mars biplane under construction at the DFW factory, 1913     42

Mars biplane No. 4, in front of the DFW factory, May 1913     46

A Rumpler Taube at the Berlin-Doeberitz military airfield, 21 April 1914     50

A Rumpler Taube shortly after takeoff, 1913/1914     54

A Rumpler Taube on its nose at the Cologne-Longerich military airfield, 1913/1914     56

A Taube     60

Front view of Taube No. A26     64

Side view of Taube No. A26     68

Close-up of an Albatros monoplane     74

A Taube ready for takeoff     78

Major Wilhelm Siegert and flying officers at the Prince Heinrich Flight of 1914     82

General Karl Heinrich von Haenisch examines an entry at the Prince Heinrich Flight of 1914     90

A pusher biplane, Otto Works, Munich     98

A French Morane Parasol monoplane     102

An Albatros twin-float monoplane on Lake Constance     110

A Lohner Aspern biplane of the Austro-Hungarian Army     118

A Lohner Aspern biplane, second version     118

# TABLES

1 German Armaments Budgets, 1909/1913     *page* 8

2 Overview of Prussian Army Aviation Agencies to 1 April 1911     16

3 Overview of Prussian Army Aviation Agencies, 1 April 1911 to 31 July 1914     34

4 Prussian Military Aviation Budgets, 1909/1914          52
5 Growth of the Albatros and Rumpler Firms,
    1911/1914                                                84
6 Prussian Army Aircraft Procurement, 1911/1913          85
7 Basic Requirements for Prussian Military Aircraft       86
8 Bavarian Army Aircraft Procurement, 1911/1913          94
9 Organization of the Austro-Hungarian Flying
    Troops, 1911                                        106

Building German Airpower, 1909–1914

# I. INTRODUCTION

From its inception in 1871 through World War I, the German Empire sought military and industrial supremacy on the European continent. Prussia was the central political entity of the new state, and the Prussian Army, the major instrument in the formation of the empire, was its military cornerstone. Forty-three years of rapid industrialization from 1871 to 1914 transformed Germany from a predominantly rural to a predominantly urban nation. The explosive growth of the coal and iron industries was only one aspect of this "industrial revolution." Germany's expanding railroad network and its canal and telegraph systems facilitated civilian and military transportation and communication. Its navy acquired a battle fleet technologically superior, though numerically inferior, to that of England, the sovereign of the waves. The empire's armaments industry, dominated by the mammoth Krupp works, was the world's best; the electrical industry had no peers in its utilization of the new source of power; and the chemical industry, particularly in the areas of synthetics and drugs, made spectacular progress.

Between the turn of the century and World War I, two important industries of the twentieth century were born—automobile and aircraft manufacture. In Germany, Adam Opel, Gottlieb Daimler, and Carl Benz began to lay the groundwork for their production of motorcars. The creation of a light, reliable combustion engine to power these vehicles suggested to inventive minds the possibility of a second mode of travel—powered heavier-than-air flight. The manned glider had aroused some interest in Germany in the 1890s, when Otto Lilienthal, a world leader in this field, had awed onlookers with his flights. However, after his death resulting from a crash in 1897, Germany fell behind. The focus shifted to America and France, where such pioneers as Orville and Wilbur Wright and Albert Santos-Dumont exhibited the interest and daring that helped them to make historic strides in the development of the airplane.

A productive interest in powered flight was not evident in Germany until 1908–1909, when small domestic aircraft firms began to appear. Aircraft assembly in the early years of the twentieth century was essentially a *Basteln*, a constructive hobby, pursued by only a handful of dedicated men. Alone or aided by a few craftsmen, one man usually designed, built, and operated his flying machine.

The machines themselves were flimsy wood and fabric kites with few metal parts. Construction was a matter of intuition, of experiment, of luck. Aeronautics was unknown to most of the early inventors. The prospects of success were dim, the physical

and monetary risks immense. Even if the machine flew or, as was usually the case, hopped, a crash was likely. The destruction of the aircraft meant the loss of the inventor's investment, possibly his fortune, and, occasionally, his life. Few men undertook this risky enterprise; fewer still realized a profit. The early pioneers in aviation came from all walks of life; businessmen, engineers, scientists, men with no profession—all were lured to the new venture. The majority of German constructors were engineers, graduates of technical institutes. In wood sheds, in basements, in rented hangars, these men created the first German flying machines.

The crucial question for these inventors was who would subsidize the development of the airplane. Only a few of the inventors had the necessary personal fortune; without it, aviation entrepreneurs had to depend on private capital from industry, business, or the great German banks. Banks such as the *Deutsche Bank* and the *Dresdener Bank* had been instrumental in the growth of German industry. Would they be interested in financing an enterprise as risky as the development of the airplane? Germany's great electric company, the *Allgemeine Elektrizitaets Gesellschaft* (AEG), which had invested in several industrial ventures with potential profitability, possessed the capital necessary to establish an aircraft firm if it took an interest in the flying machine.

But all capital was attracted by the prospect of profits, and profits depended upon the existence, either actual or potential, of

✱ *Naval Captain (ret.) Paul Engelhard, a flying instructor for the Wright Flying Machine Company, in a Wright biplane over Berlin-Johannisthal airfield on 12 August 1910. A little over one year later, on 29 September 1911, Engelhard would crash to his death at the age of forty-three in a Wright biplane at Johannisthal. Courtesy of the* Bundesarchiv, Koblenz.

a domestic or foreign consumer market. Few Germans were able to invest 15,000 to 30,000 marks in such an expensive toy, and in 1908 the airplane lacked the range and load-carrying capability necessary for transport, industry, or business. There was no private domestic market for a useful, cheap flying machine, and it was unlikely that such a market would soon develop. Besides, the superiority of French and American aircraft had enabled these countries to corner the small international market and to sell their planes even in Germany.

There remained one other source of funds that an aspiring aircraft entrepreneur might tap—the military. Although they made little headway, the Wright brothers had set this precedent in 1903 by turning to the United States Army Signal Corps with their invention. Most important inventions or industrial innovation have some military application. Better iron and steel made better armor plate and cannon, as the Krupp firm demonstrated much to its profit. The automobile was the basis for mechanized transport; the tractor would lead to the tank; and the airplane would develop into the warplane. To maintain their supremacy, the armed forces of Germany had to recognize and make good use of worthwhile technological innovation. Yet it could not be assumed that the Prussian Army, the keystone of the German military system, would from the beginning accept—and subsidize—the aircraft industry.

The Prussian Army has been accused of failing to appreciate the necessity for technological modernization. In his history of the German General Staff published in 1953, Walter Goerlitz regarded the first decade of the twentieth century as a time of progress toward the perfection of the mechanical implements of war—artillery, motorized transport, aviation. But he also discerned a hesitation on the part of the Prussian Army to exploit these new inventions. Armored cars, which were introduced in

1908, and the tank, which a Lieutenant Colonel Burstyn of the Austrian Railroad Troops offered in prototype form in 1911, never passed the experimental stage. In Goerlitz's opinion the War Ministry, that "stronghold of conservatism," was the culprit, because it determined the level of armaments through its control of the budget.[1]

As recently as 1967, Fritz Fischer condemned the army's conservatism and criticized its organization as "glaring anachronisms" in comparison with the innovative German economy:

> The strength of the army was hardly raised up to 1912; machine guns were introduced late and in insufficient numbers; the intelligence service was too small; the air arm (unlike that of France) was neglected, even for reconnaissance purposes; motorization was insufficient; the cavalry arm was too large; cavalry regiments were brigaded together with insufficient artillery; development of tanks and anti-tank weapons in the war was belated.[2]

Two German army officers writing in the 1920s and 1930s blamed traditionalism and organizational inertia for the delay in the development of military aviation. Captain Hans Ritter, formerly of the General Staff, stated that "the aircraft had the misfortune to be a purely technical creation and thus had to reckon with a certain antipathy from military circles, which had an all too abundant skepticism towards technology."[3] Major Hilmer von Buelow agreed and asserted that the army resisted any innovation that might cause changes in its organization.[4]

Yet a blanket condemnation of the Prussian Army, based on statements like these, would be misleading and incorrect. Members of the General Staff, who reckoned constantly with the possibility of war, pressed for military reorganization and sizable increases in the weaponry and manpower of the army. The major advocate of these progressive measures was Captain Erich Ludendorff, who as chief of the Second Department of the General Staff from 1908 to 1913 was adviser to the chief of the General Staff in matters of military equipment. Although Ludendorff underestimated the military potential of the armored tractor, or tank, he became an outspoken advocate of military aviation.

The Prussian War Ministry, as Goerlitz suggested, was the key to change within the German military bureaucracy. Although the War Ministry and the General Staff were theoretically equal in power at the pinnacle of the German military hierarchy, the War Ministry held the decisive position in peacetime because it was the office responsible for the budget. The General Staff was elevated to military leadership only by the pressures of war.[5] The War Ministry had to defend its budget requests for the entire imperial army before the Imperial Office of the Treasury, the Imperial Chancellor, and the imperial parliament. It therefore invariably pared the monetary requests of the General Staff. When the government cut the proposed army bills even further than the War Ministry desired, as in 1911 and 1912, the War Ministry did not effectively thwart the civilian agencies. In opposing military reorganization and an increase in the army's manpower, the War Ministry pleaded financial limitations and the fear of lowering the quality of the officers. But in fact financial considerations were less important than maintaining the composition and social position of the Prussian officer corps.

The influence of the military pervaded German life to the degree that the aristocrats of the elitist Prussian officer corps belonged to the most prestigious profession in imperial Germany. The Army showed a primary concern for the lineage, class, and social position of its recruits in order to protect the aristocratic nature of the officer corps from any "dangerous" bourgeois influences. Gordon Craig has characterized the Prussian Army as a "state within a state," pursuing its own policies for the preservation of Prussian absolutism.[6]

The aristocratic exclusiveness of the Prussian officer corps was undermined by a combination of circumstances. First, by the end of the nineteenth century, the scientific and technical aspects of modern weaponry demanded officers with a technical education. Such men came from the middle, not the upper, class, where Germany's superb system of technical institutes created a vast reservoir of talent. Second, the expansion of the Prussian Army required far more officers and officer recruits than the aristocracy could provide. Consequently, in order to attenuate bourgeois influences, the officer corps drew recruits from families of the upper bourgeoisie and demanded that the new officers accept the feudal philosophy of their new profession.[7]

In the status-conscious society of Germany, a commission in the Prussian officer corps was the sign of social acceptability. And although Germany's industrial might had created the sword with which the Prussian Army won military supremacy, and the success of the empire rested upon its prodigious economic strides, the industrialists invariably bowed in social and political matters to the old ruling class. The wealthier, educated members of the bourgeoisie attempted to compensate for their social inferiority by creating their own titles and by striving for the supreme honors—ennoblement or a commission in the reserves of the officer corps. Consequently, many bourgeois officers wholeheartedly accepted the values of their new profession and were among those who most adamantly protected the corps from bourgeois influences and the influx of middle-class recruits. Major General Franz von Wandel, the head of the War Department in the Prussian War Ministry from 1909 until 1913, was a prime example of the assimilated middle-class officer who had been ennobled for his military service. He feared that the admission of more officers from the middle class would ultimately lead to revolution.[8]

Certain Prussian officers realized not only that such fears were unfounded, but also that expansion and reorganization, which entailed the admission of more bourgeois officers, were necessary to preserve the supremacy of the German Army. Erich Ludendorff, a major advocate of these progressive measures and therefore Wandel's opponent, did not suffer from the status consciousness displayed by Wandel or by the war minister, General Josias von Heeringen. Born of a wealthy bourgeois family, Ludendorff had attended cadet school and a military academy, where he excelled at mathematics. Thoroughly devoted to his military career, he was destined for fame in World War I as *de facto* commander of the German field army from 1916 through 1918 in his position as first quartermaster general. As adviser to Chief of the German General Staff General Helmuth von Moltke before the war, Ludendorff sought to expand the military by making the fullest use of the empire's manpower, regardless of class.[9] Because Ludendorff had Moltke's ear, the General Staff and the War Ministry clashed repeatedly over the questions of expansion and reorganization.

The General Staff was likely to push for the changes necessitated by military aviation (new agencies, more officers, technical training, and the revision of tactical planning), but the War Ministry, supposedly averse to technological innovation, might veto such efforts. Thus it was at first doubtful whether the army would accept the airplane as a worthwhile addition to its arsenal and, more important, finance the development of the new industry.

The schism between the Prusso-German General Staff and the Prussian War Ministry was not the only division within the German armed forces that would affect the development of military aviation. Although the Prussian Army dominated the military establishment, two other forces—the Bavarian Army and the German Navy—maintained sufficient independence to develop their own aviation arms. Operationally and financially, the Bavarian Army was subordinate to the Prussian Army; administratively, however, it maintained a degree of autonomy. Nor had the founding of the German Empire ended antipathy between Prussia and Bavaria, and the separation between the north and the south German states was formalized in imperial institutions. Given this division, the Bavarian Army could use its autonomy to develop military aviation and to prevent any Prussian encroachment upon its sovereignty in aviation.

Discord between the Prussian Army and the Imperial German Navy had its roots in the interservice rivalry common in all lands, a rivalry exacerbated in Germany by social and ideological differences. A creation of the nineteenth century, the navy was the one truly national, middle-class German institution, and as such it enjoyed the support of liberal, industrial, and commercial Germany.[10] Under the direction of Admiral Alfred von Tirpitz, the head of the Imperial Naval Office from 1897 to 1916, the navy attempted to shift the emphasis of German military affairs from the European continent to the seas around it. This policy of promoting the importance of the navy succeeded until 1912, but it was never reflected in the military budget. Although the allocation of funds for the navy rose constantly during this period and received priority from the government, it amounted to less than one-third of the total military budget every year.[11] Here too, then, the future of aviation was far from being assured. Efforts and funds were being concentrated on the battle fleet, and the difficulty of creating a seaplane suitable for the navy seemed at the time insurmountable.

The German Army, as the dominant member of the military establishment, received the lion's share of the military budget. The size of the German peacetime standing army in 1913 was 694,000 men; the German Navy numbered 72,000 men. The growing German military budgets from 1909 to 1913, shown in table 1, indicate this imbalance:

*Table 1.* GERMAN ARMAMENTS BUDGETS, 1909–1913[*]
*(in millions of marks)*

| Year | Army Armaments Budget | Navy Armaments Budget | Total Armaments Budget |
|------|------|------|------|
| 1909 | 956.9 | 410.0 | 1,367.8 |
| 1910 | 926.0 | 450.7 | 1,367.7 |
| 1911 | 931.6 | 459.8 | 1,391.4 |
| 1912 | 1,073.4 | 472.6 | 1,546.0 |
| 1913 | 1,629.6 | 481.2 | 2,110.8 |

[*] RA, *Kriegsruestung und Kriegswirtschaft* II (2 vols., Berlin: Mittler und Sohn, 1930), 530, Table 21.

But the allocation of the budget only partially reflected the discord within the armed forces: the disagreement within the Prussian military bureaucracy between the General Staff and the War Ministry over reorganization, growth, technological innovation, and ideology; the lack of cooperation between the Prussian and Bavarian armies, which stemmed from political differences between the two states; and the interservice rivalry between the Prussian Army and the German Navy—these conflicts were major factors in the relationship of the armed forces to the aircraft industry and in their acceptance of the airplane as a weapon of war.[12]

The prevailing economic conditions in prewar Germany also affected the development of military aviation. The forty years before World War I encompassed a period of tremendous industrial expansion. *Riesenbetriebe*—enterprises employing more than 1,000 people—had absorbed most of the influx of workers, and the number of people in such factories rose from 205,000 to 879,000 between 1882 and 1907. Meanwhile, the proportion of workers in enterprises employing more than fifty persons (*Grossbetriebe*) had increased from 26.3 percent in 1882 to 45.5 percent in 1907.[13] Industrial productivity rose steadily as assembly lines and other methods of mass production began to appear, while economies of scale and the desire to control prices led to the formation of cartels. In an effort to widen their circle of power and influence, German industrialists organized trade associations, such as the Central Association of German Industrialists for heavy industry and the League of Industrialists for light industry.

The large increases in industrial production began to taper off after 1911. By 1913 a recession had gripped Germany; the economy suffered from a shortage of capital, and overproduction led to sinking prices.[14] In Berlin and other industrial cities unemployment was high, and strikes became more widespread and more violent during the last two years before the war.[15]

How this pattern of industrial development, economic fluctuation, and military contracts affected the German aviation industry is of concern here. An important measure of the industry's progress is indicated by how well prepared Germany's military aviation forces were at the outbreak of World War I. Other factors also affected the military-industrial relationship: for example, although the Prussian Army was the single most powerful institution in the German government, the Imperial Office of the Interior, under Secretary of State Clemens von Delbrueck, was in charge of the surveillance of German internal affairs and of the coordination of economic mobilization in case of war. Emperor Wilhelm II, a dilettantish dabbler in many fields who was always interested in technical advances that might enhance the glory of his reign, exerted considerable influence. His support of the German Navy had been instrumental in its development;[16] and his position as titular head of the military and his friendship with industrialists, particularly Walter Rathenau, the innovative and disseminating director of the AEG, made the emperor influential with both the military and the industrialists.

The increasing importance of public opinion and a vocal socialist movement also affected the development of the German aircraft industry. By 1912 the German Socialist party was the largest in the imperial parliament and a confirmed opponent of the military establishment. Even though the pseudo-constitutional political system of Germany was ruled by an aristocracy, public opinion carried a weight that certain enterprising members of the German industrial and military establishments did not long ignore. For example, in his drive for naval supremacy, Admiral von Tirpitz proved himself a consummate politician and manipulator. He created a news agency within the Imperial Naval Office for public propaganda and agitation and lobbied directly with the politicians in the imperial parliament for increased naval budgets. Concurrently, the manufacturers in the Central Association of German Industrialists, who stood to profit from naval expansion, formed a private association for naval propaganda, the German Naval League, on 30 April 1898. This association originally operated independently of the navy but later became a state-controlled propaganda agency.[17]

The Prussian Army took longer to realize the potential value of manipulated public opinion, no doubt because the army considered itself above the need for public backing, so secure was its position. Only in January 1912 was an Army League created with the aim of persuading the government and the people to accept

Die Euler-Flugmaschine.
Prinz Heinrich nach bestandener Flugzeugführerprüfung.

increases in the army budget. Although army officers were not allowed to join political organizations, the entire Prussian officer corps joined the Army League. The league owed its birth to Ludendorff. He asked retired Major General August Keim, a professional propagandist who had participated in the earlier campaign for an enlarged fleet, to help engage allies in his fight to force the War Ministry to accept an increase in the army budget which the General Staff proposed. Ludendorff's broader aim, however, was to maintain the primacy of the army by reducing the strength and influence of the navy. The Army League was thus a double-edged blade—to push through the General Staff's budget proposals meant the defeat of both the War Ministry and the Navy. Yet neither agency chose to protest the illegality of the membership of Prussian officers in the league. A government conference on this matter, which was attended by the chancellor, Prussian War Minister General von Heeringen, Secretary of State of the Imperial Naval Office Admiral von Tirpitz, Secretary of State of the Imperial Office of the Interior von Delbrueck, and the Prussian minister of the interior, chose to look the other way.[18]

In the contest for the acceptance of their policies, both the Prussian Army and the German Navy, as well as economic interest groups who would benefit from military and naval expansion, had deemed public support sufficiently necessary to create organizations to arouse and influence public opinion. Such associations used and intensified the popular nationalism that became increasingly rampant in Europe in the years before World War I. Precedents thus existed should the military authorities and airplane manufacturers decide to enlist public support for military aviation.

The progress of imperial German aviation was crucial not only to the security of Germany, but also to that of its one firm ally, Austria-Hungary. Among the European states, the multi-national empire of Austria-Hungary ranked second to Russia in territory and third behind Russia and Germany in population. Both Austria and Hungary were predominantly agricultural, Hungary more so than Austria. In Germany 40 percent of the population was employed in industry and mining and 35.2 percent in agriculture and forestry by 1907. In Austria in 1900 only 23.3 percent of the people were employed in industry and mining, while 60.9 percent worked in agriculture and forestry. The industrialized areas of Austria-Hungary, which centered in Bohemia, lower Austria (around Vienna), and embryonically in Budapest, were expanding before the war, and the productivity of heavy industry even grew at the same pace as that in Germany, although from a lower base.[19]

Yet what strikes the observer is the complex nature of the government of the dual monarchy, which ruled twelve different nationalities, with the Hapsburg emperor Franz Joseph reigning over two governments—the constitutional monarchy of the seventeen crown lands comprising the legal and political unit of Cisleithanian Austria, and the constitutional monarchy of Hungary dominated by the Magyars. The governmental links between the two states consisted of the emperor; the imperial bureaucracy; joint ministries of foreign affairs, finance, and defense; and interparliamentary delegations. The disadvantages of this unwieldy system, a marriage of convenience between the Magyars and the Germans, are perhaps most apparent in its effect on the army.

✱ *In front of the Euler flying school, Prince Heinrich of Prussia (fifth from the right in flying helmet), the prewar patron of German aviation, poses with his entourage and flying teacher, August Euler (second from the right), after passing his flying test in November 1910. Courtesy of Peter Grosz.*

In peacetime the Austro-Hungarian War Ministry controlled the destiny of the army, while the chief of the General Staff held a peripheral position. Although the relationship was similar to that of the two offices in Germany, the Austro-Hungarian war minister was responsible to two governments. Because the budget had to be approved by two ministers of defense and two parliaments, complications were inevitable and resulted in such things as the army's being burdened with obsolete equipment in critical areas, especially artillery. Austro-Hungarian military expenditures lagged far behind German outlays essentially because the dual monarchy was poorer and less developed industrially. In 1906 and 1914, for example, Germany, with a population of 67 million, spent 22 crowns and 43.7 crowns, respectively, per capita on the military.[20] Austria-Hungary, with a population of 51.3 million, spent 9.6 crowns and 14 crowns. The Austro-Hungarian military budgets in 1906, 1911, and 1913—306 million crowns, 566 million crowns, and 769 million crowns—meant that the dual monarchy's military expenditures, despite increases, were steadily falling farther behind Germany's. Consequently, in 1914 Germany had an army of 98 divisions and Austria-Hungary had one of 60 divisions. The German Army had 4,480 artillery pieces, of which 1,064 were heavy guns; Austria-Hungary had 2,539 pieces, of which only 168 were heavy guns. The German battle fleet weighed in at 1,019,417 tons; the Austro-Hungarian battle fleet, which was rapidly expanding from a coastal defense force, was comprised of 394,692 tons. The inability of the aggressive chief of the Austro-Hungarian General Staff, General Franz Conrad von Hoetzendorff, to secure funds from the War Ministry for

✤ *Germany's first aircraft factory, the Euler Works, located in Frankfort on the Main in the suburb of Niederrad. Courtesy of Peter Grosz.*

increases in the army's manpower and armaments drove him to the brink of resignation in 1911.[21]

The polyglot composition of the Austro-Hungarian officer corps, which was largely German and Magyar, does indicate that the army played an important role in bringing together the disparate elements in the empire's population. Yet this officer corps, which was drawn increasingly from the middle and lower middle classes, was losing the social prestige necessary to give cohesion to its widely assorted members. In 1910 the war minister reported this situation to the head of the military chancellery, Archduke Franz Ferdinand, and observed that the officer corps needed increased social prestige, better general education, and a socially more exclusive selection in order to restore its position.[22] The dual monarchy's officer corps, which historian Z. A. B. Zeman considered less militaristic than the Prussian,[23] clearly did not possess the social and political pre-eminence of its Prusso-German counterpart. Military aviation would thus develop under markedly different conditions in Austria-Hungary than it would in Germany.

Upon the outbreak of hostilities in 1914, the two empires had not coordinated their economies or even the important details of war-planning, but each army's general staff was at least familiar with the other's basic strategies.[24] Austria-Hungary, definitely the weaker of the two Central Powers, could muster an army of approximately two million men, as compared to Germany's four million troops. The Prussian Army was consequently the cornerstone not only of the imperial German armed forces but also of the armed might of the Central Powers. The two states did not react in identical ways to the introduction of aviation technology, but their responses substantially affected the development of the airplane and the industry that it engendered.

Despite the lack of successful aircraft inventors in Germany, the Prussian Army had been discussing the relevance of the airplane to warfare since the Wright brothers' initial exploits in 1903. The first opportunity for the army to make a concrete decision on heavier-than-air flight arose in 1906, when the Wrights offered to sell one of their machines to the Prussian War Ministry. At this time only the French military was pursuing aircraft development with any success. Members of the Prussian military agencies assigned to observe aeronautical developments—the engineer and fortress department of the General Staff, the engineer department of the War Ministry, and the Inspectorate of Transport Troops—discussed the offer at length, but rejected it, because they believed that the airship, not the airplane, was the key to the elimination of French aerial ascendancy. The Prussian Army's technical units, the Inspectorate of Transport Troops and its Research Unit and Airship Battalion, had been concentrating on balloon and airship development since the 1890s, and in 1909 the airship surpassed the airplane in range, load-carrying capability, and even speed.

Nevertheless, the flights of Santos-Dumont in France and the Wrights in America and the increasingly apparent interest of the French and English war ministries in the airplane prompted Captain Hermann von der Lieth Thomsen of the engineer and fortress department to warn early in 1907 of the dangers inherent in merely observing the aeronautical progress of others. The War Ministry was sufficiently concerned to assign Captain Wolfram de le Roi, an airplane enthusiast well versed in foreign developments, to the transport inspectorate's research unit. It also commissioned a private firm to examine aircraft projects, selecting the Motor Airship Study Company because of the company's close cooperation with the army in airship development, its solid financial base of one million marks, and the interest of some of its engineers in airplanes. The General Staff preferred not to wait, and encouraged the Ludwig Loewe armaments firm to secure the Wrights' patent. However, Wilbur Wright was unable to guarantee aircraft performance standards demanded by Loewe, and in August 1907, Wright offered the machine to the army through the Motor Airship Study Company. The War Ministry, though interested, wisely considered Wright's alternatives—a price of one million marks or a license fee on each airplane produced in the next seventeen years—excessive for the military value of the invention. The War Ministry consequently rejected the Wright airplane.

This initial rejection notwithstanding, French progress in aircraft development during the remainder of 1907 commanded the increased attention of the Prussian Army's technical agencies. The French inventors Léon Delagrange, Robert Esnault-Peltérie, Henri Farman, and Louis Blériot had all flown successfully before the end of 1907. In January 1908 the General Staff created a technical section under Captain von der Lieth Thomsen to follow foreign and domestic progress in aviation, motorized transport, and telegraphy. Fortunately for the development of military aviation, this section was assigned to Captain Erich Ludendorff's mobilization department in October 1908. Both he and Captain von der Lieth Thomsen advocated the simultaneous and whole-hearted promotion of airships and airplanes. However, the General Staff could influence the evolution of military aviation only indirectly, through memoranda and infrequent military commissions on the general direction of aeronautical development.

The War Ministry, which had had a transport department in charge of aeronautical and other technical fields since April 1908 (provisionally since May 1907), was the final arbiter in armament matters because of its control of the budget. It was reluctant to allocate substantial funds to technology, which it considered secondary to more basic questions of armament and manpower, because of the financial limitations imposed on the army by the navy's increasing share of the imperial budget. Although the third agency, the Inspectorate of Transport Troops, was officially independent of the General Staff and the War Ministry, in reality the ministry could influence its decisions through control of the budget and, to a lesser extent, through appointments to its ranks. Through its Research Unit and Airship Battalion, the Inspecto-

rate directed the army's daily aeronautical operations, which in 1908 focused not on the airplane, but on the Zeppelin dirigibles.

The expansion of airship aviation by 1908 had caused the Research Unit to limit its duties to the detailed examination of airship projects and inventions and the surveillance of progress in airship development, while the Airship Battalion conducted the practical development of airships for the field formations. These airship agencies were not only evaluating the potential of captive balloons and three types of motorized airships, but also constructing the army's own airship. The most famous airship, the major competition for the airplane, was the Zeppelin, which had evolved slowly since it was originally proposed by Count Ferdinand von Zeppelin in the 1890s. The War Ministry had repeatedly declined Zeppelin's first proposals, and violent disputes intermittently flared up between the two. As late as 1906 the failures of the huge dirigibles had led even Ludendorff and the commander of the airship battalion, Major Hans Gross, to declare that the Zeppelins were militarily useless. Then, in 1908, Zeppelin's ships recorded successes that swung the pendulum of army favor in his direction just when the Prussian Army began to consider the airplane seriously.[1]

The crash of a Zeppelin at Echterdingen on 5 August 1908 after a successful overland flight might have destroyed the dreams and work of its namesake. Instead, the catastrophe touched off a spontaneous popular campaign that raised over seven million marks for further Zeppelin construction. This well-publicized flight not only diverted the army's interest away from the airplane; it enabled Count Zeppelin to capture the imagination, the hearts, and the pocketbooks of the German people. Meanwhile, early German airplanes were incapable of the spectacular feats necessary to gain public support. This popular concern and the intervention of Emperor Wilhelm, who described Zeppelin as

*Table 2.* OVERVIEW OF PRUSSIAN ARMY AVIATION AGENCIES TO 1 APRIL 1911[1]

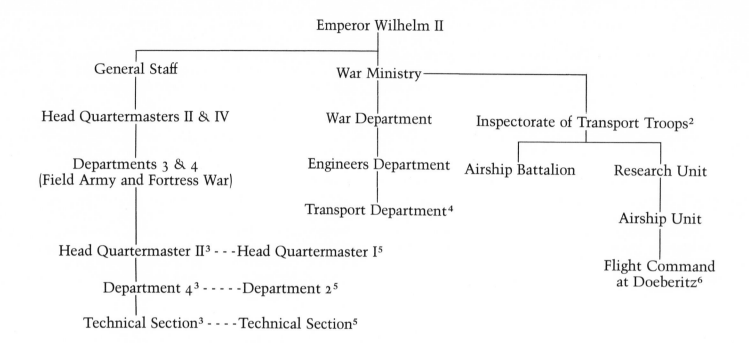

| [1]KAdL, *Die Militaerluftfahrt bis zum Beginn des Weltkrieges 1914*, 3 vols., 2d rev. ed. (Frankfort on the Main: Mittler und Sohn, 1965–66), ed. by Militaergeschichtliches Forschungsamt, II, Chart 57.<br>[2]A separate agency for technical and transport matters that was subject to the control of the War Ministry. | [3]After 16 Dec. 1907.<br>[4]After 1 Apr. 1908.<br>[5]After 1 Sept. 1908.<br>[6]After 8 July 1910. |

"the greatest German of the twentieth century" before nine years of the century had elapsed,[2] were instrumental in persuading the War Ministry to accept the Zeppelins for military service before they met its requirements. As aviation historian Hilmer von Buelow remarked, "The impressive successes of the Zeppelin still completely overshadowed the modest experiments of isolated airplane builders in Germany."[3]

Ironically, the very success of the Zeppelins was forcing the French, who were faced with the prospect of losing their aeronautical superiority, to rely increasingly on the airplane. The achievements of French civilian inventors in airplane and airplane motor construction encouraged consideration of the airplane for military purposes. The first noteworthy overland flight—Henri Farman's jaunt of twenty miles from Mourmelon-le-Grand to Reims in October 1908—heralded a new epoch in aviation. The French had quickly taken the lead in the development of light motors suitable for airplanes: Levavasseur had modified a Daimler-Benz automobile motor in 1907, and Séguin constructed the first reliable rotary engine in 1908. Hence the airplane, which began as the stepchild responsibility of the Inspectorate of Transport Troops, the Research Unit, and the Airship Battalion, acquired more importance as a tool for aerial reconnaissance and communication. As the balloon, airship, and airplane evolved, the Prussian Army accorded them different roles in strategic and tactical reconnaissance, although their similarity as technical, aeronautical inventions placed them under the same organization rubric.

Captain Wolfram de le Roi, the Research Unit's authority on airplanes, completed a report on 13 August 1908 on "The Attitude of the Military Authorities of Various States toward the Flying Machine Question and Proposals for the Introduction of Tests in the Field of Aviation Technology."[4] He noted the progress in France and America and the interest of their military authorities in the airplane. The achievements of flyers like Farman, Blériot, and Wright had awakened a lively public interest in Germany, as evidenced by the numerous articles in the daily press and technical periodicals and by the increasing number of inventions and projects submitted to the army. Awards for airplane flights, the most lucrative of which was the 40,000-mark Lanz Air Prize offered by the industrial magnate Karl Lanz, now spurred the serious efforts of inventors like Dr. August von Parseval of the Motor Airship Study Company to design successful airplanes. Despite this interest, de le Roi noted that nothing substantial had been achieved in Germany, so he recommended that the army discard its reservations toward airplanes before it fell too far behind the French.

The critical question de le Roi posed was whether the army should aid domestic inventors or begin its own tests. He recommended the latter method, supposing that the army's superior resources, if applied with a clear objective, could produce faster results than private companies. As a first step toward this goal, de le Roi proposed the erection of a workshop at the Research Unit, where the army could begin construction of its own flying machine.

The Airship Battalion disagreed.[5] In a lengthy rebuttal it conceded that the Germans had been unable to emulate the "frivolous flights" of the French and Americans (thus clearly implying that they were not worth emulating), but it found greater merit than did the Research Unit in German civilian efforts at airplane development. In its opinion the army should avoid duplicating these efforts and simply follow the American example by publishing requirements and offering prizes for military planes. The Airship Battalion also opposed de le Roi's report because the Research Unit's request for a workshop infringed upon its author-

ity and the competence of its own workshop, which it considered adequate for aircraft tests.

The inspector of transport troops, Lieutenant General Alfred von Lyncker, resolved the dispute in September in favor of the Battalion by concluding:

> The German army administration is presently of the opinion that its own work in the field of aviation technology is not yet absolutely necessary, since no type of flying machine has yet achieved the success that would demonstrate its suitability for military purposes. The solution to the problem should therefore be left to private enterprise, respectively factories, with which constant contact should be maintained.[6]

Lyncker ordered that if the army did begin experiments, the Airship Battalion, not the Research Unit, should perform them.

The War Ministry concurred with Lyncker's judgment, thus rejecting not only the recommendations of the Research Unit but also the suggestions of the General Staff, which believed that the army should begin tests immediately. The General Staff, attempting to probe all possibilities, advocated the promotion of both airships and airplanes. The War Ministry, more conservative in its estimate of the flying machine's potential and saddled with the task of defending the budget before the government, had no intention of substantially funding aircraft development. It had assumed that Germany, because of the more highly developed Zeppelin with its longer range, greater payload, and better operational safety, would not require airplanes as much as her potential opponents even if the plane acquired military value. The War Ministry certainly agreed with the General Staff's assessment in the fall of 1908 that the airplane would be a useful implement for

✦ *An Aviatik monoplane in front of the factory hangar in 1911. Courtesy of Peter Grosz.*

reconnaissance and communication. What it did not accept was that the military needed to assume the cost and risk of perfecting a military airplane. Private initiative, with a minimum of help from the army, would have sufficient time to perform this task.

Such optimism notwithstanding, Germany's private concerns had yet to produce a successful powered airplane. However, by November 1908 planes were under construction in some ten private projects around Germany, and civilian groups were becoming more involved in the support of flying machines for the army. The German Air Fleet League was formed in the summer of 1908 in an attempt to promote military aviation, just as its model, the Navy League, had promoted the fleet. In six months' time it had attracted some 3,000 members, most of whom lived in south Germany. Its first board of directors included Karl Lanz, the donor of the Lanz Air Prize, Ernst Bassermann, leader of the National Liberal party in the imperial parliament, Dr. Richard Brosien, director of the *Rheinische Kreditbank*, and retired Lieutenant General Stephan von Nieber, former commander of the Airship Battalion.[7] Organizations like the Air Fleet League, the Imperial Automobile Club, and the Berlin Society for Aviation were joining the German Airship Association (later the German Aviators Association), the controlling body of German civil aviation and Germany's largest aviation sport association. The Association, which had been founded in 1902 to foster the development of airships, was now beginning to deal with the administration of pilots' licenses, airfield and flight regulations, and other matters associated with powered heavier-than-air flight. In these roles it was granted official powers by the Prussian Ministries of the Interior and of Public Works in 1909.[8] Air-minded civilians were on the move.

The War Ministry was initially content to observe these developments; however, by the end of 1908 it felt that some projects

were worthy of more than mere notice. It consequently elected to encourage private initiative through subsidies early in 1909 by placing 15,000 marks at the disposal of a technical committee formed by the Berlin Society for Aviation, the Imperial Automobile Club, and the Imperial Aero-Club. This committee in turn granted 5,000 marks apiece to three promising inventors—Hans Grade of Magdeburg, Hermann Dorner of Berlin, and Richard Schelies of Hamburg. The technical committee was to inform the War Ministry of their progress, but there was little to report in 1909. Grade won the Lanz Air Prize with a very short flight near Berlin on 30 October 1909 and flew forty miles in early 1910 at a contest near Heliopolis, Greece. Dorner would not win acclaim for his aircraft until 1910 and 1911, and Schelies never progressed beyond the initial stages of design.[9] Disappointed at the failures of Dorner, Grade, and Schelies, the War Ministry stopped making direct subsidies to inventors and turned to yet other strategies.

On 15 January 1909 the War Ministry had reversed its decision of September 1908 and ordered the Research Unit to examine a project to build the army's own plane according to plans unveiled by master builder W. S. Hoffmann at a meeting of the German Air Fleet League in Mannheim.[10] What caused the War Ministry's change of attitude, and why did it adopt Hoffmann's plan? The answer lay with Lieutenant Colonel Hugo Schmiedecke, the chief of the War Department's transport department. The progress of German aircraft technology was slow and consequently military planes were lacking, but the French and English armies were building their own; accordingly, the War Ministry determined to take matters into its own hands. Fortunately for

✤ *An Aviatik monoplane on display at the* Salon d'aéronautique *in Paris in 1911/1912. Courtesy of Peter Grosz.*

Hoffmann, his plans and a model of his aircraft, a triplane, arrived on Schmiedecke's desk at this time. Hoffmann had presented his proposal earlier to Major Gross, the commander of the Airship Battalion, who recommended that the builder search for private subsidies and present the finished aircraft to the army. In passing, however, Gross mentioned that Hoffmann might speak to Schmiedecke and send him a model of the proposed triplane. The Ministry decided in favor of the project when it learned that several "noted specialists," among them Karl Lanz and General von Nieber, approved Hoffmann's plans.[11] As the Zeppelin Fund of 1908 had shown, the War Ministry was not immune to outside pressure.

The Inspectorate of Transport Troops, in turn, could not disregard pressure from the War Ministry. General von Lyncker had originally opposed the idea of the army's developing its own plane, stating on 26 January that it was a "deviation from the prevailing principle of subsidizing inventors with money, but otherwise leaving it to them to execute the project and furnish proof of its usefulness."[12] Nevertheless, on 18 February, Lyncker himself, accompanied by Captain de le Roi, described the Hoffmann project to a receptive emperor (with War Minister General von Heeringen present) as "the decisive step in the further development of transport."[13] Emperor Wilhelm was warned of the dangers of falling behind other powers and informed that the Hoffmann triplane would exceed in all respects the performance of the Wright machines. The emperor, duly impressed, requested that the machine be ready for imperial maneuvers in September, and the Research Unit was authorized to build the airplane. This was a logical decision considering the unit's positive disposition toward the flying machine; yet in making it Lyncker completely reversed himself, as he had previously determined to let the Airship Battalion begin any airplane

experiments. Only the War Ministry could have executed such a maneuver.

The machine was finally ready for flight on 1 March 1910, some six months late for the imperial maneuvers. Hoffmann's constant alterations and the lack of a motor had caused innumerable delays. The German motor firms were uninterested in or incapable of producing a decent aircraft motor; and so, in disgust, the army procured a French powerplant. The three-winged abomination was heavy and had neither vertical stabilizer nor a steering mechanism. With this in mind, nobody present at the trials wanted to be the test pilot, so the responsibility fell by default to Captain de le Roi. With the hesitant, untrained, and undoubtedly frightened aviation expert at the controls, the machine rose—to a height of three and one-half meters. Then it crashed, incurring minor damage. A second attempt on 18 March 1910 resulted in irreparable damage. The Prussian Army's attempt to build its own plane had failed, at a total cost of over 42,000 marks.[14]

With an originally proposed budget of 36,000 marks for airplane development in 1909, the War Ministry had squandered approximately 50,000 marks on what was never more than a doubtful proposition. Admittedly, there were no authorities in aviation design then, and guesswork played an important role in the construction of all machines. Nevertheless, the War Ministry could have chosen more experienced inventors or a reproduction of a proven foreign design. Instead it selected Hoffmann mainly because of the eminence of his backers. It is possible to attribute machiavellian designs to the War Ministry and the Inspectorate; one could claim that they purposely chose a project with little

✴ *The Gotha factory in 1912/1913. The wing of a Gotha Taube under construction. Courtesy of Peter Grosz.*

likelihood of success in order to ward off questions from the government and the public and to ensure that the army would not soon be saddled with the expense of airplane production. But these suppositions are unlikely. They could have failed more cheaply, and they need not have presented the project to the emperor so enthusiastically. No hint of such a devious design appears in the records, and it seems more likely, judging from previous indications in the areas of weapons and vehicle development, that the Hoffmann fiasco resulted from the participants' inexperience and the maladroit manner in which modifications were carried out. The failure of the Hoffmann machine persuaded the army to encourage private initiative,[15] because it had crushed the belief that the Prussian Army could easily develop its own airplane. The army had succumbed to the constant failures of these years of trial and error in aviation.

Already a number of factors that would affect the Prussian Army's acceptance of the airplane for the next few years had become evident. On the German domestic scene, civilian associations such as the Air Fleet League and the German Aviators Association were beginning to persuade the Prussian Army to adopt the airplane. The War Ministry had chosen to rely on civilian groups as intermediaries and technical advisers in its selection of inventors for army subsidies. Meanwhile, the Air Fleet League had influenced the ministry's policies by providing a forum for aspiring designers and by uniting industrialists, former military officers, and other parties interested in the development of airplanes for military purposes.

Obstacles still existed, however, mainly in the form of budgetary restrictions imposed by the War Ministry and the internal divisions within the bureaucracy. The General Staff was naturally far more enthusiastic about the airplane than either the War Ministry or the Inspectorate of Transport Troops, since it wanted

to be equipped at all costs for possible warfare. Although the War Ministry accepted the idea that the airplane had potential as a reconnaissance and communications vehicle, its concern for the budget made it reluctant to invest much in the untried airplane when airships were available. In addition, the War Ministry and the Inspectorate regarded the innovation of the airplane with different attitudes. Although the Ministry had blundered with the Hoffmann project, it had at least taken the initiative. The Inspectorate, fully occupied with daily operations and thus tending to resolve disputes between the Research Unit and the Airship Battalion in favor of the status quo, seemed content to depend on others for impetus.

Despite these hindrances, the path was clear for the expansion of military airplane development in Germany by 1909. The Prussian Army, confronted with the continuing advancement of French military aviation, had committed itself to the airplane. Its efforts to build its own flying machine or to subsidize inventors directly had failed, but, fortunately for German military aviation, a third policy was available: the encouragement of embryonic aircraft firms with whatever funding military interests and a limited budget allowed. Thus the transition was accomplished between the support of lone and largely unsuccessful inventors and the use of newly established aircraft manufacturers.

The formation of the first German airplane companies in the winter of 1908–1909 was a natural development under the circumstances. The interest of the army and of civilian groups, the prizes for airplanes—all spurred the attempts of inventors to construct flying machines. It was inevitable that, given this increasing concern for the airplane, some more enterprising inventors and interested businessmen already involved in the production of machines or motorized vehicles would found companies to enter airplane production.

✠ *The Gotha factory in 1912/1913. A Taube nears completion. Courtesy of Peter Grosz.*

The first German airplane company, the Euler Works, was founded in October 1908 on a field near Darmstadt by August Euler, a former manufacturer of bicycles and automobiles and business agent for French and German metal firms. Euler's interest stemmed from contact with his French friends Delagrange, Blériot, and Farman, all famous pilots and aircraft manufacturers. He had wanted to produce licensed copies of the French Voisin airplane, but the French government blocked his attempt to obtain the license.[16] Undaunted, he proceeded with his plans.

Although a later claim by Euler that the army had encouraged him to build the factory was never substantiated, there is indeed evidence that he obtained military assistance. On 12 December 1908, Euler wrote to the commander of the 18th Army Corps in Darmstadt requesting a field and hangar free of charge, for which he promised to train army officers as pilots. The War Ministry granted his request on 4 January 1909 with the following stipulations: Euler was required to pay for the construction of the hangar and any damage to roads on the field caused by the construction, to inform the military of his actions on the field, and to allow the army control of access to his enterprise. He could demand no payment for damages from the army, although he was liable for any he caused. In return, he received a permit to use the field for five years, and he would get six months' notice if he had to vacate the premises. The commanding general of the 18th Army Corps, General von Eichhorn, also promised orally to keep the field free of other aircraft firms for five years.[17]

When Euler found that he could not hire sufficient workers in

Darmstadt to complete the hangar, he contracted with the Twenty-first Nassau Pioneer Battalion through Eichhorn to provide the necessary men and tools. Euler provided the material, transportation, and housing for the troops, and paid the battalion 2,400 marks. The hangar was completed on 19 April 1909.[18] In his memoirs, *Luftfahrt-Erinnerungen nach 30 Jahren*, in 1939, Euler described the small establishment, so typical of the early companies:

> The factory consisted of a design office with two drawing machines, a workshop with the necessary tools: drilling and sanding machines, lathes, tool benches, etc., with electric power. The assembly-shop was fifty meters long, twenty meters wide, and nine meters high.[19]

The industrial and military center of Berlin, however, not Darmstadt, was a better location for a new industry seeking military contracts. So the next factories—the Edmund Rumpler Aircraft Construction Company and the Wright Flying Machine Company, founded in November 1908 and May 1909, respectively—were located on a state-owned field at Johannisthal near Berlin. Of particular importance was the Wright company, which the Motor Airship Study Company established to produce the Wrights' patented machine. Its capital of 500,000 marks was an extraordinarily large amount in the context of 1909 German aviation firms, and its ten stockholders included some of the most important firms in Germany: the AEG, Stinnes, Borsig, Loewe, and Krupp.[20] Although the origins of the company are obscure, the participation of the AEG led the noted aviation authority A. R. Weyl to speculate that the company was sponsored by the emperor and his friend Walter Rathenau, the director of the electric company.[21] While it is possible that Emperor Wilhelm supported the participation of his close personal friends Rathenau and Krupp in the new company, his personal sponsorship or involvement is doubtful. At best the Motor Airship Study Com-

pany may have obtained the emperor's endorsement of the enterprise through the army in order to encourage the participation of the giant firms. In any case, the involvement of the electric company and representatives of the arms industry was the first indication of large-scale capital's interest in airplanes.

In the summer of 1909, shortly after the formation of the Wright company, the Prussian Army authorized the government to sell the field at Johannisthal to a private company, which the army then subsidized with 20,000 marks annually.[22] The Johannisthal Airfield Company included among its founders two influential men: Arthur Mueller, building contractor, legal adviser to the German Aviators Association, and one of the ten shareholders in the Wright company; and retired Major George von Tschudi, former commander of the Airship Battalion. Mueller controlled the concern, since he supplied the funds; however, Tschudi became official director of the airfield company at the request of the chairman of the board of directors of the Aviators Association, Lieutenant General Stephan von Nieber.[23]

The army's 20,000 marks were insufficient to develop the property, and Mueller's company had to spend 200,000 marks for construction alone.[24] Yet the subsidy did suffice for the purposes of the Prussian Army, because it assured the army of the use of the field when necessary. Because of its proximity to Berlin, Johannisthal field became such an indispensable center for the aircraft industry by 1913 that the War Ministry, although unwilling to buy it from Arthur Mueller, increased its yearly subsidy to 40,000 marks in order to prevent the threatened collapse of the company.[25]

Of other important German firms founded in 1909 and 1910, all except *Automobil und Aviatik GmbH* (Aviatik) of Mulhausen in Alsace, which had a capital of 30,000 marks, were located at Johannisthal. Next to the Wright company, Hermann Dorner's new company with 100,000 marks, Rumpler with 90,000 marks, the Albatros Works with 25,000 marks, and Euler's factory with an unknown amount of capital were the most solidly established aircraft manufacturers in Germany.[26]

The first contractual dealings between these firms and the Prussian Army concerned the firms' offers of flight lessons for officers, not the sale of aircraft, because the army was reluctant to buy flying machines without first having its own trained pilots. Through these promotional offers the companies hoped "to get a foot in the door" with the Prussian Army in the hope of ultimately securing military contracts for airplanes. They actually had no choice but to cater to the army, since private industry and civilian transport had no use for the airplane at that early stage in its development. Dr. Walter Huth, cofounder and owner of the Albatros company, offered the War Ministry a French Latham airplane and a flying instructor on 2 October 1909 and then two French airplanes in February 1910 if the army would only pay repair costs. The Wright company also offered to train officers gratuitously on 21 February. Four days later Chief of the General Staff General von Moltke recommended to the War Minister that the army begin the systematic training of suitable officers on airplanes.[27]

A Research Unit memorandum written by Captain de le Roi on 15 March 1910 on the army's use of airplanes supported Moltke's recommendation.[28] De le Roi envisioned the airplane's being used not only for reconnaissance and communications, but also as an implement of battle to destroy slower airships by dropping small explosives or by pouring acid on them from above. He anticipated that flying shows would generate the interest and capital investment necessary for the aviation industry to solve its construction problems and overtake the French in a few years.

The most important part of his memorandum concentrated on the organizational requirements for military aviation. In his opinion only a special military organization for airplanes would ensure the conformity of airplane and motor production to military requirements. If the army did not intervene in aircraft development, their evolution would repeat that of the automobile; high-performance, fair-weather airplanes would emerge, not aircraft that would be safe and operable under field conditions. The motor vehicle had conformed to military needs only when the War Ministry had published requirements, organized a motor unit to evaluate the vehicles, and subsidized the promising machines. In de le Roi's opinion this proven procedure would force the airplane and motor industries into channels conducive to military purposes. This is the first evidence of the realization that military demands on airplanes would differ so significantly from civilian needs that the army would have to shape the industry's development according to its own ends.

De le Roi consequently recommended the creation of a combination flying school-flying unit at the Research Unit for the army to examine different aircraft and then subsidize or buy the most promising. To avoid the expense of substantial training facilities, potential army pilots would first have to earn a civilian license from the German Aviators Association. To avoid interference with private industry, the flying unit would have no production facilities and the War Ministry would choose planes entirely from the products of the German aviation industry. By awarding prizes for the motors that powered the best aircraft, the army might even encourage the cooperation of the motor industry. De le Roi thus attempted to reconcile the necessity for military airplanes with the War Ministry's thriftiness and determination to rely on private enterprise.

Despite Moltke's and de le Roi's enthusiasm, the War Ministry drove a hard bargain with Huth, who committed Albatros on 8

July to place two French aircraft and one engineer at the disposal of the Research Unit. The army assumed no responsibility to buy the planes or to pay for their use, but Albatros had at least gained a foothold with the army. At any rate Huth, by sending his chauffeur and aviation mechanic Simon Brunnhuber as the "engineer"[29]—an obvious affront to the immense pride of the Prussian officer—must have gained some satisfaction. On 8 July the Research Unit appointed de le Roi head of the new Flight Command at Berlin Doeberitz, where four officers completed pilot training successfully on the Albatros machines by mid-September. In the meantime, for want of facilities at Doeberitz, six more officers had been assigned to the Albatros factory for training by December.[30] Huth's initial bargain paid even handsomer dividends later; the army bought the two planes for 24,108.25 marks apiece when it recognized the necessity of owning the planes for which its pilots were trained.[31] Nevertheless, the Research Unit refused an offer from Albatros in October to train large numbers of pilots, for four reasons: it was not yet certain of the aircraft's military value; it doubted the ability of Albatros to train a large number of pilots; it preferred to keep the training in its own hands; and it feared a monopoly for Albatros would diminish the army's control over its own flight program.[32] The army's determination to control aeronautical development by preserving competition among the firms and thus preventing a monopoly in the aircraft industry—a policy it would later pursue in its granting of airplane contracts—appears here for the first time with regard to pilot training.

The success of the Albatros training program did elicit the

Inspectorate's recommendation that the army buy its own planes as soon as possible, for which task the War Ministry appropriated 110,000 marks.[33] The uncertainty about the military merits of the airplane, the fears that high speed made observation from aircraft impossible (German airplanes in 1910 were barely capable of fifty miles per hour at full throttle) and that piloting demanded acrobatic skill—all militated against a larger military investment in aircraft.[34] By April 1911, the end of the 1910 fiscal year, the War Ministry had purchased only seven airplanes, including those from Albatros, at a total cost of 135,894.75 marks.[35]

In the opinion of some observers, it was this failure to obtain many orders, rather than any flaws in the industry's technical ability, that kept the German aircraft industry from catching up with the progress made in France.[36] Yet the facts about German airplanes and the industry at this time show that the army's circumspection was warranted. The best firms reproduced successful American and French designs. Wright copied the Wrights' machine; Aviatik, the Farman; Albatros, the Farman and Sommer planes; and Euler, the Voisin. They bought the French aircraft and attempted to duplicate them without a license, since the French firms had no German patents on their inventions.[37] The resulting copies, however, were invariably inferior to their French prototypes, because without the license German firms lacked detailed knowledge of construction procedures and materials.

French pilots and airplanes held every international flying record. Louis Blériot flew the English Channel on 25 July 1909. The records achieved at the Reims Air Week in August 1909—a top speed of fifty miles per hour, altitude of 500 feet, distance of 100 miles, and duration of three hours four minutes—so impressed Major Detloff von Winterfeld, the German military attaché in Paris, that he labeled them "astounding" and declared that aviation, even if its practical usage remained uncertain, had left the

✱ *The Gotha factory. A biplane under construction. Courtesy of Peter Grosz.*

stage of childish amusement.[38] The German duration record of 1910, set in an Aviatik Farman in October, was only fifteen minutes sixteen seconds longer than the record set at Reims in 1909, while the French records of 1910—a speed of seventy-five miles per hour, altitude of two miles, and a distance of 365 miles—had long since surpassed that level. French pilots dominated the German contests in 1909 and early 1910—the Berlin Flying Week, the Frankfort Flying Week, and the Johannisthal International Flying Week—and carted away the 10–40,000 marks prizes so needed for German aviation.

Hilmer von Buelow asserted that the flight competitions in 1909 and 1910 gave a powerful stimulus to the German aircraft industry and private aviation.[39] Approximately thirty aircraft companies did spring up within a short time, but most of them quickly collapsed for want of markets, capital, and military support. The stimulus was not sufficient to sever the German aircraft industry's dependence on foreign designs or to nurture its substantial growth, nor was it enough to lure the German motor industry to the production of aircraft engines. The German motor industry's neglect of aircraft motor development until late 1910 was a prime cause of the relative backwardness of the German airplane industry. In 1910 the Argus company introduced the first German airplane motor, while Daimler, Benz, and *Neue Automobil Gesellschaft* (NAG) began construction of lightweight powerplants for airplanes. Of course, at the Paris air show of 1911 the French displayed thirty-six aircraft engines. Since the German motor industry preferred to concentrate on the profitable world automobile engine market, where it was a leading competitor, the airplane firms were dependent on the French Gnome or Antoinette motors or on Austrian Austro-Daimler engines. The French thus dominated German aviation by default.

The Germans ended the French dominance of their flight contests with a simple expedient—they barred foreign competitors. The Johannisthal contests held in August and October 1910 were national flying weeks, open only to planes built entirely (except for their engines) in Germany.[40] The War Ministry, which co-sponsored these contests with the Johannisthal Airfield Company and the German Aviators Association, had probably instigated this change, since it certainly intended its prizes of 18,000 marks and 34,000 marks for the German, not the French, industry. The Prussian Army's desire for a self-sufficient national aircraft industry caused it to close out competition and to accept French aircraft and inferior copies of French airplanes as long as they came from German companies. For this reason the War Ministry, the Inspectorate, and the Research Unit declined an offer from the French aircraft manufacturer Henri Farman to erect a factory on German soil. All three agencies feared that support of the Farman company would discourage and damage domestic aircraft factories and possibly make the army dependent on the French airplane industry—an intolerable situation in the event of war.[41]

The General Staff knew that the French Army was already buying planes and training pilots at the end of 1909 and that by the fall of 1910 the French War Ministry had ordered some 100 aircraft from the larger French factories for delivery before 1 March 1911. Hence Moltke recommended in the fall of 1910 that the army create a military aviation agency before the next five-year army bill and then purchase the most modern machines for pilot training. He wanted army aviation parks and an army aviation command as the Inspectorate's central aviation agency for pilot training, guiding the aircraft and motor industries in the army's interests, and evaluating technical progress and new airplane designs.[42]

As usual the War Ministry considered the General Staff's far-reaching plans premature,[43] but it could no longer ignore the increasing superiority of French aviation. Consequently, it proposed on 19 September 1910 an examination of German airplanes at maneuvers attached to the October Johannisthal national flying week. For this task the War Ministry, the General Staff, and the Inspectorate of Transport Troops agreed to recall the aviation commission that had evaluated the airship in 1909. The Cologne Commission, composed of War Ministry department chiefs Colonels Schmiedecke and Werner Voigts-Rhetz, General Staff Lieutenant Colonel Erich Ludendorff, the director of the Research Unit Colonel Wilhelm Messing, and the Inspectorate's adjutant Captain Karl Gruetzner, convened on 21 October 1910.

The commission's final report,[44] completed in January 1911, noted French superiority, the primitive beginnings of Russian military aviation, and the slow development of German aviation technology despite the airplane's proven military suitability for reconnaissance and communications. Although only German companies copying foreign designs had shown any success, the War Ministry still preferred to rely on private industry. The Commission did design a new organization for the transport troops for the fiscal year beginning on 1 April 1911. Military aviation would become the province of an Inspectorate of Aviation and Motor Vehicles, which in turn would be subordinate to a General Inspectorate of Military Transportation. While this reorganization signified the increasing importance of technical matters, it entailed the continuation of the marriage of convenience between military transportation and aviation, and not the establishment of an independent, authoritative aviation agency along the lines of Moltke's proposal. To fund this expansion, the commission proposed an allocation of 450,000 marks, including 130,000 marks for the procurement of five or six planes and 100,000 marks for awards and subsidies for aircraft technology.

This allotment, which the War Ministry could augment, was an increase over the 36,000 marks and 300,000 marks allocated in 1909 and 1910, respectively, for airplane development. Yet in comparison with the total budget for aviation (including airships—3,194,050 marks in 1909 and 3,849,550 marks in 1910—and with the total army budgets of over 900,000,000 marks in both years, these funds were insignificant and insufficient to finance any substantial advances in military aviation.[45] Mobilization under these conditions would require the army to commandeer all suitable private aircraft and the factories to deliver wartime replacements as needed with no financial assistance from the military.

The provisions of the commission's report illustrate the lack of a solid, consistent attitude within the army toward airplanes. Despite the interest of the General Staff and of officers like Captain de le Roi of the Research Unit, the army could not bring itself to accept the airplane unreservedly. The most critical indication of this hesitation was the lack of funds allocated for airplanes by the War Ministry. The necessity to preserve German superiority in airships and the War Ministry's overweening concern for the budget hindered a more positive encouragement of the aircraft industry. The War Ministry and the Inspectorate of Transport Troops did not consider airplanes sufficiently important to merit the investment of substantial funds, so they sought to encourage the best output from the industry for the smallest possible input of military investment. The War Ministry had helped the aircraft industry get its start, but its reserve and consequent limited aid and contracts were not conducive to more than the modest growth of a German aircraft industry despite its recognition of the advisability of a strong domestic industry. The caution of the War Ministry and the Inspectorate toward the airplane, which was justified by the embryonic state of the industry but unjustified to

the extent that it was based on groundless fears about high speed and acrobatic pilots, did give the army a definite advantage in its dealings with the industry. In addition, the absence of a civilian market forced the firms to keep military guidelines in mind as they developed their flying machines.

The few productive aircraft companies still resembled the workshops of artisans rather than actual industrial factories, but they were growing in number and size. The years 1909 and 1910 were a time of waiting for the Prussian Army and a period of struggle for the nascent airplane industry. Only if the War Ministry and the Inspectorate saw fit to increase their faith in the airplane and to award larger contracts to the manufacturers would future difficulties for the airplane industry be averted.

## THE RELATIONSHIP ESTABLISHED, 1911

During 1909 and 1910 the aircraft industry was launched, and the Prussian Army organized its aviation agencies. The exact nature of the relationship between them was defined and further elaborated in the course of the next year. The army would have to decide to what degree its policies would foster the growth of the airplane industry, and, because of the absence of private markets, its decision would determine the survival or demise of the industry.

The first indications were that the army's stance toward aviation was favorable. The Cologne Commission's reorganization of the Transport Troops took effect on 1 April 1911. The Inspecto-

✱ *In top hat and tails "the Flying Dutchman," Anthony Fokker, pilot and aircraft entrepreneur extraordinary, confers with the pilot of a Fokker Spinne at the Fokker flying school in Schwerin in 1913. Courtesy of Peter Grosz.*

rate of Transport Troops was elevated to the General Inspectorate of Military Transportation, with an Inspectorate of Military Aviation and Motor Vehicles as its subordinate agency. General von Lyncker became inspector general, and Colonel Wilhelm Messing, the former director of the Research Unit, became inspector. The Inspectorate's Instruction and Research Institute for Military Aviation replaced the Flight Command at Doeberitz, and the Research Unit became a direct subordinate of the General Inspectorate.[46] However, this improved organizational scheme did not define precisely a division of authority between the War Ministry and the General Inspectorate; military policy toward the aircraft industry would be determined jointly by the two agencies.

There were advantages as well as disadvantages under this system of dual command. For example, the military bureaucracy had declared its intention in 1910, when dealing with the Albatros company, to foster interfirm competition. Obviously, if one company secured a monopoly position the military would no longer be able to choose the best aircraft at the best prices, nor ultimately to control the rate of growth of military aviation. Yet in 1911 and early 1912 it was the War Ministry's ability to interfere at will in the affairs of the General Inspectorate that prevented the Prussian Army's dependence on a single company.

The General Inspectorate and the Inspectorate of Military Aviation and Motor Vehicles maintained an impartial stance toward the various firms with one exception—an unexplained predilection for the Albatros Works. Since the relationship between the General Inspectorate and Albatros seems to have been entirely legitimate, the favoritism must have stemmed from Albatros's position as one of the first and best firms producing military aircraft. When the partiality of the Inspectorates toward Albatros became too flagrant, the War Ministry intervened to restore the balance, as the following incidents indicate.

*Table 3.* OVERVIEW OF PRUSSIAN ARMY AVIATION AGENCIES, I APRIL 1911 TO 31 JULY 1914[1]

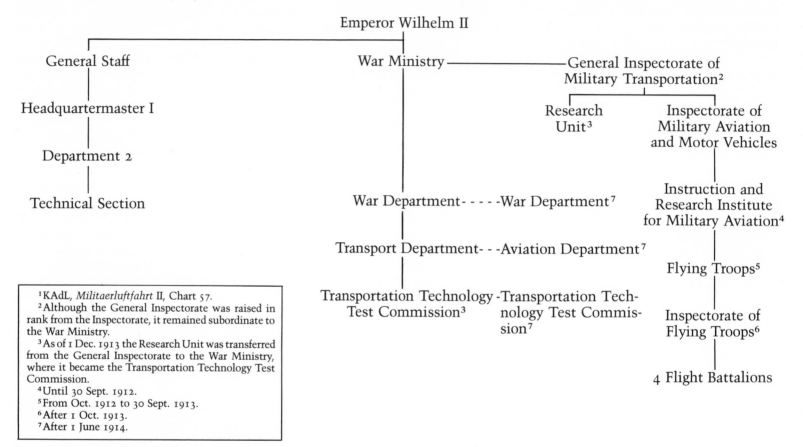

Emperor Wilhelm II

General Staff

War Ministry ——— General Inspectorate of Military Transportation[2]

Headquartermaster I

Research Unit[3]

Inspectorate of Military Aviation and Motor Vehicles

Department 2

Technical Section

War Department - - - - War Department[7]

Instruction and Research Institute for Military Aviation[4]

Transport Department - - - Aviation Department[7]

Flying Troops[5]

Transportation Technology Test Commission[3]

Transportation Technology Test Commission[7]

Inspectorate of Flying Troops[6]

4 Flight Battalions

[1] KAdL, *Militaerluftfahrt* II, Chart 57.
[2] Although the General Inspectorate was raised in rank from the Inspectorate, it remained subordinate to the War Ministry.
[3] As of 1 Dec. 1913 the Research Unit was transferred from the General Inspectorate to the War Ministry, where it became the Transportation Technology Test Commission.
[4] Until 30 Sept. 1912.
[5] From Oct. 1912 to 30 Sept. 1913.
[6] After 1 Oct. 1913.
[7] After 1 June 1914.

The army sought to eliminate middlemen from its dealings with the airplane industry because of the resulting rise in prices. Consequently, at the urging of Albatros in the summer of 1911, Colonel Messing refused to deal with *Luftverkehrsgesellschaft* (LVG), a small aircraft company owned by the ubiquitous Arthur Mueller.[47] According to Otto Wiener, the business director of the Albatros company, LVG was merely a sales agent for Albatros. Captain de le Roi, formerly of the Research Unit and now in Arthur Mueller's employ, had allegedly persuaded Wiener that the army preferred to deal through him and LVG rather than directly with Albatros. Albatros, however, supposedly reserved the right to sell directly to the army if the army so desired, in which case LVG would receive 750 marks for each plane. What Wiener neglected to explain was that LVG had become Albatros's sales agent by saving it from collapse in the spring of 1911 after the army had rejected Albatros's request for a subsidy. LVG had bought four Albatros planes for 100,000 marks, covered the company's sales expenses, and financed its participation in three large contests so that Albatros could continue production. Since then LVG had bought three French Morane monoplanes and built workshops for the production of its own aircraft.

After Captain de le Roi explained the actual situation to Colonel Schmiedecke of the War Ministry's transport department, the department supported LVG. Schmiedecke concluded that despite LVG's role as a sales agent for Albatros, its expenditures on Albatros and its later independent development indicated considerable financial resources and potential for expansion at a time when most German aircraft factories lacked both.[48]

The victory of an LVG pilot in an Albatros-LVG aircraft in the Circuit of Germany Flight in July forced a resolution of the question. The army was committed to order the victorious airplane, but from whom, Albatros or LVG? When Albatros re-fused to give LVG another airframe, Schmiedecke, while saying that the plane would have to come from LVG, suggested that it need not be an Albatros type. But Messing maintained that the army was committed to order an Albatros type from LVG, or the contract would be void. In November, however, he consented to purchase any plane that LVG offered if it met the army's standards, so the Inspectorate bought a modified Farman on 20 December 1911 and, "to erase any impression of prejudice," ordered two more soon thereafter. The War Ministry, and with it LVG, had triumphed.[49]

In another attempt to undermine his company's competition, at the end of January 1912 Otto Wiener sent the Inspectorate copies of letters from the *Deutsche Flugzeugwerke* (DFW) and Rumpler which asserted that the Aviatik firm was a French firm with a French staff. The French automobile company Peugeot allegedly held 800,000 or 900,000 marks of Aviatik's 1,000,000 marks capital.[50] By discrediting Aviatik, Wiener hoped that Albatros could replace it as the supplier of airplanes for the new air stations at Strasbourg and Metz in Alsace-Lorraine. On 20 January 1912, four days before he relayed the incriminating letter to the Inspectorate, Wiener proposed to the War Department's transport department the establishment of a branch of Albatros equipped for a minimal annual production of twenty-four aircraft on a maneuver field selected by the army. Military orders of fewer than twenty-four aircraft would necessitate a subsidy gradually increasing to 400,000 marks for an annual order of less than six planes.[51]

Although twenty-four aircraft was a rather large order from a single firm in 1911 (the army bought only twenty-nine planes the entire year), General von Lyncker and Colonel Messing, assuming that the information on Aviatik was reliable, found the offer attractive. Messing, who proposed to replace Aviatik with Albatros as the only firm on the western border, desired to order as many planes as possible from Albatros in order to lower the subsidy and to take advantage of Albatros's reproduction of the promising French Breguet design. Since Lyncker likewise could not refuse the offer of such a "capable and reliable" firm as Albatros, he merely amended Messing's proposal by limiting the subsidy to five years and by withholding the right to repair the planes in military workshops; he further provided for withdrawal of the subsidy if the planes did not meet army requirements.[52]

Upon investigation of Wiener's accusations, however, Colonel Schmiedecke and Major General von Wandel, the head of the War Department, discovered that all of Aviatik's shareholders were Alsatians and that the general commanding the 14th Army Corps in Alsace where Aviatik was located considered them quite trustworthy. The War Department had rejected an offer from Aviatik to build a branch factory because of the General Inspectorate's reservations, but it now refused to assume the responsibility for eliminating Aviatik as a supplier and consequently causing the factory's collapse on such trumped-up charges. Furthermore, the transport department believed that a subsidy to establish another firm in west Germany was unnecessary, since it was negotiating for the formation of an airplane factory in Aachen and was certain that other established airplane companies would make competitive offers if notified of the situation. The War Ministry promptly declined Albatros's offer, and Wandel gently reprimanded the General Inspectorate for not handling its business with Albatros more carefully.[53] What was obvious to the War Department, and should have been to the General Inspectorate, was that Albatros, as a competitor standing to gain by the elimination of Aviatik, might use questionable methods. Messing was enraged, and undoubedly embarrassed, since the initial recommendation had been his. What angered him even more was that

the War Department was negotiating for the construction of the factory in Aachen without informing the Inspectorate.[54] In any case, the Albatros plot had failed, although it had momentarily shaken the army's faith in Aviatik.

This last clash and the reprimand so aroused the General Inspectorate that it proposed in February 1912 that the War Department's transport department should allocate the funds to buy the number of aircraft it desired and leave the selection of type and factory and the assignment of planes to flying stations to the General Inspectorate. The War Department did not accept the proposal, since it would have had to relinquish any direct control over procurement. It merely acknowledged the desirability and necessity of maintaining closer ties with the General Inspectorate.[55]

Thus in this instance the institutionalized system of checks and balances within the Prussian Army was healthy for the army and the industry because it preserved competition. Without this system Albatros might have gained a monopoly and the army would have been placed at a distinct disadvantage. With the exception of these instances of partiality toward Albatros, the General Inspectorate zealously policed the competitive nature of the airplane industry, guarding against the formation of cartels or syndicates that might weaken the army's position.

The military's concern for retaining its control and for the preservation of competition also influenced the Inspectorate's first contacts with the Convention of Aircraft Industrialists, a central agency representing the aircraft industry. The convention had been formed within the Association of German Motor Vehicle Industrialists on 26 March 1911 by eleven firms, among them Albatros, Aviatik, Dorner, Euler, Grade, Harlan, Rumpler, and Wright. These firms joined the motor vehicle industrialists, rather than an aeronautical association, for a number of reasons:

the manufacturers regarded the airplane, like the automobile, as the progeny of the motor; the firms, with the exception of the Wright company, had developed independently of the airship industry and other aeronautical associations; and August Euler, the driving force behind the formation of the convention, had been an automobile manufacturer. The member companies elected Euler as chairman, Richard von Kehler, the business director of the Wright company, as his deputy, and Edmund Rumpler as secretary.[56]

The association was intended to protect the economic interests of the aircraft industry. The formation of trade associations to protect and further the interests of particular groups had been only recently established in German society. In German economic life the individualism of the "bourgeois era" had yielded to the collectivism evidenced by the formation, during the depression of 1873, of the first large groups of businessmen with common interests. The depression ran its course, but these groups remained.[57] The formation of the association of airplane manufacturers was consequently a logical development, marking the transition of the aircraft industry from an "individualistic" state to one characterized by the more collective representation of its needs.

Another reason for banding together was that the manufacturers wanted to influence air show regulations, which had previously been formulated by the sponsors, such as sport associations and newspapers, with little regard for the manufacturers' wishes and profits. The industry's representatives had been unable to influence the German Aviators Association concerning the rules of the Southwest German Overland Flight. Because the air shows presented the industry with small profits in return for large outlays and losses, the convention ruled that its members could participate in these competitions only with its prior consent.

Disregarding this regulation would mean punishment for breach of contract. The companies would participate *en masse* in contests which they considered to their benefit in order to end the previous dissipation of the industry's influence resulting from the participation of one or two firms in every little show or contest. They hoped that the threat of their boycott of contests would enable them to influence contest rules and, in contests which the army cosponsored with the aviation associations, to deal directly with the army.

By presenting a unified front the industry also hoped to win concessions from Arthur Mueller's Johannisthal Airfield Company, which had recently trebled their rent with impunity because no firm could afford to leave the geographical center of the German aircraft industry. Because construction of hangars, sheds, and factories on the airfield was the exclusive domain of the Mueller construction company, the firms were even more indebted to Mueller. What the manufacturers feared most was that Mueller might dissolve the company and demand the liquidation of the aircraft firms or their transferral to his ownership if he ever found himself in financial difficulties. For this reason the convention asked the Imperial Office of the Interior to purchase the field for 1,500,000 marks, the amount of a subsidy Mueller had requested from the government to prevent the collapse of the company in early 1912. Their request went unheeded, as did Mueller's for a subsidy, since the government had no intention of spending such funds on the airfield company. Finally, the convention attempted to eliminate the techniques of cutthroat competition by preventing firms from stealing one another's patents and employees.[58]

There was no reference to any need for protecting the industry's interests in its relationship with the army. Initially the convention did not even interfere in the military-industrial relationship,

and only on 14 September did General Secretary Curt Sperling of the Association of German Motor Vehicle Industrialists inform General von Lyncker of the convention's existence as a central agency for the industry. Sperling asserted that the convention would facilitate the close military-industrial cooperation necessary to overtake French aviation by offering a channel through which the military could influence the industry.[59] Yet the Research Unit interpreted the convention's first intervention in its affairs, when the general secretary suggested moving aircraft trials from Doeberitz to Johannisthal and awarding subsidies to companies, as unwarranted interference.[60]

This latent hostility erupted in January 1912, when LVG, which was not a member of the convention and was on poor terms with the members because it was owned by Arthur Mueller, accused the Convention of being a syndicate in a letter to the Inspectorate. The army would benefit, according to the letter, by giving large contracts to LVG, which could transact business more freely since it was not beholden to the convention.[61] Colonel Messing reacted quickly with short, threatening letters to members of the convention, in which he concluded:

> The observation of that firm [*LVG*] that it can deal freely and unrestrictedly with the army because it remains outside of the syndicate could lead to the conclusion that the syndicate is directed against the army.
>
> The Inspectorate would sincerely regret this, because it would then be forced to take countermeasures in the army's interests. It therefore kindly requests an explanation.[62]

The firms, well aware of the seriousness of the situation, replied immediately, all vehemently denying that the Convention was directed against the army.[63] As Edmund Rumpler succinctly explained, "No reasonable man saws off the branch he sits on." Opposition to the army, the major customer and supporter of aviation technology, would be absurd. On the contrary, the industry most fervently desired to keep the army's trust in their cooperative venture to develop German aviation. Richard Goetze, business director of the Dorner Aircraft Company, was certain that the entire industry realized implicitly the necessity of working hand in hand with the army, since to do otherwise would mean virtual suicide.

Richard von Kehler and Georges Chatel, business directors of the Wright and Aviatik companies, respectively, explained that the Convention was not a syndicate, which Kehler defined as "a union of manufacturers or sellers that gives its members specific guidelines on prices for their products and punishes their noncompliance with penalties for breach of contract." The association had never set prices or placed the penalty of breach of contract on any of its member's sales. Nor had it set prices for the training of military personnel at the factories. The manufacturers had discussed the training prices among themselves after an earlier conference with the Inspectorate, but only to achieve clarity. The Convention had placed no penalties, regulations, or price limits on the training of officers or on planes destined for the Prussian Army.

Rumpler even declared that all of the Convention's strivings were "directly in the interest of the army," since the army's aim—a healthy, powerful airplane industry that would be sufficiently strong to meet any emergency demands—coincided with that of the industry. The members of the Convention, in Rumpler's opinion, were just as unrestricted in their dealings with the military as any outsider, and LVG's products were neither more capable nor cheaper than theirs. He regarded LVG's accusa-

✠ *Fokker Spinnes at Anthony Fokker's flying school in Schwerin in 1913. Courtesy of Peter Grosz.*

tions as an underhanded attempt to ingratiate itself at the expense of the other firms. In explaining his colleagues' reasons for forming the Convention, Rumpler particularly emphasized their difficulties with the Johannisthal Airfield Company.

The Convention had no intention of challenging the Prussian Army, because the manufacturers agreed with the army's policy of free competition. The firms would not restrict their competition substantially, since the number of army contracts was insufficient to support them all. The Convention did not attempt to confront the army's consumer monopoly with a producer monopoly of the syndicated industry; instead, it limited its action to such noncontroversial measures as delivery guidelines in its relationship with the army. The fact that its members accepted the necessity of free competition eroded any real influence that the Convention might have wielded in bargaining with the army; the manufacturers still acted as individuals. In their business with other trade organizations, however, they considered themselves a collective, an industry, because in these cases a unified approach was imperative, attainable, and clearly in the interest of all the member firms.

The risk of reprisals also lessened the likelihood that the firms would take any important concerted action against the army. The General Inspectorate was capable of drastic countermeasures, the worst of which would have been to stop issuing contracts for a limited period of time. Despite its desire to encourage the industry, the General Inspectorate did not yet value the military worth of the airplane so highly that it would tolerate attempts by the manufacturers' group to force concessions from it.

In a sense, however, the army's anxiety over the Convention was justified. Although the development of military aviation was their mutual goal, the specific interests of the industry did not in fact coincide with those of the army. The Inspectorates were interested in a slower rate of expansion and fewer contracts than the aircraft industry. Most basically, the divergence resulted from their opposite roles—the army as customer and the industry as producer and seller. In any dispute between the army and the industry, the disunity among the firms gave the army a key advantage. A consensus or lessening of the competition that the aircraft manufacturers' association might provide would undermine the military's strong position. In the future the Convention might become the focal point for any opposition of the aircraft industry to the army's policies. In spite of the industry's small size and scope and the fact that the army considered it far from vital, the Inspectorate recognized the Convention's potential as a future unifier of opposition to the army's control and warned the manufacturers early that it would countenance neither interference from nor collusion among them. Competition was to reign within the industry.

The General Inspectorate's policies on pilot training, on aircraft procurement and repairs, and on the industry's employment of foreign designers and businessmen helped to preserve competition among the firms, as did its continued practice of reproducing foreign aircraft; there were even a few new entries into the field of aircraft production at this time.

After its creation in April 1911 the Instruction and Research Institute trained most army pilots, although officers could learn to fly at the factories if they or the firm paid. Because of the growing need for pilots, after 1 February 1912 the factories whose planes were used by the army began the training, which the Institute completed. The flight training of each officer cost the army 5,000 marks, a source of income to the firms second only to airplane contracts. Because crashes in pilot training were frequent and sometimes costly, the Inspectorate also agreed to pay the cost of repairs on training planes if the company could prove that the officer pilot trainee was to blame for the damage. The General Inspectorate, making certain not to become dependent on one firm, spread the first consignment of officers rather evenly among the firms: Albatros received twelve; Rumpler and Aviatik, eight apiece; LVG and Euler, five apiece; the Harlan company, four; and Dorner, two.[64]

The airplane procurement relationship between the Prussian Army and the firms began with the manufacturers' advertisement of the aircraft, since the army made no attempt to seek them out. If the Inspectorate knew beforehand that a plane's performance was inferior, it declined the offer outright. On the other hand, if the plane showed promise and the Inspectorate needed more airplanes, the Instruction and Research Institute invited the company to present the plane for trials at the army field at Doeberitz. If the airplane passed the tests, the Inspectorate and the firm settled on a price and signed a contract, which included the army's right of construction inspection.[65]

Certain procurement regulations, though based on the premise of competition, favored the larger firms. The Prussian Army ordered one prototype of the prize-winning planes of certain large contests like the Circuit of Germany Flight, the Saxon Flight, the Upper Rhine Flight, and the Kiel Week. The largest factories—Albatros, Rumpler, and Aviatik—did best in these contests, not only because their aircraft were good, but also because they had the money to raise the army of automobiles, technicians, master craftsmen, and laborers for repairing and refueling aircraft at forced landings.[66] In the fall of 1911 the smaller firms were placed at a further disadvantage in securing military contracts when the Inspectorate reserved the right to raise its requirements for airplanes whose construction and delivery took from two and one-half to four months.[67] These regulations were designed to keep the army's airplane fleet up to date, but their primary side-effect was to hasten the decline of smaller firms.

After the army took delivery of the planes, the factories still had to repair them, because the military had neither the personnel nor the facilities to perform extensive repairs.[68] The Inspectorate conceded in June 1911 that it could not keep abreast of repairs on the increasing number of army machines, yet it feared that an increased reliance on the factories risked straining the budget.[69] In September the War Department's transport section, preferring to rely on the industry, refused to increase military repair facilities in order to avoid unnecessary competition with the industry.[70] This factory arrangement worked well, but only with the relatively limited number of airplanes in the peacetime air fleet.

The army assumed a protective stance toward the domestic aircraft industry in relation to international competition. It continued to bar foreign competitors and to buy foreign aircraft from German firms, which were using French, English, and Austrian airplanes as production prototypes and then selling them to the army. Rumpler made his fortune producing the Taube, a plane created by the Austrian Igo Etrich, and LVG copied the French Farman and Nieuport aircraft for its first successful types. Albatros bought two Morane monoplanes and a Breguet biplane as prototypes in 1911 and then sold the Breguet to the army.[71] In November, DFW of Leipzig, which used a Farman and a Nieuport as production models, announced its entry into competition for military contracts.[72] In early 1912 the German Bristol Works was founded in Halberstadt with 200,000 marks capital to produce under license the planes of the English Bristol and Colonial

Aeroplane Company. The offer that the army greeted most enthusiastically came from Walter Rathenau, the director of AEG, who volunteered to buy a Breguet with patents for 300,000 or 400,000 marks and then to produce them in the AEG factory if the army would buy twenty-five the first year. Although General von Lyncker wanted AEG to enter airplane production, he believed that the General Inspectorate could not afford such a large commitment to a new, untested firm. The matter was resolved when AEG built such a successful unlicensed copy of the Breguet that it began construction of an aircraft factory near Hennigsdorff, five miles north of Spandau, near Berlin.[73] Saving the expense of a patent meant that AEG no longer needed guarantees of military contracts to take the risk of aircraft production. The duplication of successful foreign airplanes thus enabled existing firms to profit from the technical expertise of more experienced builders and encouraged new companies to enter production, while the army learned the characteristics of foreign aircraft and gained a more competitive domestic aircraft industry.

The army was not disturbed when foreign nationals held important positions in the domestic aircraft industry, so long as they maintained no foreign connections that might damage the industry in wartime. Otto Wiener, Albatros's aggressive business director, was Austrian, as were Edmund Rumpler and some of the stockholders of the Rumpler firm, although Rumpler, a resident of Germany for twelve years, was applying for German citizenship.[74] LVG began full-scale production so successfully in February 1912 because it had hired the famous Swiss designer Franz Schneider from the French Nieuport firm. The Dutchman Anthony Fokker founded his first factory in February 1912 in partnership with two Germans, who served as figureheads to offset any liability caused by Fokker's foreign nationality.[75] That Fokker soon became sole owner of the Fokker Airplane Construction Company without surrendering his Dutch citizenship indicates the army's lack of concern about the employment of productive foreigners in the industry.

While such new firms as DFW, LVG, and Fokker were beginning production in the winter of 1911–1912, older companies were expanding. On 15 December, for example, August Euler opened a new factory of five large hangars and workshops sufficient for thirty airplanes in Frankfort on the Main. The extremely patriotic tone of his letter announcing the new factory to the army reflects the general "national awakening" in the fall of 1911 in Germany that resulted from the Moroccan crisis of the previous summer.[76] Because of the crisis, Edmund Rumpler increased the capital invested in his factory from 120,000 marks to 354,000 marks in anticipation of military contracts.[77]

Thus the aircraft industry, expecting more contracts from the Prussian Army, was growing rapidly. But contracts were not forthcoming, because the War Ministry and the General Inspectorate remained ambivalent toward the airplane. Although many of the army's policies encouraged the growth of the industry, the most critical measure of its support—the number of contracts awarded—reveals that such encouragement was limited. The Prussian Army procured only twenty-nine planes at prices ranging from 17,800 marks to 25,000 marks (including engines) from April 1911 to April 1912, and Albatros and Rumpler alone supplied twelve and ten of them, respectively. The Prussian Army had nineteen flyable airplanes in the summer of 1911 and thirty by the end of the year.[78] This situation disturbed Major Thomsen of the General Staff, who believed that the airplane was

✳ *The DFW factory. A Mars biplane under construction in 1913. Courtesy of Peter Grosz.*

simpler to handle, service, house, and prepare for flight, and was faster and harder to shoot down than the airship.[79] The General Staff consequently advocated that the airplane be given priority over the airship in meetings of the Cologne Commission in June and September 1911.

The first conference of the Commission passed a supplementary credit of 1,300,000 marks to establish and equip two air stations at Metz and Strasbourg, although the resulting contracts were obviously insufficient to fuel a national airplane industry. In the second meeting, Ludendorff asked that part of the budget designated for airships be reallocated to supplement the 3,391,000 marks proposed for airplanes in 1912. Although the War Ministry and the General Inspectorate did consent to use a proposed airship battalion for airplanes, they still refused priority and more funds to heavier-than-air craft. In the opinion of War Minister General Josias von Heeringen, the airship remained safer, had a longer range, and was more suitable for reconnaissance than the airplane.[80] In November 1911, when Chief of the General Staff General von Moltke requested a total of 116 planes on the army rolls by October 1912, the War Ministry intended to procure only an additional thirty-four by that date, which would mean a total of sixty-four. When the Ministry decided in March 1912 to increase its procurement to ninety-one by October 1912, Moltke's demands had long since increased.[81]

The General Inspectorate intended to concentrate its meager orders with the producers of the best aircraft in order to ensure the operation of a sufficient number of capable firms in case of a mobilization emergency. As the agency supervising the industry's mobilization and exemptions in time of war, the Inspectorate would contact Rumpler, Albatros, Aviatik, and Euler for airplanes and airframes, while all aircraft factories would be required to place their plant and material at the army's disposal.

The army General Commands in the areas where factories were located commissioned qualified officers to exempt directors, important engineers, and skilled workers so that the factories could maintain maximum production in wartime.[82] In the meantime, while peace reigned, Colonel Messing had no intention of increasing the Inspectorate's orders merely to support a larger industry. This policy, in combination with the blossoming of new factories lured by the hopes and rumors that the Prussian Army was ready to spend huge sums on airplanes, resulted in a depression in the airplane industry by early 1912.[83]

There was little hope for factories, including established ones, who could not develop successful airplanes. Two aircraft companies—the Dorner and Wright firms—were in particularly dire straits because of their inability to produce a successful airplane and the resulting forfeiture of army contracts. Although they lingered until later in 1912, both the Dorner and Wright companies received their critical blows in the winter of 1911–1912.

The crash of the Dorner company's best airplane and the death of its renowned pilot, Georg Schendel, on 6 June 1911 dashed any hope of victory in the Circuit of Germany Flight, upon which future military contracts depended. Dorner wrote to foreign and German financiers during the winter in an unsuccessful attempt to raise the capital necessary for the company's survival. Under these circumstances, the failure of his airplane to pass the army trials in December 1911 was to be expected. The firm was in the red 36,862.69 marks by August 1912, and new sources of capital were nonexistent. A company meeting on 22 August 1912 liquidated the Dorner Aircraft Company.[84]

Like the Dorner company, the Wright company was in severe difficulty by early January 1912. The belief of the East German writer K. D. Seifert[85] that the Wright company, because of the participation of the AEG and the trust of the emperor, achieved a "truly extensive production" of one hundred planes in five years seems unjustified because the Wright company pleaded in January 1912 for military contracts to prevent its collapse. The contracts, however, were not forthcoming, since twice, in mid-1911 and in early 1912, the company failed to deliver airplanes for scheduled acceptance trials at Doeberitz field. Overtaxed by the high cost of its license, which amounted to 200,000 marks in cash and 200,000 marks in shares of its 600,000 marks capital, the Wright company fell behind the rest of the German aircraft firms.[86] Finally, at the end of 1912 the ownership of the Wright company was transferred to *Luftfahrzeuggesellschaft* (LFG), a firm connected to one of the Wright company's original shareholders, the Motor Airship Study Company.

Even thriving established factories like Rumpler and Albatros and newer successful ones like DFW and LVG requested in early December that the Prussian Army send them officers for pilot training during the winter. Otherwise, they would have to release their workers and close, because they had not received sufficient contracts to maintain their growing plants. Messing agreed to assign more officers to the factories for training only because he recognized that the industry might collapse, but he still had no immediate intentions of placing orders.[87] Since the industry had no market other than the military, this refusal to issue substantial contracts exacerbated its problem of lack of demand. There was no civilian market for airplanes, in that most civilian pilots were actually financed by the firms themselves, and prizes from the air shows were insufficient to support a company. After the pilot's share, which was usually one-third of the contest award, and the damages and losses were deducted from the prize money, company profits were at best meager. In any case, the same firms that received military contracts usually won the contest.

The blame for the dismal circumstances in the airplane industry has been laid at the door of German private interests and the government, particularly the military. Compared with their French counterparts, German private interests contributed little to airplane development.[88] Rather than assume the risks involved in the development of the airplane from its earliest stages, private capital preferred to wait until the army's interest assured it of a profitable investment. The German military was not the enthusiastic customer that the French authorities were.[89] While an energetic airplane industry already existed in France, the energies of capable pilots and engineers lay fallow for want of money in Germany, as Major Georg Neumann later observed. While the French had recognized the potential of the airplane as an instrument of warfare and had proceeded to spur its development with contributions and contracts, interest in airplanes in Germany remained remarkably dormant in exactly the circles that were indispensable to its survival.[90]

However, Neumann's assertions were not entirely correct. Civilian interest in military airplanes was not dormant, but growing rapidly.[91] By 1912 the German Air Fleet League had some 12,500 members, and its leaders were influential army and navy officers, businessmen, and administrators. Meanwhile, the German Aviators Association, to which the Air Fleet League belonged, had grown to comprise some seventy member associations with approximately 60,000 members. The Air Fleet League was pressing for a national fund for the airplane industry as of July 1911, and the Aviators Association, through its contest prizes and the popularization of the airplane by the contests, was furthering the cause of the airplane and the aircraft industry, however poor their efforts were in comparison with the French. Despite the general interest, private capital had preferred to wait until the military showed an interest in the airplane.

While the French military allocated 9,700,000 francs[92] for aviation in 1911, the Prussian Army granted 2,252,000 marks for airplanes of a total aviation budget of 4,382,600 marks.[93] The smaller investment in the German aircraft industry certainly reflects, in part, the inferiority of its airplanes, as compared with those of the French. In addition, the War Ministry and the General Inspectorate, though interested in airplanes, felt that other considerations (e.g., the preservation of Germany's superiority in airships) merited equal concern and funds. In any case, the army could not support all of the existing firms. If it had spread its contracts over the entire industry, the individual firms would not have sufficient work. However, not even the smaller number of top producers could survive on so few contracts. Yet time was of the essence, as the German aviation historian Hilmer von Buelow recognized later:

> The basic question at this time, so critical for the existence of the airplane industry, was whether the army would recognize in the airplane an instrument of warfare and thus rapidly promote military aviation, or whether the prevailing emphasis on the continued development of the airship would remain dominant, in which case military aviation, and the airplane industry, would perish.[94]

This bleak picture notwithstanding, military aviation and the airplane industry had come a long way since 1908. The industry was growing, and the Prussian Army's organizational development and policies toward the industry showed its slowly increasing interest in the airplane. The War Ministry and the General Inspectorate preferred to wait for German firms to develop a successful warplane before they invested substantial funds in the new technology. Meanwhile, they fostered interfirm competition in order to prevent the army's dependence on any one firm and to secure the best aircraft. A huge investment in the aircraft industry and standardization on a particular model at such an early stage of development would have been unnecessarily wasteful, since airplane types changed so rapidly in those years.

Yet the Prussian military bureaucracy may have erred in the other direction, that of economy. Had these agencies been less conservative about the airplane, the relative backwardness of the German industry might have served as incentive for them to invest more funds. Such a policy would certainly have contributed toward their stated goal of a strong national aircraft industry. Yet nothing, whether the General Staff's urging, reports on French aviation, or pleas from the firms, seemed to shake the War Ministry and the General Inspectorate from their policy of strict frugality. The industry needed more money to develop warplanes; the War Ministry and the General Inspectorate insisted on making their investment of substantial funds contingent on the prior existence of these warplanes. As of March 1912, there seemed no way out of the impasse.

✠ *In front of the DFW factory. The completed product—Mars biplane No. 4 in May 1913. Courtesy of Peter Grosz.*

# III. THE GROWTH AND MOBILIZATION OF NORTH GERMAN MILITARY AVIATION, 1912–1914

The Chief of the German General Staff, General von Moltke, was disappointed with the Cologne Commission's decision to proceed slowly with airplane development under the guidance of the General Inspectorate, but he could only reply, "We will not overtake the French in this manner."[1] Despite his attitude and the predicament of the airplane industry, the War Ministry and the General Inspectorate were clearly unwilling to promote a faster expansion of military aviation.

In a conference held on 18 April 1912, the War Ministry, the General Inspectorate, and the Inspectorate of Military Aviation and Motor Vehicles translated this general intent into specific guidelines for their relationship with the airplane factories. Present were Major General Messing of the Inspectorate, Lieutenant Colonel Paul Meister and Captain Karl Gruetzner of the General Inspectorate, and Colonel Schmiedecke and Majors Ernst Hasse and Ernst von Wrisberg of the War Department. They first reaffirmed the War Ministry's ultimate control over procurement and the stipulation requiring the General Inspectorate to obtain the Ministry's agreement when selecting aircraft firms for military deliveries. They reckoned then that the army's annual needs in 1913 and 1914, though greatly increased, would not exceed 200 airplanes. Calculating an average profitable annual productivity of from 30 to 35 aircraft per factory, the conferees estimated that this demand would support only six factories, or less than half the existing firms in Prussia. The War Ministry consequently sent the following letter to the Convention of Aircraft Industrialists on 6 May 1912:

> Given the constant increase in the number of aircraft factories, the fear that only a part of the factories can secure an assured existence under the present circumstances seems well-founded. In the immediate future it must be reckoned that the army will be almost the sole customer in the airplane market. At this time it cannot be perceived whether the interest in aviation, if it spreads, will lead to the dissemination of the airplane in our sports life. According to the French precedent, only a limited use in this area can be assumed in the beginning.
>
> Therefore, in the opinion of the War Ministry, it seems in the interest of the national aircraft industry that any further formation of aircraft factories occur only if they are large scale, well provided with capital, and build only types that are assured of success. The War Ministry recommends that the association [the Convention] impress this upon its circles.[2]

The Convention, which naturally agreed with these sentiments, published the warning in the official journal of the German Aviators Association, the *Deutscher Luftfahrer Zeitschrift*.[3]

With these three stipulations—large scale production, sufficient capital, and successful aircraft—the army attempted to dissuade small entrepreneurs from entering aircraft production. By the same token, the existing airplane manufacturers hoped to ward off the disaster possible if their number increased faster than military contracts could support them. The army's policy naturally tended to reinforce the industry's trend toward consolidation and to hasten the demise of individual small-scale builders, as the latter well knew. The illustrious German aviatrix Melli Beese, who owned a small flying school and workshop in Johannisthal, published a "Cry of Distress from German Aviation" in the newspaper *Vossischer Zeitung* of 14 September 1912 which concluded:

> Naturally the existing large firms do not want to have their comfortable, profitable mass production disturbed, and therefore they fight tooth and nail against any potentially capable technical competition.[4]

Such a statement, though partially true, gave too much credit to struggling inventors, most of whom were neither technically capable nor competitive. The larger firms were absorbing most of the innovative designers, who could thus continue their work unhampered by financial problems. Despite protests, the heyday of the small builder and solitary inventor had already yielded to the age of the larger, more stable firm with sufficient capital and technical manpower to experiment and develop more sophisticated aircraft while surviving the rigors of competition.

Reports in June and September 1912 noted that airplane companies still suffered from a lack of army contracts. In March 1913 the outlook remained unfavorable for the industry.[5] There were two interrelated reasons for this situation: the army's policies and the continued growth of the aircraft industry.

The War Department's transport section acknowledged in August the demands "from many sides" to hasten the development of military airplanes in Germany, but it gave three reasons for its inability to do this. First of all, the major determinants of the rate of growth were the War Ministry's and General Inspectorate's considerations of troop quality and organizational priorities. They concurred that since the Prussian Army lacked the trained flying instructors and service personnel necessary for a faster expansion, haste would result in a lowering of standards and quality.[6] It is conceivable that the notion of troop quality concealed a more basic reason of the War Ministry and the General Inspectorate for a moderate pace of development. Officer quality was essentially defined by War Minister von Heeringen and the head of the War Department General von Wandel in terms of social position and ideological outlook,[7] and a precipitous growth of military aviation might have brought about an unassimilable influx of bourgeois officers into the army.

Secondly, the General Inspectorate undoubtedly feared that a faster expansion of military aviation might make the new sector large enough to merit an independent agency, as Moltke was suggesting. Nevertheless, the outbreak of the Balkan War caused the War Ministry to replace the Instruction and Research Institute in April 1912 with a provisional Flying Troops command with central offices in Berlin and subordinate stations on Germany's eastern and western borders. Because the General Inspectorate had initially opposed this measure, the War Ministry replaced its chief of staff, Lieutenant Colonel Meister, with Colonel Schmiedecke of the War Department's transport section.[8] Major Albert Oschmann, formerly transport officer of the Metz garrison, in turn replaced Schmiedecke as head of the transport section. Meister's removal probably did little to affect the attitude of the General Inspectorate, because Messing, the chief of the In-

spectorate of Military Aviation and Motor Vehicles, was the key figure in the General Inspectorate's decisions on military aviation. Messing, however, was too powerful to be dislodged because of his rank and general importance to military aeronautics. Anthony Fokker declared that Lieutenant Franz Geerdtz, the adjutant of the Inspectorate, urged the speedier growth of aviation, but the older officers thwarted him.[9]

The provisional Flying Troops became permanent on 1 October 1912 and one year later achieved the status of an Inspectorate of Flying Troops with four battalions. The creation of this Inspectorate as the airplane agency under the Inspectorate of Military Aviation and Motor Vehicles denoted an increase in the importance of military aviation, but still no separation of aviation from transport. Although the officers of the Flying Troop battalions petitioned in December 1913 for a separate agency directly under the General Inspectorate with direct connections to the high command (i.e., the General Staff), the General Inspectorate refused, in part because it feared a loss of control over military aviation.[10] Only on 1 June 1914 did the War Ministry take the first step toward detaching aviation from transport by creating a separate aviation department in the War Department.

The third reason for a slow development of military aviation was "the lack of flyable airplanes, . . . continued crashes, and . . . the insufficient capability of the industry."[11] Since the War Ministry attributed much of this to the motor industry, after August 1912 the General Inspectorate would order the motors itself and dole them out to the firms, in the hope that the motor firms would deliver more punctually to the army. To grant more contracts to the industry under such circumstances made no sense to the War Ministry. The army was attempting to help the industry improve its airplanes in order to make them a safer, more reliable tool of war, but the industry would need time to achieve this. Consequently, until a certain plateau in the development of flying machines was attained, the army would place orders sufficient to fill out the formations, the reserves, and the training organization. Oschmann's contention that this careful systematic approach to the expansion of the airplane forces would assure success in the attempt to overtake the French was supported by General von Wandel, who recalled the setbacks in the navy's U-boat program caused by its unwarranted haste.[12]

The War Ministry and the General Inspectorate consequently refused to increase their orders merely because factories requested more in order to remain profitable. The General Inspectorate specifically refused to finance the expansion of its largest suppliers for fear that it might become dependent on them and thus hinder the "healthy development of competition."[13] In November 1913 the Inspectorate of Flying Troops considered the issue of too many contracts in general disadvantageous because designs changed so quickly that the army might be saddled with a surplus of obsolete airplanes.[14]

It is notable that money was not one of the major deciding factors listed by the War Ministry and the General Inspectorate. In December 1912 the war minister requested supplementary funds for aviation, since he then considered it possible to expand the aviation forces at a faster rate than originally estimated. The imperial treasury accepted these demands as a part of the military budget for 1913, and the expansion of the transport troops and aviation forces surged ahead financially, as table 4 shows.

✱ *A Rumpler Taube at Berlin-Doeberitz military airfield on 21 April 1914. Courtesy of the* Bundesarchiv, Koblenz.

Once the decision was made to move ahead more quickly in aviation, the War Ministry was able to secure the funds from the treasury, the chancellor, and the imperial parliament. It is evident, then, that bureaucratic, technical, and personnel considerations were the major determinants of the growth of military aviation, with budgetary considerations a secondary factor.

*Table 4.* PRUSSIAN MILITARY AVIATION
BUDGETS, 1909–1914[*]
*(in marks)*

| Year | Total Annual Appropriation (Airships and Airplanes) | Portion for Airplanes |
|---|---|---|
| 1909 | 3,194,050 | 36,000 |
| 1910 | 3,849,550 | 300,000 |
| 1911 | 4,382,600 | 2,252,000 |
| 1912 | 7,023,150 | 3,391,250 |
| 1913 | 31,267,350 | 15,612,000 |
| 1914 | 52,525,950 | 25,920,000 |

[*] KAdL, *Militaerluftfahrt*, I, 264; II, Chart 106.

Meanwhile, the successful airplane manufacturers exhibited a steady drive toward concentration, although new firms continued to sprout. The factories constantly expanded in hope of encouraging more contracts, although their growing production facilities could never be fully utilized in peacetime. Rumpler, for example, informed the army on 24 October 1912 that he had invested 350,000 marks in his plant to double his production capacity to four or five planes weekly, or from 200 to 250 annually. Of course, he would need the army's cooperation (i.e., contracts) to preserve his firm's peak capacity for mobilization. In mid-1913 the worth of Rumpler's factory reached nearly one million marks, as he actively responded to "repeated military suggestions" that the factories be prepared for "expected extraordinarily increased demands in time of mobilization."[15] Such expanding older firms were joined by new ones. The army's contracts increased from 24 in 1911 to 130 in 1912 and 432 in 1913, but so had the number of its airplane manufacturers, from 7 in 1911 to 9 in 1912 and 11 in 1913.[16] The abundance of factories consequently compensated for the increase in contracts.

Nevertheless, the War Ministry and the General Inspectorate adhered to their policy of May 1912 by encouraging the entry of large diversified industrial enterprises, because they believed that such companies could maintain their aircraft production indefinitely even without sufficient contracts[17] and consequently relieve the army of any responsibility for their livelihood. This attitude conditioned the response of the General Inspectorate to large companies like AEG in early 1912 and the *Gothaer Waggonfabrik* (Gotha) in early 1913. Although the War Ministry and the General Inspectorate encouraged AEG to enter production in 1912, they extended no commitments in return. When Gotha offered to establish a richly equipped airplane factory whose capacity could be expanded or deflated as necessary, the General Inspectorate gave its approval. It even rejected an attempt by Albatros to undercut the new proposal with an offer of a flying school and factory on the same airfield. Yet, after the formation of the factory's new airplane department, the General Inspectorate's policy was to demand business-as-usual procedures, avoiding commitments and leaving the firm to compete on equal terms with the others. By late October 1913, Gotha was in a predicament similar to that of the other airplane factories, requesting contracts in order to keep its aircraft workers employed.[18] Its pleas notwithstanding, the Gotha factory delivered the substantial number of thirty-six airplanes to the Prussian Army in 1913, and by February 1914 the War Ministry rated it seventh and AEG ninth among the top eleven north German aircraft firms.[19]

The increasing competition finally prompted the general secretary of the Union of German Motor Vehicle Industrialists to write the General Inspectorate on behalf of the Convention of Aircraft Industrialists in February 1914.[20] General Secretary Sperling warned that the anticipated formation of new airplane factories would lead to overproduction; so he requested another press notice from the army similar to the one of 6 May 1912 stating that new aircraft factories were unnecessary and could not count on contracts. The army refused. Major General Messing stated that the circumstances in 1914 were entirely different from those in 1912 and denied that the industry was so highly developed that it could not benefit from the competition of new firms. In any case, the army alone, not the factories, decided which firms received contracts.[21] General Adolf Wild von Hohenborn, who had replaced General von Wandel as head of the War Department, observed that even if the present factories could fulfill current needs, the demand might increase in the future. The War Ministry thus reserved the right to include progressive new firms in its orders and refused to hinder the formation of new airplane companies or to withhold contracts from new factories.[22]

When the firms' direct approach failed, they had other methods of trying to secure more contracts from the army. Although the Convention of Aircraft Industrialists usually asked the army to limit its orders to established firms, in at least one case it resorted to its own measures without the army's approval. In June 1913 the motor factories could not deliver punctually to certain new firms that did not belong to the Convention, because members of the Convention had cornered the market by securing prior rights to large production series of their engines. General Karl Heinrich von Haenisch, who replaced General von Lyncker as general inspector in 1913, concluded that certain members of the Convention were attempting to establish a blockade of motors in order to make the military authorities more dependent on them. The General Inspectorate thwarted this attempt simply by executing more rigorously its policy of the summer of 1912. It ordered the motors directly from the engine factories and distributed them to the airplane manufacturers. Now serial delivery of motors to the army's airplane factories could not occur without the army's consent. As this incident showed, any measures taken by the industry without the army's consent had the inherent drawback that the army could always take countermeasures once it discovered the plan.[23]

Influential personages were useful as members of founding committees and boards of trustees of the airplane factories. An even better way to bridge the gap between the industry and the army was to employ somebody intimately acquainted with the military, preferably a former army officer. In 1913 one airplane company openly advertised for the services of a former officer with good contacts to represent it in its dealings with the army. In the imperial parliament the Social Democrat Gustav Noske condemned such methods as unfair ploys of the airplane industry to secure contracts from the army.[24] There is no concrete evidence on the results of such methods, but one can surmise that while the endorsement of an influential person undoubtedly helped a firm establish itself financially, its survival depended basically on the success of its airplanes. The Prussian Army attempted to deal impartially even with firms of the size and importance of AEG, and the division of authority between the General Inspectorate and the War Ministry provided an administrative safeguard against favoritism.

Yet an incipient scandal in mid-1914 indicated that ways might

exist to circumvent the army's defenses against partiality. Two former employees of the Albatros company informed the army that Albatros was presenting gifts worth over 200 marks to its officer pilot trainees for them to recommend the firm to the army. They intended to place an article in the newspaper *Die Welt am Montag*, since the regulations stated that only a pin worth 36 marks could be given to the pilots upon completion of their course at the factories. Although the officers in question swore that they had received no gifts, Albatros was certainly capable of resorting to such sales procedures in view of business director Wiener's attempt in 1912 to undercut Aviatik.[25]

The aircraft industry was left with one tactic to pry more contracts from the Prussian Army—the threat of contracts with foreign governments. The superiority of French airplanes and their domination of the European market had originally closed foreign markets to the Germans. Only in early 1914, when German airplanes had begun to wrest world records from the French, were they able to compete on the international market. In April 1914, Austria-Hungary and Turkey sent military missions to Germany to purchase aircraft for their armies. More important were inquiries from Russian enterprises, which had previously clung to the coattails of the French with the exception of a few isolated firms.

The first example of industrial connections with Russia came to light in January 1913, when an anonymous "true patriot" informed the War Ministry that the Wright company was training three Russian officers and had received large contracts for aircraft from the Russian government. A Wright company engineer

confirmed that the Russian government had ordered 6 airplanes, but said that further orders of 18 and 250 aircraft had been canceled.[26] The authenticity of this claim, in view of the poor performance of Wright airplanes and the Russian Army's ownership of superior French machines, is doubtful. The Wright company apparently initiated this contact in order to elicit more contracts from the Prussian Army. Its dealings with the Russian government coincided with its unsuccessful attempt in December 1912 to secure a contract for 12 planes a year from the Prussian Army and permission to build a factory-flying school in Posen for the eastern flying stations.[27]

In 1914 Russian companies did inquire about airplanes at Aviatik and DFW, two of the most competent German firms. In February a consortium in Odessa asked Aviatik to establish a branch there, and in May the Russian airplane factory E. Anatra of Odessa asked DFW to sell it one of DFW's new biplanes for licensed construction. Aviatik informed the Inspectorate of Military Aviation and Motor Vehicles that it would act according to the decision of the General Inspectorate, because its livelihood depended on the Prussian Army. Messing's answer that the General Inspectorate would dislike the idea seems to have satisfied Aviatik. In any case it had already decided to decline the offer. If the consortium offered again, however, Aviatik intended to request a decision directly from the General Inspectorate. DFW desired to sell the plane to Anatra, although it promised to present all new models first to the Prussian Army and, if requested, to curtail foreign sales.[28]

The Prussian Army's reaction to the offer to Aviatik demonstrated the success of this method of securing more contracts. The Inspectorate of Military Aviation and Motor Vehicles felt that Aviatik's participation in the Russian enterprise was undesirable but doubted that Aviatik would continue to subordinate

✱ *A Rumpler Taube shortly after takeoff from the Cologne-Longerich military airfield in 1913/1914. Courtesy of the* Bundesarchiv, Koblenz.

its interests in this way. Since the army had no power to prevent a firm's participation in a foreign undertaking in peacetime, Major General Messing proposed to the General Inspectorate that Aviatik be encouraged to build a branch inside Germany in order to reserve its production for the German military.[29] The army naturally could not afford to lose its best producers or their products to potential enemies; therefore it had to induce them to limit themselves to domestic production. A threatened cancellation of contracts risked the loss of the firm, and, however remote the possibility of such a development, Messing preferred not to risk it. The Russian offers thus had potential value to the firms as a lever to pressure more contracts from the Prussian Army, but the outbreak of hostilities in August 1914 curtailed further bargaining. Otherwise, if the army had not given Aviatik more contracts, the firm undoubtedly would have participated in the Russian venture. Large armaments firms like Krupp supplied equipment to the Russians right up to July 1914 on the grounds that this was the only way to experiment and maintain capacity given the War Ministry's limited number of contracts and its reliance on its own technical institutes.

Thus despite the rise of Prussian military aviation from 1912 to 1914, the aircraft industry never received sufficient contracts to fill its capacity because the number of firms grew apace, encouraged by the Prussian Army. Ironically, the army's very desire to have productive capacity available, coupled with its unwillingness to finance the industry's expansion, was causing firms to seek additional orders from other sources. Knowledge of this situation is essential to the comprehension of the developments

✱ *A Rumpler Taube on its nose at Cologne-Longerich military airfield in 1913/1914. Courtesy of the* Bundesarchiv, Koblenz.

discussed in the following chapters, because the north German airplane industry's search for additional markets figures prominently in all of them.

## THE NATIONAL AVIATION FUND AND SPORT AVIATION

Fund-raising campaigns to supplement defense budgets in times of national crisis have occurred in several states in the twentieth century, including imperial Germany. Two national campaigns played an important role in the development of German aviation before World War I: the Zeppelin Fund in 1908 and the National Aviation Fund in 1912. Since the Zeppelin Fund had been instrumental in persuading the Prussian War Ministry to accept the Zeppelins for military service before they met its requirements and had also provided Count Zeppelin with the money to found a new airship company,[30] the lesson that substantial voluntary contributions could influence the course of military-industrial relations was not lost on certain observers.

At the nadir of the fortunes of German military aviation and the aircraft industry, a proclamation announced on 21 April 1912 the creation of a National Aviation Fund for German aviation, "because the active support of the entire nation is due the men, who, as pioneers in a great new cultural task, risk their lives in the patriotic endeavor to secure for Germany in this area an equal place in the universal struggle of nations." In this "hour of national danger," Germany had to protect her reputation for preeminence in applied science and assure her honored place in history by making the German nation "the powerful motor that would drive her planes to victory" in time of peace and war. Recalling the tremendous enthusiasm engendered by the earlier Zeppelin Fund, the announcement concluded with the rousing slogan "For the People! By the People!"[31] Although Clemens von Delbrueck, the secretary of state of the Imperial Office of the Interior, described the proclamation as "devoid of chauvinism,"[32] its emphasis on such terms as "culture" and "struggle of nations" is a prime example of the conscious German nationalism of the era of imperialism preached by professors and other propagandists. A cartoon in the magazine *Kladderadatsch* portrayed a winged Germania soaring above a uniformed Gallic cock glaring up from a dungheap.[33] Postcards, medals, parades, photos—all celebrated the feats of German aviators, as organizations like the Aviators Association and the Air Fleet League strove to arouse interest in the fund.[34]

The National Aviation Fund was significant for German military aviation, the airplane industry, and aeronautical technology because it affected the airplane, the machine of the future, and not the airship, the creation of the transitional era from lighter- to heavier-than-air powered flight. The Fund merits particular attention because it presents an opportunity to observe the critical interaction of the German public, civilian interest groups, and agencies of the civilian government in military-industrial affairs.

Unlike the Zeppelin Fund, its predecessor and model, the National Aviation Fund's campaign was not spontaneous. The idea of the campaign had occurred to August Euler,[35] whose former flying pupil, Prince Heinrich of Prussia, had become the patron of German aviation. It is quite likely that Euler broached the idea to the military and civilian authorities on the occasion of the Universal Aviation Exhibition, which was held in early April in Frankfort on the Main.[36] The exhibition's honorary committee included not only such notables as War Minister General von Heeringen, Secretary of State of the Imperial Naval Office Admiral von Tirpitz, General von Lyncker, Colonels Messing and Schmiedecke, but also Dr. Heinrich Albert and Dr. Theodor

Lewald, higher bureaucrats in the Imperial Office of the Interior, who would later serve on the Fund's committees and board of trustees.

Under Prince Heinrich's patronage an imperial committee of men from business, government, and industry sponsored the proclamation and the campaign. The retired secretary of state of the Interior, Count Arthur von Posadowsky Wehner, the banker Franz von Mendelsohn, and Dr. Albert became, respectively, president, treasurer, and business director of the imperial committee. They turned immediately to the imperial German government, specifically the Office of the Interior, for support, a logical choice considering the presence of Posadowsky Wehner and Albert on the committee and the precedent of the office's representation on the honorary committee of the Universal Aviation Exhibition.

Secretary of State Clemens von Delbrueck personally took the matter in hand, because he considered aviation so important that Germany could not afford the "unpleasant impression" that a failure of the Fund would create, particularly in foreign countries. Delbrueck knew that a structured national organization would have to substitute for the spontaneous mass participation of the Zeppelin Fund, since the Aviation Fund lacked a popular personality like Count Zeppelin and a catalyst like the dramatic crash of the dirigible LZ – 4 at Echterdingen. He wrote the governments of the German states to secure their cooperation, and a network of Fund committees was established by May 1912. Some cities had amassed independent contributions of almost 500,000 marks and were reluctant to merge them with the Fund. At Delbrueck's suggestion, Emperor Wilhelm had these contributions transferred to the National Aviation Fund with the promise that the army would name the planes bought with the money after the cities. In order to encourage contributions from the German royal families, the emperor sponsored a national aircraft motor competition with 50,000 marks from his private treasury, and the imperial committee invited Prince Regent Luitpold of Bavaria and Duke Ernst Guenther of Schleswig-Holstein to join its ranks. The government was inextricably involved in the Fund.[37]

The campaign was praised by all—with the exception of one vocal minority. In the session of the imperial parliament of 14 May 1912, the Social Democrats opened a scathing attack on the Fund with the statement, "Now we have not only a militarism on land, but also one in the air." In their opinion German "militarists," like those in other nations, were transforming a potential means of transportation into a weapon for mass murder. "Irresponsible advisers and agitators" were employing the new "airfleet patriotism" to press for more armaments and to defray the costs with the people's contributions, since the money collected would be given to the War Ministry and the Imperial Naval Office. The socialists also objected to the solicitation by certain aircraft companies (specifically Albatros) of a minimum contribution from their workers, to the contributions of profits from the canteens of German warships, and to collections from soldiers—actions which violated the voluntary nature of the Fund.[38] Their protests did not affect the course of the Fund.

The imperial committee reported in December that it had received 7,234,506.29 marks. Sizable donations had come from Germans as far away as Buenos Aires and Shanghai. 1,975,306.78 marks had been contributed for specific purposes: 1,060,018.81 marks for the Prussian Army's procurement of airplanes, 577,000 marks for an aviation research institute, and 338,287.97 marks for miscellaneous ends, with 5,212,199.51 marks remaining unassigned.[39]

The imperial committee entrusted the distribution of the unassigned five million marks to a board of trustees of from forty-five to fifty men in December 1912. Posadowsky Wehner, Mendelsohn, and Albert became, respectively, president, treasurer, and business director of the board; thus the top three officials of the imperial committee became the top officials of the board. In order to ensure that the board would dispose of the money according to the wishes of the government, Posadowsky Wehner arranged for the German chancellor to appoint ten members of the board and nonvoting advisers from the military and the civilian government. These appointments would assure the "necessary consideration of the transcendent military interest" in the distribution of the Fund.[40] The official representatives of government agencies—the Imperial Naval Office, and the Prussian Ministries of War, Commerce, Public Works, and the Interior—came as nonvoting advisers to give the Fund the appearance of a civilian enterprise.[41] Members of the Imperial Office of the Interior on the board—Drs. Lewald, Albert, and Trautmann—held their positions of first vice president, business director, and permanent representative of the business director as private citizens, just as did the few military men who were voting members of the board (for example, the now Major General Wilhelm Messing, chief of the Prussian Inspectorate of Military Aviation and Motor Vehicles).[42]

The German Aviators Association and the Convention of German Aircraft Industrialists, as the organization representing the airplane industry, also helped select the board. Euler, the chairman of the manufacturers' association, and Sperling, the general secretary of the Union of German Motor Vehicle Industrialists, were the most important representatives of the aircraft industry's interests. Thus a cross section of military men, government officials, and industrialists controlled the distribution of the National Aviation Fund.

The board of trustees promised openly that the contributions

would not be used to relieve state funds, thus implying their use either as a financial basis for civilian aviation and the aircraft industry or as a supplement for the military aviation budget. The key board positions held by civilian and military bureaucrats and their statements in private about the "transcendent military interest" suggested that military aviation would reap the major benefits from the board's execution of its self-appointed tasks. An examination of these tasks will determine whether in fact the Fund's priorities entailed aid primarily for military aviation or for the aircraft industry and civilian aviation. The National Aviation Fund provided the money for army airplanes and airbases, the German Research Institute for Aviation, pilot training, and the administration and prizes for airplane competitions and record-setting flights.

The Prussian Army bought sixty-two airplanes before August 1914 with the donations contributed for military aircraft (1,060,018.81 marks, plus interest and further donations). This money went directly to the army and never passed through the Fund treasury, although it was labeled part of the Fund. The army distributed the sixty-two extra contracts among its manufacturers in its effort to promote a competitive industry.[43] Following the wishes of the contributors, the army used this part of the Fund to promote military aviation, while the industry profited indirectly from the contracts granted to specific factories.

The army also indirectly controlled 120,000 marks given by the Fund for a network of twenty airfields around Germany. Officially the board awarded the money to the German Flight Association of Weimar, which had been founded on 1 March 1912 to create these bases for overland flights. It was understood, how-ever, that the Association, whose first vice president was the ubiquitous Major General Messing, would cooperate fully with the military authorities.[44]

On the other hand, the formation of the German Research Institute for Aviation, the culmination of two years of parliamentary agitation for an aeronautical agency, seemed designed to foster civilian aviation technology and the aircraft industry. In response to the original proposal from the Catholic Center party in 1910, Secretary of State of the Interior Clemens von Delbrueck had promised that the government would consider the matter. Inquiries from the National Liberal party in 1911 passed unnoticed. Only when the Fund granted 577,000 marks for the institute did the imperial parliament, undoubtedly encouraged by Delbrueck's description of the institute as a civilian enterprise with no connection to the military, then unanimously ratify a supplement of 250,000 marks for the agency.[45] The institute was to serve as a completely independent central agency for aeronautical research, and in this capacity it would perform practical tests on theoretical investigations, distribute the results in order to prevent unnecessary duplication, and encourage new research. The institute's contract with the Johannisthal Airfield Company bound the company to maintain the airfield until 1929 and thus helped assure the industry of a secure future. Its laboratories would solve technical and scientific problems that were beyond the capacity of the airplane firms.[46]

Despite Delbrueck's promises, the institute soon discarded its civilian emphasis, since the industry itself was oriented toward military aviation. In 1913 the institute offered to help with military aircraft acceptance tests, and by March 1914 it had contracted with the Prussian Army to perform its trials and research.[47] The army thus became the institute's major employer. The institute's preferential consideration of military needs hindered the broadest

✠ *A Taube. Courtesy of Peter Grosz.*

possible development of aviation technology and occasionally conflicted with the interests of the aircraft industry.

The board of trustees considered its first task to be the basic training of pilots to meet the needs of the aircraft industry and the army. Although the program was supposed to satisfy the demands of civilian aviation and the industry for pilots, these very same trainees would be placed at the army's disposal in time of mobilization. The pupils had to have a secondary education and to be fit for military service if they were not already reservists. There was no place for the civilian who simply wanted to learn how to fly, even if he could pay. The reservists had to enter the flying troop reserves and participate in four three-week maneuvers in the next two years, while the others committed themselves to enter the flying troops on 1 October 1913. By October 1913, 71 field pilots had been trained, 29 reservists and 42 others. After 1 October 1913 the requirements were relaxed to allow any person over eighteen years of age, without regard for his draft status, to enter the flying troop reserves if deemed suitable (e.g., equipped with technical training). By August 1914 the Fund had financed the training of 186 field pilots, and many more applicants underwent training but did not complete the requirements.[48]

The selection and training of Fund pilots were the complete responsibility of the aircraft factories, who also trained army officer pilots. The pupils learned to fly on military machines, since the board of trustees required a certificate of ownership of a military aircraft and previous experience in pilot training from the firms. The companies earned 8,000 marks for every trainee who passed the field pilot examination, but they would have to bear the training costs of those students who failed the field pilot test. August Euler, perhaps in order to divide the responsibility and costs of the training, had wanted the army's help in pupil selection,[49] but the army refused to have anything to do with the Fund's pilot training program.

Later, in the fall of 1913, the Convention of Aircraft Industrialists sought the army's cooperation in coordinating the training of army officers with that of civilian pupils sponsored by the Fund. Dr. Albert, the board's business director, asked the War Ministry if the army's inspection officers at the factories could check on Fund pupils, since the program was in the army's interests. The Inspectorate of Military Aviation and Motor Vehicles and its subordinate, the recently created Inspectorate of Flying Troops, refused. Instead they complained that the training of civilians interfered with that of army officers. On 20 March 1914 the Fund curtailed its pilot training program because it could not afford to pay officials to supervise the factory schools. Any contracts still in effect when the war began were immediately dissolved. The Prussian Army, while ultimately benefiting from the project as much as the industry, had contributed nothing to it and indeed was instrumental in its demise.[50]

Yet it was the final endeavor of the National Aviation Fund—its sponsorship of aircraft competitions through the German Aviators Association and thus supposedly of sport aviation—that held forth the prospect of immediate benefit to the sagging aircraft industry. Sport aviation, in which individuals or private groups owned and flew aircraft, did not exist in Germany to any notable extent. Lacking a private market for airplanes, the industry concentrated on producing relatively large, slow, and stable airplanes to meet the military requirements and neglected the development of cheaper, smaller, and lighter aircraft that private individuals could afford. As the German Aviators Association described the situation, the principle dominating other sports, that the sport lead the industry and not vice versa, was impossible to follow in aviation because of the tremendous expense entailed in securing and maintaining an airplane. Civilian aircraft were military types owned by the aircraft factories, which trained and paid private pilots to fly for them. The aircraft industry itself was the practitioner of the sport, and only the organization and funding of competitions were left to sport associations.[51]

Nevertheless, the highly developed organization of aviation sport associations represented by the German Aviators Association might have provided the basis for a domestic market for small private sport aircraft. As the official controlling body of German civil aviation and Germany's largest civilian aviation group, this association was the key to the development of the market. In contrast with the industry and individual flyers, it had been subsidized by the National Aviation Fund, enabling it to sponsor contests to popularize sport airplanes and possibly to buy airplanes until prices dropped to a level within the reach of the private consumer. Moreover, the Association professed to believe that the healthy competition of sport aviation would help maintain and develop the aircraft industry.[52]

The absence of sport aviation was considered by many, among them Secretary of State Delbrueck and the chief of the Bavarian Army's agency in charge of aviation, General Karl von Brug, to be the basic reason for the underdevelopment of German aviation.[53] In Delbrueck's opinion, the formation of the aircraft manufacturers' association, which "locked the factories and pilots into an economic organization," prevented the freedom necessary for sport aviation. General von Brug believed that the lack of intensive civilian participation in aviation was to blame for the industry's lagging growth and recommended that the Fund promote sport as well as military aviation. Delbrueck and Brug were justified in decrying the lack of civilian sport aviation; both erred, however, in attributing the cause either to the industry or to a lack of civilian participation. An examination of the contests held with Fund money reveals a subtler yet more pervasive factor contributing to the nondevelopment of sport flying.

The contests and air shows, though ostensibly intended to promote sport flying, actually prevented the development of civilian aviation and did less than they might have to help the industry and aviation technology. They involved distance and reconnaissance flights for military aircraft—slow, stolid, two-seater monoplanes and biplanes. They therefore served the army as maneuvers for its pilots and observers and as military acceptance tests for the industry's airplanes. The industry, however, was not so fortunate. The interval between contests was insufficient for firms to incorporate their acquired knowledge in new models. The contests unnecessarily duplicated the Fund's awards for individual distance and altitude records, and the over-concentration on expensive, exhausting overland flights no longer served the development of aviation technology.[54] The prizes were insufficient to compensate the industry for its expenditures and losses, since a disproportionate amount of the Fund's grants went to the Aviators Association for administrative costs.[55] Soon even these moderate rewards escaped the industry. By August 1913 the army pilots, who were superior to most civilian pilots, could accept the monetary prizes, which were often awarded to the top group of pilots in order to assure the army of the money. Since the officers flew for honor, the prize money flowed directly into the military treasury instead of to the industry, which financed the civilian competitors. The Prussian Flying Troops took these competitions seriously; victory for army flyers had to be assured by any and all means, because defeat would reflect upon the honor of the Prussian officers.[56]

One of the original goals of the Convention of Aircraft Industrialists had been to alter contest regulations in their favor. Consequently, the aircraft manufacturers group had entered the German Aviators Association in 1912 in order to make the industry's interests felt in that critically important body. For annual dues of 200 marks any firm that had produced three successful aircraft could become a member of the Convention and thus of the Aviators Association. August Euler, still the chairman of the Convention, and F. Rasch, the national business director of the Aviators Association, publicly portrayed the goals of the Convention and the Association in a positive light—the strengthening of the industry in order to overtake the French, the preservation of free competition, the prevention of contests damaging to the industry, and its corollary, the promotion of profitable contests.[57]

In late 1912 the Convention persuaded the Association to allow only its members to participate in Association air shows, a decision that was openly criticized in the Association for hindering competition. Yet Rasch, who was clearly willing to do whatever the Convention desired in order to keep it in the Association, excused the new regulation as a product of economic necessity. In reply to the criticism, Euler emphasized that the new rule applied only to large contests (i.e., those with more than seven entrants), denied that the new regulation limited free competition, and affirmed that the industry was solidly behind the new measure by praising the "outstanding unity" within the Convention.[58] Euler's distinction between large and small contests was meaningless, because the Association could ill afford to promote contests with fewer than seven entries. Yet the criticism within the Aviators Association that the new rule would hinder competition

was valid, because the Convention intended to limit the number of flying shows to the point where large and small firms could compete equally. However, Euler defined competition not in terms of the number of flying shows but in terms of the number of firms participating in each event.

The Convention pursued this policy because it was composed largely of the smaller, weaker aircraft companies, who would be the first to disappear given the tendency of unbridled competition toward monopoly. Euler and other small and medium sized companies had watched earlier as successful growing firms, themselves included, had forced lesser competitors out of business. Now they themselves were in danger of being routed by even larger, more successful companies. Euler and the Convention were attempting to decrease the number of instances of competition in order to preserve as many firms as possible.[59]

To influence contest regulations through the threat of a boycott, however, the Convention had to ensure the participation of all the major airplane manufacturers. The stipulation that only members of the Convention could participate in Association air shows was designed to do exactly that—force all the firms into the Convention. The large firms outside the Convention, Albatros and LVG, were in a quandary. They were too few to influence such matters outside the Convention, because it contained such productive firms as Rumpler and Aviatik. Yet within the Convention, even if they joined forces with its larger members like Rumpler and Aviatik, they would still be outnumbered, since each of the eleven member firms received one vote regardless of size. The intermediate stage of the aircraft industry's development—the technical and financial ascendancy of larger companies in the face of the continued numerical superiority of smaller firms—thus enabled Euler to pursue successfully a policy protecting the interests of the smaller aircraft companies.

✠ *Front view of Taube No. A26. Courtesy of Peter Grosz.*

A dispute over the rules of the third Reliability Flight on the Upper Rhine, more commonly called the Prince Heinrich Flight of 1913, precipitated the first crucial test of the convention's real power and influence in the Aviators Association. The contest, which was held the week of 10–17 May in honor of the patron of German aviation, was designed to measure the performance of the participating airplanes and to give the army experience and knowledge about aerial reconnaissance. Military airplanes were flown by officer pilots, and private aircraft—basically the same types but owned and sponsored by the industry—by civilians. After acceptance tests for the civilian airplanes, the contest consisted of three days of "reliability flights," in which the total flight time of each plane determined the winner, and two days of reconnaissance tests.

Prior to the contest, the Convention had complained to the Southwest Group of the Aviators Association, the organizers of the competition, about the absence of entry fees and acceptance tests for army airplanes. Baron von Oldershausen, the chairman of the Southwest Group, refused to drop these special privileges for the army.[60] The army pilots, as expected, won the top prizes. In October, Euler informed Oldershausen that the industry had decided not to participate in the Prince Heinrich Flight of 1914 unless it received assurances from the General Inspectorate that officers would be forbidden to participate in future contests. The industry's economic interests were at stake here, and it needed the prize money so desperately that it was willing to challenge the army indirectly over the question of officer participation in the contest. When Oldershausen replied that the General Inspectorate and Prince Heinrich himself desired civilian-military competition, Euler requested that the Southwest Group call a conference of the Convention, the General Inspectorate, and the Southwest Group to discuss the matter. Yet, within three weeks

on 14 November 1913, Oldershausen informed the General Inspectorate that a conference would not be necessary because the industry had agreed to participate in the Prince Heinrich Flight.[61] Clever maneuvering, if not outright deceit, on the part of the military had made the Convention its foil, as an examination of the sequence of events leading up to the November announcement reveals.

An anonymous article entitled "Should we remain active in sport aviation?" which appeared in the important German aviation magazine *Flugsport* on 15 October 1913,[62] aired the industry's desire to develop sport aviation and small, light monoplanes with engines under fifty horsepower. According to the author, military aviation stifled the development of sport aviation and light, fast airplanes because the army's control of the market and influence on the rules of the flying contests had led the industry to develop only heavy military aircraft that were too expensive for the private consumer. But now that the army had its standard aircraft and a sufficient number of aircraft manufacturers, the time had come to promote sport aviation and light aircraft, which even smaller firms might build profitably. In response to such encouragement, the Convention proposed a speed contest for such airplanes in August or September 1914 in order to have time to develop the planes.

When the General Inspectorate learned that the industry was not only considering a boycott of the Prince Heinrich Flight but also planning a contest of its own, the Inspector General, General von Haenisch, recommended that the speed contest be scheduled as part of the Prince Heinrich Flight in May 1914 in order to force the industry to compete in the reliability flight. The Convention then proposed a compromise to the Southwest Group: it would participate in the Prince Heinrich Flight in May if the Southwest Group persuaded the army to support a speed contest in September. At the request of the Southwest Group, aided by Prince Heinrich, the General Inspectorate withdrew its proposal for a May speed contest, and the industry committed itself to compete in the Prince Heinrich Flight. The General Inspectorate, however, never agreed to support the September speed competition, because it believed that speeds of more than seventy miles per hour were unnecessary and would only make observation more dangerous and difficult. Not only did General von Haenisch refuse to grant military funds for a speed contest, he also recommended to the National Aviation Fund's board of trustees, which was willing to grant 200,000 marks for the event, that none of their funds be allocated for such a competition.[63]

August Euler tried to explain that a speed contest would aid aeronautical progress and thus inevitably benefit military aviation; in his view the army should at least support private endeavors if it was unwilling to take the risks. Although he convinced many important civilian aeronautical societies, such as the Imperial Aero-Club and the Berlin Society for Aviation, nothing deflected the General Inspectorate from its intransigent stance. The industry was powerless, because it had already relinquished its only lever against the General Inspectorate and the Aviators Association, the threat of nonparticipation in the Prince Heinrich Flight.[64]

Euler, having lost the major confrontation, attacked the aspects of the Prince Heinrich Flight that the industry still found most disagreeable: the lack of entry fees for military airplanes, the closure of registration three months before the opening of competition, and the awarding of the top prize to the best group of entries rather than to the best single entrant.[65] His complaints, however, were to no avail. The Southwest Group and the General Inspectorate agreed on the regulations and the aim of the contest—the development of an all-weather warplane for the army.

General von Haenisch's precondition for military participation was the group prize, which ensured the victory for the army. The General Inspectorate explained its demand for an early end to registration as insurance that private entries would be well tested and safe.[66] Actually, Major Wilhelm Siegert of the Flying Troops proposed the stipulations to make certain that the army pilots received no surprises during the competition. Siegert feared that in order to win the competition the factories might surprise the army's regulation machines with special designs, a situation which he likened to a race between a cart horse and a thorobred.[67]

After November 1913 the General Inspectorate, having won the industry's participation in the Prince Heinrich Flight of 1914, withdrew from the dispute, but the clash between the Convention and the Southwest Group continued. At a meeting of the Aviators Association in February 1914, General Secretary Sperling of the motor vehicle industrialists, speaking for the Convention, warned the Association that the industry saw little need to cooperate with it if it could not protect the industry's interests.[68] The warning only exacerbated the conflict. Euler declared that the Prince Heinrich Flight of 1913 had caused losses for the industry that considerably outweighed the prizes it won.[69] In reply to this statement in March 1914 the chairman of the contest, Dr. Ludwig Joseph of the Southwest Group, accused the industry of vastly exaggerating its losses in the 1913 contest.[70]

Euler's opinion was actually upheld by an Aviators Association memorandum[71] written after the war when tempers had cooled. The memorandum blamed the failure of the Convention to secure the influence that the leaders of the industry and the national Aviators Association desired for it on local associations like the Southwest Group, who refused to grant the industry more than an advisory role in the planning of sport shows. It also admitted that the profits from these air shows swelled the coffers

of the local associations, while manufacturers frequently went into debt. Although considerable prizes had gone to the industry, the sport organizations had accumulated tremendous sums by defraying most of their expenses from contributions that might have been used as prizes instead of from their own treasuries.

Even after the Convention walked out of an Association meeting on 23 March, the Southwest Group pursued the attack, questioning the validity of Euler's statements and implying that he had imposed his will on the other members of the Convention.[72] In the meeting of the board of the Aviators Association on 18 April 1914, Euler and Sperling gave notice that the Convention and its parent union were quitting the German Aviators Association at the end of the year.[73]

The Southwest Group's reply in 1914 to the industry's announcement did not acknowledge any errors on its part. Ludwig Joseph did explain, however, why the group had disregarded the industry and inadvertently why a sport aviation market could not exist in Germany. The Southwest Group had attempted to cooperate with the industry, but a basic difference of opinion over the importance of military interests made a split inevitable. As long as there was no aviation sport, the duty of the sport associations was to serve the cause of national defense, and the Southwest Group was proud to be the army's "obedient servant."[74] Joseph neglected to reflect, of course, that sport aviation could not exist without the support of the Association. In any case the Association, as he implied, was merely adhering to the policy of the General Inspectorate, which wanted all efforts focused directly on military aviation. The Southwest Group had taken it upon themselves to represent the General Inspectorate's interests, which they construed as their own, to the aircraft industry. The industry, which could not afford to antagonize the army despite the difference of interests, could only complain to the General Inspectorate that the Convention preferred to conduct its business directly with the army without "profiteering middlemen who should have been devoting their efforts to the promotion of sport aviation."[75]

The outcome of the Prince Heinrich Flight, held from 17 through 25 May 1914 and labeled the greatest aviation event of 1914,[76] was anticlimactic. Nine of the top twelve finishers were army officers; the best a civilian could do was to take fourth place. The triumph of the General Inspectorate and the Southwest Group was complete. The industry's attempt to promote a domestic sport aviation market had been blocked by the army's pervasive influence in the aviation sport organizations, which saw their duty in servility to the cause of military aviation, not in the promotion of civilian sport aviation.

The National Aviation Fund obviously catered to the Prussian Army. As Delbrueck confided to the emperor, its primary goal was to increase German power in military aeronautics. Thus the army and the navy, with whom the board of trustees cooperated, were the real beneficiaries.[77] This priority, however, did not go uncriticized. Hans Grade, one of the pioneers of German aviation, condemned the distribution of the Fund as irrelevant and even disadvantageous to aeronautical progress. An entrepreneur whose initial achievements had given way to failure, Grade felt that the Fund should have compensated the factories directly for their risks and losses.[78] In the opinion of the newspaper *Frankfurter Sportzeitung*, the Fund should have aided firms not employed by the army.[79] These objections suggest that an alternative distribution of the Fund would have been preferable—direct subsidies to factories. Yet Fund regulations expressly forbade direct

✠ *Side view of Taube No. A26. Courtesy of Peter Grosz.*

subsidies to the aircraft firms. The board of trustees had decided to help indirectly only successful factories (i.e., those producing for the army) and to ignore, or if possible destroy, the small workshops "that sprouted like peas from the earth."[80] Before examining the overall effect of the Fund on German aviation, one must conisder whether the alternative of direct subsidies was worthwhile or even possible under the circumstances.

Direct subsidies to the firms would have had certain disadvantages. Productivity could not be guaranteed in return for the money, and for this reason the Prussian Army had refused subsidies to its aircraft manufacturers as early as 1911.[81] Granting funds to the multitude of small workshop "factories" not employed by the army would have been wasteful and the selection of recipients difficult. In any case, as the board perceived, the day of the small workshop and the lone inventor was past. Direct subsidies to the aircraft companies were consequently not a wise alternative.

Direct subsidies were also unlikely because of such Prussian Army policies as the publicized decision of the conference of the War Ministry and the Inspectorates on 18 April 1912 to support only large, financially sound factories. The board of trustees could not fly in the face of the military decision.

The Prussian Army could determine the priorities of the National Aviation Fund without assuming any responsibility not only because of its omnipresent influence and its advisers on the Fund's board of trustees, but also because of men like August Euler, Ludwig Joseph, and, behind the scenes, Clemens von Delbrueck. Since the industry was completely dependent on the military for its livelihood, Euler and the other manufacturers placed the army's interests above, or equated them with, those of the industry.[82] When their interests clearly clashed, as they did in 1913–1914 over the question of sport aviation, the Prussian Ar-

my's influence effectively blocked the aircraft industry's efforts to promote sport flying. Ludwig Joseph and the Southwest Group, in their concern for national security, considered support of the army's aviation policies their patriotic duty. Delbrueck, like former Secretary of State Posadowsky Wehner, the president of the board of trustees, emphasized the Fund's benefits to the military in his correspondence with the emperor because the army was the apple of Wilhelm's eye and the most powerful element in the German government. Given such pervasive military influence, an alternative mode of distribution of the National Aviation Fund is perhaps too much to expect.

Aviation historians have considered the National Aviation Fund the "turning point" in prewar German aeronautics. It "crowned the pre-history of military aviation" by giving the aircraft industry the money to overtake French aviation by 1914 and "the real and decisive impetus to enlarge itself to the size essential to meet the demands of the coming war."[83]

These evaluations are essentially correct, since the National Aviation Fund provided the decisive impetus for the development of German military aviation and thus indirectly for the German aircraft industry. The psychological effect of popular support and the injection of seven million marks at such a critical time was of inestimable value. Civilian aviators, stimulated by the Fund's rewards for record-setting distance and altitude flights, had wrested both records from the French by the beginning of World War I.[84] The Fund's significance in monetary terms is striking when one considers that its contributions equaled almost twice the Prussian Army's budget for airplane facilities and procurement in 1912 (3,391,250 marks) and slightly less than one-half that for 1913 (15,612,000 marks). As this almost five-fold increase in allocations for aviation shows, the Fund probably had a catalytic effect on military aviation. The army had ordered only 26 airplanes from Germany's eight largest airplane factories in 1911; but in 1912 it received 129 planes from them, and in 1913 it received 432. The 62 aircraft purchased with Fund contributions thus amounted to one-half the army's total contracts for airplanes in 1912, or to approximately 8 percent of the total orders from 1912 to August 1914.[85]

August Euler had calculated correctly that substantial popular support and funds could encourage the Prussian Army's increased reliance on the airplane to the benefit of the airplane industry. The German government, in particular the military, could use the supposedly "civilian" venture to transfer part of the armaments burden from the military budget to the people through a "voluntary tax." Contrary to promises about the Fund's civilian nature, the government from the outset had intended to use the Fund's contributions to develop military aviation. For this reason the East German historian Gerhard Wissmann has accused the imperial German government of deceiving the people, of leading them to believe that they were aiding technological progress through contributions to civil aviation, while the Fund's initiators and executors intended to employ it to develop the aircraft as a weapon and to train pilots for the army.[86] Perhaps some people were deceived. Nevertheless, the contributions for warplanes and the open complaints of those who disagreed with the Fund's priorities indicate that the majority of the informed populace was aware of the Fund's true purpose, whether they approved of it or not. What had happened was that the German government, the Prussian Army, and the aircraft industry had exploited the patriotic temper in Germany to supplement substantially the budget for military aviation in preparation for the war they believed was inevitable.

At the same time, the National Aviation Fund was, in a sense, a "turning point" at which history failed to turn. It was a missed opportunity for the development of sport aviation in Germany, and, for the industry, a failure to establish a supplementary domestic market that would have given it needed contracts and perhaps a degree of independence from the Prussian Army. Ironically, the pursuit of profit had linked the industry closely to the Prussian Army. Now, when it sought to weaken this attachment in pursuit of further profit, it was unable to escape the clutches of a system in which the army's sway was unchallenged.

## MILITARY CONTROL AND INDUSTRIAL MOBILIZATION

The crucial question regarding the relationship of the Prussian Army with the north German aircraft industry between 1912 and 1914 is their readiness for war in 1914. Although this question has been studied since the "Great War," previous answers remain unsatisfactory because of insufficient research and the debatable manner in which the question has been posed.

Postwar German analysts depicted German industry in general as being unprepared for the war of 1914–1918. According to Karl Helfferich, a former director of the *Deutsche Bank* and of the imperial treasury, the official military and economic circles responsible for the German wartime economy generally considered the war danger of little importance, did not reckon with a long war, and thus could not conceive of the organizational preparations necessary for modern war. There was no overall plan for the economy; proposals for an economic general staff were stillborn.[87] Journalist Arthur Dix, a prewar advocate of industrial mobilization, observed that the General Staff considered economic preparations for the war the province of the War Ministry, which in turn left such problems to the Imperial Office of the

Interior. This last agency, however, paid little or no attention to matters of industrial mobilization.[88]

The first two volumes of the Imperial Archive's (*Reichs-Archiv*) official history of the 1914–1918 war, *Kriegsruestung und Kriegswirtschaft*, corroborated these interpretations. Secretary of State of the Interior Clemens von Delbrueck was concerned more with the welfare of the entire country than with the narrower sphere of industrial mobilization. The army had no overall view of the factories producing war material and neglected to determine until shortly before the war whether private industry had sufficient stocks and supplies. The German mobilization plans dealt mainly with worker exemptions, because military leaders believed that every deferment meant a weakening of the army's manpower. The army was prepared to increase the production of its own factories and workshops only, plans which clearly had no effect on airplane procurement, and to receive increased deliveries from some of its private producers in case of war.[89]

Yet Arthur Dix had advised the army in the *Vierteljahrsheft fuer Truppenfuehrung und Heereskunde* of July 1913 that modern warfare required planned industrial mobilization. The more complicated the technical apparatus involved, the more necessary were provisions for the factories' retention of skilled workers in a mobilization. In Dix's opinion the age of modern technology demanded close military-industrial cooperation in order to maintain vital industries, such as the automobile and aircraft factories, at their operational peak.[90]

Such perceptive warnings were isolated and supposedly unheeded,[91] for authorities on prewar German military aeronautics have agreed that German military aviation and the aircraft industry, like the entire industrial establishment, were unprepared for World War I. The Military Science Department of the German Air Force (*Kriegswissenschaftliche Abteilung der Luftwaffe*), which began the official history of German prewar and wartime military aviation during the interwar years, concluded initially in an unpublished volume that the aircraft industry had barely survived, much less developed, before the war. According to this interpretation, a few firms were housed in factories with high-quality machines, but the majority resided in primitive workshops or barracks. The industry's basic source of funds, military contracts, was insufficient to support the number of competing firms. Consequently the high risks and doubtful profitability of aircraft production deterred the investment of private capital, and frequent failures made even the aircraft manufacturers reluctant to invest in costly equipment.[92] According to the wartime chief of the German air forces, General Ernst Wilhelm von Hoeppner, the army's small peacetime demands had not equipped the airplane plants for the serial fabrication necessary to replace wartime losses, and mobilization plans entailed no increase in aircraft production.[93] Hilmer von Buelow emphasized that the outbreak of hostilities interrupted plans for development of the aviation troops and aircraft industry at an early stage and concluded that there was "no more conclusive proof of Germany's unpreparedness for a war than this deficient level of armaments of the German aviation troops in July 1914."[94]

Unfortunately, these interpretations are based partially on meaningless criteria for preparedness. They concluded that Germany was unprepared for the magnitude of the war that occurred and that the early interruption of plans for developing military aeronautics was a critical indicator of Germany's unreadiness. But a discussion of whether the German armed forces were ready for a war the size of which was unforeseen and unparalleled becomes an essay in futility. The answer can only be no, because no European government was prepared for the long and total war of armies and nations. National survival in World War I depended more on the ability to mobilize the nation's resources after the war had settled into a stalemate than on prewar preparations. The question that must be posed and answered is how well Germany was prepared for the expected brief conflict of movement and decisive battles.

That the outbreak of war caught German military aviation in the early stages of its planned development does not affect the answer to this question. All armed forces must remain in a state of constant evolution based on long-range planning if they are to maintain their efficiency. The war interrupted plans for the expansion of all European armed forces, and some armies were poorly equipped in categories more basic than aviation. The French military's neglect of heavy artillery, for example, could not be offset by its emphasis on élan and attack. As a technological aid of the German land forces, the airplane was naturally secondary to basic armaments in 1914. Therefore, contrary to Buelow's assertion, unreadiness on the part of the aircraft industry and aviation forces would not prove that the rest of the military was unprepared.

In any case, earlier accounts lack detailed analysis of the aircraft industry and of its relationship with the Prussian Army according to an analytical framework for evaluating industrial mobilization. To rectify such errors and omissions, the following discussion will examine the development of the north German aircraft industry and its relationship with the Prussian Army with an eye to their readiness for wartime mobilization. The analytical scheme used to evaluate their readiness for mobilization comes from a book entitled *Kriegswichtige Industrie im System der Wirtschaftspolitik*, written in 1937 by Justus Schmidt. That the book was published during the Nazi era does not detract from the general applicability of the criteria for mobilization, criteria that may well have been formulated by the author in light of the experience of World War I.[95]

According to this framework, the preparation of a militarily important industry for war would necessitate state control and direction in three spheres: the political, which entailed the exclusion of foreign capital and workers; the technical, which focused on the surveillance of quality by the military procurement agency; and the economic, which aimed at the state's dictation of prices to the industry and the creation of surplus industrial capacity through the military's distribution of contracts and subsidies. The army had taken care of the political aspects to its satisfaction, as indicated by its rejection of the French Farman firm's offer to establish a factory in Germany in 1910 and its examination of the Aviatik firm's capital backing for French influence in 1912. It was not concerned if foreign nationals worked in the German industry, and it allowed for capital investment in the aircraft industry by Austrian citizens. To determine whether the Prussian Army's relationship with the north German aircraft industry fulfilled the economic and technical prerequisites for mobilization, one must examine the effect of the pilot training program and aircraft procurement on the industry and their relationship from 1912 to August 1914.

In its policy of pilot training the General Inspectorate considered the interest of both the army and the industry. The decentralization of the army's pilot training program at the various factories hindered surveillance and the application of uniform standards, and experience had given the General Inspectorate the impression that the firms were more interested in profit than in providing the best military training. The factories trained military and civilian pilots together and thus increased the time and cost of training, and to prevent unnecessary damage to the aircraft they forbade the army pilots to fly in bad weather and to practice

gliding. The General Inspectorate had continued to rely on the factories only because it refused to spend more money on a military training program. The system of pilot training established in 1912, in which the factories would conduct the first stage of training and the Training and Research Institute and the military air stations the second, had never operated in practice because the stations did not have enough instructors or material to complete the training punctually. The factories consequently were responsible for completing the second stage of training for many pilots.[96]

In the summer of 1912 Hermann Behrens, the owner of the German Bristol Works, offered to establish a private flying school under military control, an offer the General Inspectorate and the War Ministry gladly accepted. The Halberstadt Military Flying School, founded in August 1913, could train at least forty-eight pilots annually at a cost of 8,000 marks each, approximately 2,000 marks less than the current price at the factories.[97] The number of officers trained at the factory schools consequently declined to the point where the army planned in December 1912 to send only eight student pilots apiece to Albatros and Rumpler. However, the War Ministry's decision in late 1912 to hasten the pace of aeronautical development led to the realization that more flyers would be necessary; and so in April 1913 the army turned once more to the factories of Albatros, Rumpler, AEG, Fokker, Gotha, and the Emil Jeannin Aircraft Company. Instead of creating another military flying school, the General Inspectorate resorted to the simple expedient of ordering these factories to remodel their schools after the one in Halberstadt in December 1913. Henceforth, the training programs of these schools were subject

to military control and would train only army pilots.[98] Since these schools would complete the training, the burden of this task had been lifted from the air stations, which were still not equipped to handle the increased number of personnel.[99]

Instead of establishing sufficient army flying centers to remove the responsibility of flight training from the factories, the General Inspectorate had taken the half measure of using private enterprise under military control to train army officer pilots. This solution benefited both the army and the factories: the army saved money while securing suitable military flight training, and the firms preserved a source of livelihood second only to aircraft contracts. With regard to mobilization readiness, the army's policy may not have produced as many pilots as a systematic all-military program might have, and it lacked uniformity and efficiency, but it did ensure military control over another aspect of factory life while producing sufficient numbers of pilots.

The army's goal of control in order to secure military interests was just as evident in the War Ministry's and the General Inspectorate's policies on aircraft procurement. The perfect illustration of this tendency toward increasing military authority over the aircraft industry in all facets of their relationship—even in matters of technology and construction—is found in the history of the Prussian Army's procurement of the Taube, the most popular German monoplane design of the prewar era.

The creator of the Taube, the Austrian designer Igo Etrich, had intended to establish a firm in Germany in 1910 to sell his successful monoplane to the Prussian Army, but his father demanded that he forgo aircraft production in order to manage the family textile plant. Acceding to his father's wishes, he sold the rights to licensed production in Germany to Edmund Rumpler, the Austrian owner of the Rumpler factory in Johannisthal, on 21 June 1910. The popularity of the Etrich-Rumpler Taube in Prus-

✠ *Close-up of Albatros monoplane. Courtesy of Peter Grosz.*

sian military circles made Rumpler's fortune and reputation. Then Rumpler discovered that the bird-like wing for which the Taube was famous was conceived by a Professor Ahlhorn, and so he dropped Etrich's name and ceased to pay the license fees. After several unsuccessful attempts to persuade Rumpler to abide by their agreement, Etrich dissolved their contract and withdrew his patent application for the design in Germany. Since the design was no longer protected, other German firms could now construct unlicensed copies of the Taube.[100]

In 1912, Igo Etrich and his father founded the Etrich Flying Works near Libau in Silesia in order to compete with Rumpler in Taube sales to the Prussian Army. General Messing postponed a decision on procurement from Etrich in May because the Inspectorate of Military Aviation and Motor Vehicles was unsure of the legal aspects of the Etrich-Rumpler dispute. Messing observed, however, that Rumpler, because of the absence of competition, had not improved upon Etrich's original design while constantly increasing his prices.[101] Nevertheless, the Taube remained the best German military monoplane.[102]

Although Etrich's new factory delivered no aircraft to the Prussian Army, its formation probably planted in Messing's mind the seed of a policy of Taube procurement designed to promote competition among the army's aircraft manufacturers. In late September 1912 the Instruction and Research Institute suggested that the army set the industry on a course designed to perfect a warplane.[103] In mid-November the Inspectorate promoted competition and channeled the industry's efforts by ordering the Taube at lower prices from other firms.[104] At the end of November, General von Lyncker informed the War Ministry that the General Inspectorate expected a general decrease in aircraft prices when competitive production began.[105]

Euler and Albatros began Taube construction in late 1912, and the Inspectorate could report in early January 1913 that the increased competition had already lowered the prices of Taube replacement parts. In the future it intended to improve the quality of Taube construction and to force prices down even more by further increasing the competition.[106] One way in which the Inspectorate achieved this goal was to use Taube contracts to ease the entry of new firms into airplane production. The Prussian Army took delivery of thirty-six of the monoplanes from Gotha in 1913, and by June the army had included two other new firms— Jeannin and LFG—in its orders of Taubes.[107] Older firms, among them DFW, Aviatik, Fokker, and Bristol, received Taubes as prototypes for future construction by October 1913. The competition in Taube construction also increased competition in biplane construction, as Rumpler began biplane production before the end of 1912 to keep pace with Albatros, which was now building both monoplanes and biplanes. The army thus used Taube construction to lure more firms into aircraft production, to achieve lower prices, and to channel efforts toward its own production goals.

The General Inspectorate's policy of granting Taubes and biplanes to firms as production prototypes[108] led to standardization and licensed production. In May 1913, Messing had opposed the introduction of standardization because he feared it would arrest changes and improvements in the detailed construction of airplanes. The introduction of norms other than those already in effect on motor type, certain construction materials, gas tanks, and propellors was premature.[109]

Yet, in practice the Inspectorate was fostering standardization on two types of airplanes. The first was the tractor biplane, suitable for reconnaissance and capable of using shorter fields and carrying a heavier load than the monoplanes; the second, the Taube, faster and somewhat more stable, and better suited for communications. In October 1913 the Inspectorate of Flying Troops, despite the knowledge that the French were developing four types of aircraft and that specialization would be necessary in the future, recommended the desirability of one standard airplane for the Prussian Army.[110] However, after conferences with the Inspectorate of Flying Troops and representatives of the industry in March 1914, the War Ministry's recently established Transportation Technology Test Commission[111] recommended the development of three specialized types—a high-speed, long-range model to be evolved from existing aircraft, then a light plane and a heavy, long-range type to be developed through future competition.[112] The Inspectorate of Military Aviation and Motor Vehicles believed, however, that the procurement of specialized airplanes would create problems of production and supply that would dwarf its present difficulties with differences in manufacturer and model. Faced with a choice between specialized types to meet military-technical demands and standardization to meet organizational-bureaucratic necessities, Messing granted immediate priority to the latter and postponed the competition for the light aircraft until November 1914 and for the heavy one until sometime in 1915.[113] The army was left, in effect, with the Taube and the tractor biplane as its basic types.

Licensed production was an unexpected, though perhaps unavoidable, result of the General Inspectorate's granting of production prototypes. Although the army apparently had no intention of instituting formal licensed production, Emil Jeannin complained on 11 November 1913 that DFW had delivered an exact copy of the Jeannin steel Taube to the Prussian Army. This was not the first objection, because LVG had questioned the legality of the army's delivery of one of its biplanes to Euler for reproduction in September. Admittedly, the question of aircraft patents was unsettled, but the army had no right to dispense airplanes for duplication or even modification without some form of compensation to the original creator. Rather than risk legal complications, the Inspectorate of Flying Troops decided on 15 November to institute a policy whereby it paid the original manufacturer a license fee for each copy delivered by other firms.[114] Standardization and licensed production were clearly aspects of the Prussian Army's increasing control over the production of the aircraft industry in order to obtain better military airplanes.

Ironically, a fatal misconception of the requirements for the Taube on the part of the War Ministry and the General Inspectorate led to even greater military control of the technical aspects of airplane production. The Taube was at the peak of its popularity in the summer of 1913. However, the General Inspectorate had made a fateful decision at the beginning of 1913 that would soon send the fortunes of the birdlike machine plummeting. It had decided upon a new requirement for military airplanes, one recommended by the War Ministry as early as 1911—transportability. The demand for transportable airplanes stemmed from the concept that the airplane, because of its limited range and durability, would be built to be incorporated into the columns of a maneuverable land army. A premium was placed on the time and labor necessary to assemble and dismantle the machine and the ease with which the army could transport it by truck. The General Staff's opposition to this approach in 1911, which was based on the idea that the airplane should follow the troops in the air, was disregarded. The first Taubes delivered to meet this requirement for a competition in May were unsuccessful. Nevertheless, the War Ministry and the General Inspectorate refused to drop the

idea and held a conference with the aircraft manufacturers in June in hopes of removing the deficiencies. Rumpler and Albatros felt that they could solve the problem by the next delivery in August. In the heat of competition, they preferred to risk failure rather than forgo the contracts.[115]

The firms took the risk, but unfortunately the pilots and observers of the Prussian Army paid for it. On 4 September 1913, Lieutenants Helmuth von Eckenbrecher and his observer died in the crash of a Rumpler Klapp-Taube. Crashes usually passed relatively unnoticed. But Eckenbrecher had been engaged to the daughter of the influential general director of agriculture in East Prussia, Wolfgang Kapp, and Kapp complained to the emperor.[116] The army responded to the general public reproach that its demands for collapsibility were responsible for the crash by removing planes of the model flown by Eckenbrecher from service and then, after fall maneuvers, calling an army commission to investigate the cause of the crash.

The commission, which met from 21 September to 2 October 1913, was headed by Major Wilhelm Siegert and composed of one engineer and three lieutenants of the flying troops. The commission blamed the crash largely on "a lack of expert designers" in the aircraft industry. Business was apparently more important to some firms than the safety of army flyers. The commission singled out Rumpler as "unworthy of the army's trust," for a short time after the crash the firm had produced a modified Taube that was approximately 1.3 times stronger than its previous models. It recommended to all firms that they check their workers and subcontracted piecework better. It advised the army that ease of transportation would have to be subordinate to safety, and that its

prices were too low and delivery times too short to allow careful work. Henceforth, stress tests, entailing the application of sand to the parts of an airplane until they ruptured, were to be performed periodically on aircraft upon delivery from the factory. Such tests, which had been developed according to the theories of the scientists and engineers of the Scientific Society for Flight Technology and the German Research Institute for Aviation, were used for the first time in the commission's investigation of the Taube.[117]

After examining the army's biplanes, the commission compiled a list of "Rules and Suggestions for the Aircraft Factories" on materials, construction techniques, and measures to be incorporated in future military aircraft. It also proposed that the army flying troops train more officers in raw material examination, and conduct further experiments in close cooperation with the Research Institute. At the urging of the director of the Institute, the Imperial Office of the Interior recommended such cooperation to the War Ministry. Consequently, the General Inspectorate, approached from two directions, first permitted the Research Institute to investigate the causes of all army airplane crashes at its own cost and later, in April 1914, engaged the Institute under contract to perform the army's scientific work, technical tests, and experiments in aviation.[118]

The September crash also encouraged the War Ministry to check the methods of aircraft acceptance and purchase. Before this incident the General Inspectorate and its subordinate agencies had conducted pilot training and the testing, procurement, and deployment of aircraft, while the War Ministry had limited itself to control of the finances and the acceptance or rejection of the General Inspectorate's procurement proposals. Now, the War Ministry established a Transportation Technology Test Commission on 1 December 1913 as its subordinate agency for the control of the procurement of all transport vehicles, including airplanes.

✠ *Taube ready for takeoff. Courtesy of Peter Grosz.*

As such it officially replaced the Research Unit of the transport troops. Now the War Department had a direct voice in aviation procurement through the Test Commission, as it already had in weapons and artillery through similar commissions. Although disputes over the delineation of authority between the General Inspectorate and the Test Commission led to time-consuming disagreements among the Commission, the War Department, and the General Inspectorate,[119] the establishment of the Commission and the army's close cooperation with the German Research Institute for Aviation gave the Prussian Army more influence over the technical aspects of airplane production, which hitherto had been the province of the aircraft industry. This influence was formalized in the "Construction and Acceptance Regulations" formulated by another commission convened on 8 June 1914 and composed of the War Department, the General Inspectorate, the Inspectorate of Military Aviation and Motor Vehicles, the Inspectorate of Flying Troops, and the Transportation Technology Test Commission with representatives of the industry present.[120]

The General Inspectorate made increasingly vigorous attempts to make the firms conform to its will in the latter part of 1913 and in the first half of 1914. Its treatment of the Euler and Rumpler companies illustrates this tendency, replete with personal overtones in the case of the influential Euler.

Because of the airplane industry's relative insignificance on the scale of arms industries, the use of business position or highly placed acquaintances in order to receive better treatment from the army as it increased its technical controls was less a possibility for the aircraft manufacturers than for large arms companies. Euler was the only builder whose personal financial independence and whose various positions of leadership in the Convention, the Aviators Association, and the National Avia-

tion Fund enabled him to revert to this expedient. His turgid estimation of his importance, which led him to declare to the army that in one hundred years one would not be able to discuss the development of German aviation without mentioning his name, caused him to list his accomplishments and contacts to Messing on 6 September 1913 in an attempt to remove certain difficulties with the army.[121]

According to Euler, Captain Job von Dewall of the Darmstadt air station had initiated a personal vendetta against him, insulting him and rejecting his aircraft for minor reasons, because Euler had refused to accept the blame for the crash of one of his planes that had resulted in the death of two officers. Second, a dispute between Euler and the new inspector general, Lieutenant General von Haenisch, over the lowering of his prices for pilot training had resulted in the cancellation of all pilot training at the Euler factory and unleashed a feud between him and Haenisch. As if this were not sufficient trouble, Euler then accused the General Inspectorate and Haenisch of undercutting his license for production of the French Gnome motor in Germany by refusing to buy his Gnomes while encouraging the German motor firm Oberursel to secure the license from the French factory.

Euler's letter to Messing, instead of easing the situation, provoked the wrath of Haenisch. Various friends informed Euler that Haenisch intended to destroy him and that the army would accept no more of his aircraft. Euler's next production series of fourteen biplanes, after undergoing three trials at the Darmstadt station, was subjected to the exhaustive scrutiny of a special Inspectorate of Flying Troops commission in mid-November 1913. When the army finally accepted the airplanes, Euler had been forced to lower his price from 348,750 marks to 247,300 marks. In late May 1914 the General Inspectorate also delayed acceptance of and then payment for his licensed production of the

LVG biplane. Euler finally had to beg for mercy; he was on the verge of releasing half of his employees and was even prepared to sell his factory.[122]

Euler's influential friends and important positions had meant nothing to the Prussian Army, and the General Inspectorate may have humiliated him purposely in order to make that evident to him. The dispute and Euler's ensuing difficulties were common knowledge; thus none of his associates had the excuse of unawareness. If anybody did intercede for Euler, the act has never come to light. The loss of individuality and initiative involved in licensed production undoubtedly severely injured the pride of a pioneer like Euler, and only the failure of his own designs forced him to accept licensed production and the accompanying personal humiliation.

After the Flying Troops commission singled out Rumpler as unworthy of the army's confidence, the General Inspectorate subjected Rumpler to similar, though less harsh, treatment. Although the Rumpler firm was successful, it received negligible orders until it proved itself capable of faultless deliveries. With threats of cancellation of orders and harassment over minor problems, the General Inspectorate held Rumpler to guarantees of careful work. As Rumpler discovered much to his dismay, the costs of careful work and close examination of the airplanes were much increased. In early 1914 he was forced to request an increase in parts prices and contracts in order to avoid firing some of his skilled workers.[123] The army had brought Rumpler to his knees and shown that it controlled his survival as an airplane manufacturer. On the other hand, its disfavor stimulated better construction and general progress in Rumpler's development of military aircraft. His new monoplane introduced in March 1914 was a vast improvement on the old Taube, and his 1914 biplane was also successful.[124]

The army's increased technical control over the airplane industry had both positive and negative effects on the development of the monoplane. It definitely forced the firms to improve their construction techniques and the safety of their aircraft. Under the pressures of competition or even cancellation of orders, a stronger Taube built with steel tubing had become operational by the end of 1913. Increased military controls thus meant improvement in detailed construction techniques and progress in the evolution of the particular aircraft selected by the army.

However, in a much larger sense standardization at such an early stage in the development of the monoplane meant, as Messing had foreseen in May 1913, a certain degree of ossification, a stifling of the creativity of the airplane industry. Most manufacturers concentrated solely on profitable production and relinquished preparations for that inevitable time when the Taube would be obsolete. Only isolated designers, among whom the Dutchman Anthony Fokker was the best, constructed new monoplane types during the era of the ascendancy of the Taube. Of course, the firms had little choice if they desired profits. The army's monopolization of the consumer market enabled it to channel the talents of the aircraft industry in the direction of military interests.

The Prussian Army consequently entered the war in 1914 with two standard aircraft types—the Taube monoplane and the tractor biplane. Although the Taube was approaching obsolescence because of its heavy weight, slow speed and rate of climb, and long take-off run, Major Wilhelm Siegert, who was emerging as one of the most dynamic and imaginative of the Flying Troops' officers, regarded it as an ideal type for strategic long-range reconnaissance. It was a superbly stable airplane whose single wing would enable a free field of fire for an observer's machine gun. However, the biplane's better speed and rate of climb, shorter

takeoff run, and steadily increasing stability made it the mainstay of the Prussian Army's aviation forces. As early as the 1911 maneuvers, observers had achieved better results in biplanes because the lower wing was smaller in chord and better positioned than a monoplane's single wing. In Siegert's opinion the biplane was destined to become the standard type, although its upper wing would obstruct the forward field of fire of a machine gun. Other types considered by Siegert were a pusher biplane, with the observer in the nose and the engine behind the pilot, and a parasol tractor aircraft, with a single wing mounted above the fuselage. Both models would offer good observation and firing ability, but in a crash, the rear-mounted engine of the pusher biplane could smash the crew into the ground. In any case, whatever the potential of these two planes, it would have to be realized by the airplane industry.[125] Thus one cannot avoid the conclusion that if the tractor biplane was destined to become the Prussian Army's standard type, this destiny was owing as much to the stagnation in the evolution of the monoplane and to the absence of other types, which the army's policy of standardization had encouraged, as it was to the progress made in biplane performance.

As the Prussian Army awarded more contracts and fostered competition, the aircraft industry grew. As of February 1914 it bought planes from eleven manufacturers, who were, in order of their capability, Albatros, Aviatik, LVG, Rumpler, DFW, Euler, Gotha, Jeannin, AEG, Fokker, and LFG.[126] By World War I the

✠ *Major Wilhelm Siegert (center), commander of Flying Battalion No. 3, chatting with flying officers at the Prince Heinrich Flight of 1914. Siegert, dynamic and imaginative, became inspector of flying troops in 1916. Courtesy of Peter Grosz.*

industry had outgrown Johannisthal. Albatros founded the East German Albatros Factory in Schneidemuehl in April 1914. Fokker had relocated his factory in October 1913 to Schwerin in Mecklenburg because Lieutenant Geerdtz of the Inspectorate of Military Aviation and Motor Vehicles arranged terms favorable to Fokker with the city and airfield administration and then offered Fokker a three-year contract for pilot training if he left the overcrowded field at Johannisthal.[127]

Fokker may have been the only successful aircraft entrepreneur who preferred not to enlarge his plant. According to A. R. Weyl, the Dutchman lacked a proper understanding of economy, which he interpreted as investing as little as possible in equipment, and continued to rely on earlier haphazard workshop measures. The one technician and two draftsmen in his design office at the end of 1913 were "practical people" with no specific qualifications or aeronautical experience. Nevertheless, he delivered twelve aircraft of his own design to the army in 1913, and by the end of 1914 his factory had a staff of ninety-five workmen and fifteen technicians and designers.[128] Even greater expansion was common among the successful older factories, as shown in table 5.

Although firms founded after 1911 accounted for part of the aircraft industry's expansion, most of it was owing to the success of older firms in achieving the status of *Grossbetriebe* (firms employing fifty or more workers). Albatros had introduced limited serial production as early as January 1912, and LVG, Rumpler, Aviatik, Gotha, and AEG followed suit in 1913.[129] Although mechanization and serial production were thus common in larger factories, the aircraft industry still used the pattern of work arrangement known as *Platzarbeit*, in which "machines were grouped by type . . . and the pieces were moved from one post to another until they were finally brought together for fitting in the assembly shop. . . . The more successful enterprises gave entire floors, or even separate shops, to a single type of tool."[130] The layout of the Rumpler company in later 1914 exemplified this arrangement. It comprised a five-story factory, assembly halls, its own electric power plant and telephone office, and a railroad loading station. The factory was arranged in the following manner: in the cellar, a workers' dressing room; on the first floor, company headquarters; on the second, the drill, lathe, mill, and tool construction workshops; on the third, a workshop for the construction of small parts; on the fourth, a workshop for larger parts such as undercarriages; and on the fifth floor, the coppersmith and sheet metal shops.[131] *Platzarbeit* and the reliance on skilled craftsmen were the hallmarks of early aircraft production, before increased demand and precision necessitated the more efficient assembly-line method of production.

The growth of the industry indicates that the best firms profited, if not substantially. Average prices of monoplanes rose from 19,500 marks in 1911 to 23,500 marks in 1913; of biplanes, from 25,500 marks to 26,000 marks to account for the rising costs of materials and motors. If the War Ministry's calculation of 1912 that 30 to 35 contracts annually would keep a company profitable remained accurate, then Rumpler and Albatros, with 48 and 46 contracts, respectively, profited in 1912. In 1913 Rumpler, Albatros, Aviatik, LVG, and Gotha, with 66, 85, 98, 88, and 36 deliveries to the Prussian Army, surpassed the minimum, while Jeannin with 26, Euler with 27, and LFG with 20 deliveries came reasonably close. Dividends rose: Albatros's grew from nothing in 1911 to 4 percent in 1912 and 8 percent in 1913, while LVG showed dividends of 10 percent in 1913, one year after its formation. Of course, much of the profit was put back into the plant, as evidenced by the rise in value of Rumpler's plant from 15,000 marks in 1908 to 1,400,000 marks in 1914, and of Aviatik's capital from 30,000 marks in 1910 to over 1,000,000 marks in 1914.[132]

Table 5. GROWTH OF THE ALBATROS AND RUMPLER FIRMS, 1911–1914 *

| | Albatros | | Rumpler | |
|---|---|---|---|---|
| Year | Employees | Number of Planes Produced | Employees | Number of Planes Produced |
| 1911 | 115 | 12 | 80 | 11 |
| 1912 | 250 | 46 | 200 | 48 |
| 1913 | 320 | 85 | 245 | 67 |
| 8–1–14 | 500 | | 290 | |
| 1914 | 745 | 338 | 400 | 110 |

* KAdL, *Militaerluftfahrt* III, 316–17 (App. 70); Ernst Heinkel, *Stuermisches Leben*, ed. by Juergen Thorwald (Stuttgart: Mundus-Verlag, 1953), 53.

The airplane industry's dependence on the Prussian Army was advantageous because it was sheltered from the fluctuations of the German economy. The years 1911–1914, described by historians Fritz Fischer and Kurt Stenkewitz as a time of economic recession, capital shortage, and labor unrest,[133] saw a period of growth for the airplane industry. These circumstances partially explain why private capital shied away from the embryonic airplane, which lacked the load-carrying capability and the reliability to suit it for commercial purposes. But a market which hinged on the constant, ever-increasing needs of national defense could attract the available capital in a tight capital market. Even the introduction of minimum wages by the unionized Berlin workers, which forced the firms in Johannisthal to increase their wage payments in early 1914,[134] probably had little effect, because the average hourly wage in August 1914 of the best-paid skilled workers in the Berlin aircraft factories—the lathe hands—was .92 marks.[135] The industry's connection to the Prussian Army was the key to its growth.

The firms' expansion in anticipation of a future war made their

potential output in peacetime much higher than the army required. Early in 1914 the army estimated that its best eight firms
could produce 103 to 112 aircraft monthly,[136] or one-quarter of
the army's orders for the entire year of 1913. The surplus industrial capacity stipulated in the analytical scheme for mobilization
was available.

By 1914 the Prussian Army's dealings with the north German
aircraft industry fulfilled the hypothetical political, economic,
and technical prerequisites for industrial mobilization, and the
industry was completely harnessed to the army. The War Ministry and the General Inspectorate had not relied on any overall
blueprint for conquest of the industry; the domination grew out
of their successful pursuit of military interests in their transac-
tions with the aircraft manufacturers. They had achieved
haphazardly what the analytical scheme of 1937 determined
needed to be done purposefully and according to plan.

The Prussian Army's actual mobilization plans for the aircraft
industry in 1914 focused on the exemption of personnel and the
procurement of raw materials. The General Inspectorate suggested the preparation of a supply of finished motors, a planned
delivery quota to permit the industry's accumulation of raw
materials, and a plan for the exemption of skilled workers. The
Inspectorate of Flying Troops would regulate the factories'
supplies and production. The Aviatik factory would be moved
from Mulhausen to Freiburg. The necessity for exemptions did
occasion disagreements: the factories pushed for as many exemptions as possible, while the General Staff and the War Ministry
believed that every deferment meant a weakening of the army's
strength. Because there were no legal provisions to guarantee that
exempted workers would remain at their assigned tasks, elements in the German Army, in particular the Bavarian Inspectorate of Engineers, which would direct the mobilization and

Table 6. PRUSSIAN ARMY AIRCRAFT PROCURE-
MENT, 1911–1913*

| Year | Data |
|---|---|
| 1911 | 11 monoplanes, at prices from 19,000 M. to 20,000 M. |
| |     10 Rumpler |
| |      1 Harlan |
| | 17 biplanes, at average prices of 25,000 M. |
| |     12 Albatros      1 Lᴠɢ |
| |      2 Aviatik       1 Wright |
| |      1 Euler |
| 1912 | 60 monoplanes, at average prices of 21,000 M. |
| |     48 Rumpler     2 Bristol |
| |      7 Harlan      1 Dorner |
| |      2 Aviatik |
| | 79 biplanes, at prices from 25,000 M. to 27,000 M. |
| |     46 Albatros     8 Lᴠɢ |
| |     13 Euler       3 Dꜰᴡ |
| |      9 Aviatik |
| 1913 | 183 monoplanes, at prices from 22,000 M. to 25,000 M. |
| |     66 Rumpler   12 Fokker |
| |     37 Albatros    3 Euler |
| |     36 Gotha      2 Mars |
| |     26 Jeannin    1 Lꜰɢ |
| | 278 biplanes, at prices from 25,000 M. to 27,000 M. |
| |     98 Aviatik    24 Euler |
| |     88 Lᴠɢ      18 Mars (Lꜰɢ) |
| |     48 Albatros    2 Aᴇɢ |

* KAdL, *Militaerluftfahrt*, III, 319 (App. 71).

exemptions of the Bavarian industry, preferred labor conscription. The army could therefore dole the conscripts out to the factories, which in the fondest dreams of certain officers[137] might even be directed by army officers, and then force the men to work without the right to strike.[138]

*Table* 7. BASIC REQUIREMENTS FOR PRUSSIAN
MILITARY AIRCRAFT

| | Range (kilometers) | Speed (kilometers per hour) | Altitude (meters) | Climb (meters/minutes) |
|---|---|---|---|---|
| Summer, 1907 | 50 | 60 | 1,000 | |
| Fall, 1910 | fuel for 4 hrs. | 60 | | |
| Fall, 1911 | fuel for 4 hrs. | 80 | | 500 in 15 |
| Fall, 1912 | fuel for 4 hrs. | 90 | | 500 in 10 |
| Fall, 1913 | fuel for 4 hrs. | 90 | | 800 in 15 |
| June, 1914 | fuel for 4 hrs. | 90 | | 800 in 15 |

Although these mobilization plans were incomplete as of August 1914, the war did not catch the aviation troops unawares. The urgency of the international situation in July prompted the General Inspectorate to order 220 airplanes on 4 July without awaiting the ratification of the War Ministry. Of the 220, 42 were ordered from Albatros, 40 from LVG, 30 from Aviatik, 36 apiece from AEG and Gotha, and 18 apiece from DFW and Rumpler.[139] These firms in turn immediately placed extensive orders for raw materials and parts.[140]

The German airplanes, which by this time held international altitude and distance records, were equal to or better than those in other European armies. On 14 October 1913, Viktor Stoeffler flew more than 1,400 miles in one day in an Aviatik "Arrow" biplane. Richard Boehm, flying an Albatros biplane on 11 July 1914, estab-

lished a world record for nonstop flight of twenty-four hours twelve minutes that was not broken until thirteen years later. Finally, only two weeks before the war, on 14 July 1914, Heinrich Oelerich set a world altitude record of over 25,000 feet in a DFW biplane. These records are indisputable evidence that the army had succeeded in its aim of developing a rugged, dependable two-seat reconnaissance craft with a reliable water-cooled inline engine. All of these airplanes were military types powered with the army's standard 100-horsepower Daimler engine, as the Daimler factory had captured a monopoly share of the motor market. The engine problems that had plagued the army in 1912 had been surmounted; by 1914, 150- to 200-horsepower power plants were available and installed in naval seaplanes. The army's planes were equipped with only 100-horsepower engines because the military authorities, who were concerned with reliability and not with speed, and who did not have the navy's problem of the additional weight of floats, were satisfied with the smaller engine. Indeed, in 1914 they were anxiously awaiting the development of an 80-horsepower rotary engine by the Oberursel firm for use in light airplanes.

The General Staff intended to use aircraft primarily for reconnaissance. However, in addition to secondary duties as a messenger and artillery spotter, the airplane was potentially an attack weapon. Major Siegert of the Flying Troops expected air-to-air combat and anticipated the use of the airplane against troops in the field as a bomber and ground-strafer. In light of these ideas, the General Staff had ordered by the middle of 1913 that some planes be equipped with five- and ten-kilogram bombs. By 1914 the General Staff was examining the possibility of arming some craft with light machine guns, which had been available since early 1913. Although the French had displayed such armed planes at the Paris air show in 1913, the Prussian Army delayed in developing such "destroyer" aircraft because of its concentration on reconnaissance. August Euler had proposed such a *"Zerstoerer"* in 1910, but machine guns at that time were far too heavy for the flimsy airplane. Even in 1913 and 1914 the machine gun's weight reduced the maximum altitude of military craft, and it was not until during the war that the airplane realized its potential as a weapon.

When World War I began in August, the Prussian Army's aviation arm had the same number of effective first-line airplanes as the best of its opponents. The vaunted French could muster approximately 300 front-line planes of a variety of types among its 600 machines; the English only had some 160 airplanes; and the Russians some 400 aircraft, most of which were French and only half of which were fit for service. The Prussian Army went to war with 450 airplanes, 270 biplanes, and 180 monoplanes, of which 295–320 were fit for active service.[141] Given the expectations of a short war and of the small role airplanes would play, the north German aircraft industry and the Prussian Army were at least as well prepared to commence hostilities as any of their counterparts in other European states.

The consensus among authorities on prewar German military aviation—the belief that Prussian military aviation and the north German aircraft industry were not prepared for war—is thus not supported by the facts. These previous interpretations have permitted the tremendous expansion of military aviation and the industry during the war to overshadow their equally important, if quantitatively smaller, prewar development.

In 1916 the Convention of Aircraft Industrialists contended that the most important strides in aviation had occurred before the war but had gone unnoticed because of the relative lack of interest in the airplane. The industry, though small, was fully developed in matters of aviation technology, and its wartime development consequently consisted of an increase in production because of wartime contracts. Although this assertion is clearly an exaggeration, since the industry was far from fully proficient in technological matters by 1914 and made great strides in aviation technology and manufacturing procedures during the war, it lies closer to the truth than those portrayals of a completely undeveloped primitive airplane industry.

The productive companies and designers of the war years had all begun their work before 1914; so too had the army's architects of the wartime expansion of military aviation, Hermann von der Lieth Thomsen and Wilhelm Siegert. This continuity was of the utmost importance because the development of early airplanes was generally a matter of intuition, experience, and experiment, rather than scientific theory translated into reality. Nevertheless, science and aviation technology were becoming increasingly linked as the connections of the Scientific Society for Flight Technology and the German Research Institute for Aviation with the army and the industry indicated. The best firms were profitable, progressive, and expanding in the prewar years; those that fell by the wayside were simply too small, poor, technically barren, or unlucky to survive the competition. In turn the successful firms clearly owed their prosperity to the Prussian Army, however ambivalent the War Ministry and the General Inspectorate appeared toward the airplane, because private capital did not invest substantially in the industry until the military showed an interest in the airplane as a weapon. Given these circumstances, the army deserves credit for the fact that the industry developed as fast as it did, even if its production was naturally geared entirely to military ends. The crucial basis for the great expansion of Prussian military aviation and the north German airplane industry between 1914 and 1918 was laid in the years from 1908 to 1914.

## IV. GERMAN NAVAL AND BAVARIAN AND AUSTRO–HUNGARIAN MILITARY AVIATION, 1909–1914

As the attempt to create a civilian sport aviation market indicated, the north German aircraft industry was actively searching for supplementary markets between 1912 and 1914. Yet the possibility of such markets for the industry existed within the very structure of the German military establishment.

Although the Prussian Army dominated the imperial German military establishment, the Imperial German Navy and the Bavarian Army maintained sufficient independence to develop their own aviation arms and consequently to procure their own airplanes. The navy was an autonomous military institution. Nevertheless, it had to compete with the Prussian Army for its portion of the defense budget. Funds for the fleet rose constantly from 1897 to 1912, ultimately accounting for one-third of the total military budget.

The existence of a Bavarian Army with some independence from the Prussian military machine stems from 1871, after Bavaria, which was second only to Prussia in size and importance in the German Empire, had fought with Prussia against France in the Franco-Prussian War. Consequently, in order to create the German Empire at the Versailles Conference in 1871, Bismarck granted Bavaria and its ruling dynasty, the Wittelsbachs, certain privileges in return for their support of the Prussian Hohenzollerns as the ruling dynasty of the empire. These privileges—an independent railway and postal system, limited diplomatic independence, and a degree of legal, financial, and military autonomy—gave Bavaria a semblance of independence within the confines of the empire without threatening Prussian dominance. The Prussian War Ministry, not the Bavarian War Ministry, controlled the Bavarian Army's budgetary allocation, and the Prusso-German General Staff directed the operations of the Bavarian Army in wartime. Nevertheless, the latter retained considerable administrative autonomy, which it fought jealously to preserve against Prussian encroachment.

The administrative autonomy of the Bavarian Army and the increasing budgetary allocations for the German Navy had obvious significance for the north German aircraft industry; here were two substantial potential markets as yet untapped. Given their difficulties after 1911, would the airplane manufacturers seek to exploit these possibilities?

The Imperial German Navy showed its first official interest in airplanes on 26 October 1910, when Admiral Alfred von Tirpitz, the Secretary of State of the Imperial Naval Office, issued the order to begin airplane tests.[1] For an investigation of the airplane's suitability for the navy, the Dockyard Department of the Naval Office allocated 100,000 marks on 3 December for the coming year, an amount which Tirpitz later raised to 200,000 marks. Since the department recognized the airplane's potential for observation, reconnaissance, and even the destruction of airships, it planned to persuade the airplane industry to undertake overwater flights and to train some naval officers to fly landplanes. Through these flights it hoped to determine the usefulness of army aircraft for naval tasks, since it had no seaplanes at its disposal. The scheme entailed no orders for planes, since the navy had yet to establish the requirements for a seaplane. To set these standards, the Naval Office also ordered the Imperial Dockyard at Danzig to develop a seaplane. The dockyard consequently assigned the task to a Lieutenant Max Hering, naval master builder Coulmann, naval engineer senior grade Karl Loew, and Lieutenant Walter Langfeld as test pilot. Their task was to develop floats, not entire aircraft, since, to the navy, the seaplane meant a plane that that could land at sea in an emergency. These men officially formed the flight test station at Danzig at the end of 1911.

In the meantime the navy continued to seek contacts with the aircraft industry. In May 1911 the Naval Office attempted to persuade the German Aviators Association to encourage test flights over water. Such urgings were to no avail. The Hermann Dorner company did offer to try, but only if encouraged with a subsidy. Since Dorner had recently experienced a series of failures in landplane development and probably hoped to recoup some of his attendant financial losses, the navy wisely requested results

first. Because of their inland location and the fact that landplanes were easier and more profitable to construct, the aircraft firms were reluctant to accept the challenge and expense of seaplane development.

The navy had little money to make its proposition more attractive; it was therefore dependent on the progress made by the industry and the Prussian Army in the development of landplanes, and consequently its first three machines were planes with floats attached at the dockyard. The first was a monoplane built by Engineer Loew and a Lieutenant Fritsch with Rumpler's help and placed at the navy's disposal in August 1911, and the other two were Albatros biplanes delivered in October 1911. In July 1912 the second Albatros floatplane became Germany's first true seaplane and amphibian, as it staged a water takeoff from the Baltic Sea. The Dockyard Department, already satisfied with its three acquisitions, had decided in December 1911 that it would work closely with aircraft firms to develop a seaplane for the German Navy. However, the requirements that it submitted to eleven firms on 15 March 1912—a two-seat amphibian with performance equal to that demanded of army craft—probably only increased the reluctance of the aircraft manufacturers to enter naval aviation. The industry needed more contracts, but the technical difficulties and consequent high cost of seaplane production discouraged full cooperation with the navy.

Naval inventories listed only five flyable airplanes in July 1912, with the ironic result that the National Aviation Fund was funding the construction of several naval air bases which would have no planes. Nevertheless, the Naval Office rejected a request from the Imperial Dockyard at Danzig in July for permission to build its own seaplane, because it considered the financial outlay and risks too great and preferred to depend on the output of German

private enterprise. The Naval Office did acknowledge the possibility that the Dockyard might copy a successful plane developed by private industry, but the dockyards at Kiel and Wilhelmshaven were to serve only as aircraft repair stations and their personnel as members of airplane acceptance commissions. The navy chose to employ its facilities mainly for the development of special aids to naval aviation, such as aircraft radios. As of August the Dockyard Department planned to have only thirteen planes in 1913, of which it estimated that six would be flyable at any given time.

By the fall of 1912 the Imperial Naval Office was using its limited funds to sponsor airplane development in two ways. After representatives of the Naval Office had watched the Glenn Curtiss seaplane perform well at the international seaplane competition held in Monaco in late March 1912, the Office had ordered the Dockyard Department to arrange for the procurement of the plane through a German firm. The Curtiss craft was ordered in July through the *Allgemeine Flug Gesellschaft* (AFG) and accepted by the navy in September. In addition to purchasing successful foreign designs, the Naval Office began to sponsor contests and trials promoting the development of floatplanes and flying boats. In the first contest at Heiligendam in September, the six machines that were entered failed to meet all the requirements for amphibious aircraft, although they all demonstrated a capability to operate from land or water. Nevertheless, the competition laid the foundation for further cooperation between the industry and the navy. The firms actually improved their planes during the contest, and four of them—Rumpler, Albatros, Ago,[2] and Aviatik—later offered to deliver seaplanes that would fulfill the navy's requirements. The last three manufacturers were invited to aircraft trials at Putzig in October 1912, and the navy bought the only plane to pass the tests, the Albatros floatplane, with 30,000 marks contributed for that purpose by the West Prussian Provincial League of the German Air Fleet League. In November following this acquisition the Naval Office appointed an engineer from the Dockyard Department as permanent liaison to Albatros to begin the construction of new seaplanes.

Because of the difficulties in building a production seaplane to meet naval requirements, the navy's new performance stipulations in January 1913 dropped a major impediment to the industry's interest in seaplane construction, the demand that every airplane have amphibious qualities. Seaworthiness, not the ability to operate from land and water, became the major prerequisite, since the best amphibian was worthless if it sank in the turbulent waters of the North Sea.

The Imperial Naval Office sent the new guidelines first to DFW, Rumpler, Albatros, Aviatik, LVG, and to a most significant newcomer—*Flugzeugbau Friedrichshafen* (FF). Until this time naval orders had gone primarily to firms producing for the Prussian Army. Now, in FF, the navy had acquired its first manufacturer specializing in seaplane construction and, consequently, some degree of autonomy from the Prussian Army in aircraft procurement. The firm had been founded in 1912 by Friedrich Kober, Count Zeppelin's oldest friend and co-worker. Kober had persuaded the count to help him found a small company to build seaplanes, and in an old Zeppelin hangar on Lake Constance, Kober had completed his first successful seaplane, a modified Glenn Curtiss design, in the fall of 1912.[3] After February 1913, FF and the navy collaborated so well on the design and construction of seaplanes that the firm on Lake Constance became the largest supplier of naval airplanes in the 1914–1918 war.

✠ *General Karl Heinrich von Haenisch (second from the right), inspector general of military transportation in 1913 and 1914, examines an entry at the Prince Heinrich Flight of 1914. Courtesy of Peter Grosz.*

This first example of differentiation between army and navy aircraft manufacturers was followed later in 1912 with the founding of the Oertz firm, which specialized in the construction of flying boats, and in 1914 just before the outbreak of war by the *Hansa Brandenburgische Flugzeugwerke* (Hansa Brandenburg), which became Germany's second largest wartime manufacturer of naval airplanes. This last firm was something of an anomaly, albeit a successful one, because it was founded by an Italian magnate of the Austro-Hungarian monarchy, Camilio Castiglioni, who already owned two aircraft factories, the *Motorluftfahrzeuggesellschaft* (MLG) in Vienna and the Hungarian Aircraft Works in Budapest. Castiglioni persuaded the German Ernst Heinkel, formerly an outstanding designer with LVG and Albatros, to become his chief designer and, with such solid financial and technical foundations, began production for the German and Austro-Hungarian armed forces soon after the outbreak of hostilities.[4]

With the formation of companies in 1912 devoted entirely to seaplane construction, the navy was undoubtedly encouraged to commit itself more fully to aircraft, although it continued to rely on the airship for aerial reconnaissance and communications. On 1 April 1913 the Imperial Naval Office established an Aviation Section and on 3 May a Naval Flying Unit. That it would still have to coax the industry along was nevertheless evident in the preparations for a high-seas flight scheduled for 29 June–5 July 1913. The navy wanted to hold the contest on the high seas, off the coast of the Baltic or North Sea, but the industry refused, pleading its inability to develop planes capable of flying from the open sea. The contest was held on Lake Constance. As of August naval inventories listed ten airplanes, although the Naval Office had expected to have twelve by that time. And when only Ago and Albatros participated in the naval trials of August 1913, the Naval Office recognized the necessity of promoting seaplane construction much more actively.

Since the flying-boat design was popular in England and America, although the floatplane was preferred by German naval pilots, the Naval Office on 1 November 1913 commissioned FF, Oertz, and Albatros to construct a flying boat and simultaneously ordered a Glenn Curtiss and an English Sopwith flying boat through AFG as models for the German industry. The Curtiss boat had severe difficulties with the high seas during its acceptance tests in January 1914, and the Sopwith boat was never delivered. An Austrian flying boat was procured from MLG and was received, tested, and accepted in June. Of the German airplanes only the FF model showed any promise by mid-1914, but by then the floatplane, by virtue of its superior performance, had gained preeminence. An English Avro floatplane that the Naval Office had also bought through AFG in the fall of 1913 had demonstrated superior performance at the fall maneuvers of the German high-seas fleet. The Naval Office consequently recommended that select firms copy the Avro plane, and from these copies came the first serial orders for naval airplanes. In February 1914 the Naval Office ordered ten Ago, five FF, and five Albatros floatplanes. The first contract for a shipboard airplane went to AEG in March 1914, and although production difficulties were to delay fulfillment of all these contracts, the expansion of naval aviation was under way.

In order to popularize the cause of naval aviation and to test the seaworthiness of German naval airplanes, the Imperial Naval Office planned to hold the Baltic Sea Flight 1914 at Warnemuende in cooperation with the National Aviation Fund, the Imperial Office of the Interior, the German Aviators Association, and the city of Rostock. As the Naval Office planned to order the victorious airplanes in small quantities, eleven firms, among them

Albatros, Ago, FF, Hansa Brandenburg, AEG, Aviatik, and Rumpler, entered twenty-six planes in the contest, which was planned for 1–11 August 1914.[5] The sponsors, however, had not reckoned with one eventuality: the declaration of war on 1 August abruptly halted the proceedings. The navy hastily commandeered all twenty-six entries, many of which were worthless, and rushed away, enthusiastic but ill-equipped for what lay ahead. As of 1 August 1914 the navy had twenty-four planes at its stations, many of which were not seaworthy and none of which could be considered more than a training airplane.[6] Between 1911 and August 1914 it had bought thirty-nine airplanes—sixteen Albatros, nine Ago, six FF, and four Rumpler models, with one each from AEG, Gotha, Oertz, and MLG. Almost one-quarter of these, nine aircraft (three Albatros, four FF, one Ago, and one MLG) had been acquired between April and June of 1914. Because these seaplanes were heavier and stronger than landplanes, they generally used from 150- to 200-horsepower inline motors, the best of which were the 6-cylinder, 150-horsepower Mercedes and the 150-horsepower Argus.

English seaplane forces, which would confront the German Navy in the North Sea, had also undergone their greatest prewar expansion during the first half of 1914. Although few in number, the English craft were far superior in performance and seaworthiness to any the Germans possessed. Given England's traditional concentration in naval affairs, this superiority was to be expected; yet in both England and Germany only the war prompted the speedy development of the seaplane to a truly reliable weapon of naval warfare.

By August 1914, German naval aviation had advanced only slightly beyond the experimental stage. Technical difficulties were numerous, and the navy's reliance on the airship and its small budget for airplanes slowed the development of a seaplane force. In addition, the navy would never be completely independent of the Prussian Army and its airplane manufacturers, because it would later need landplanes as much as floatplanes. Nevertheless, the navy's considerable achievements in airplane development laid the foundations for future strides. The Imperial Naval Office had determined the basic organization and facilities needed for airplanes, it had settled on the floatplane as its fundamental airplane type, and it had established close contact with firms specializing in seaplane production in order to remove the technical difficulties of construction. And the navy intended to continue this progress, since the Dockyard Department proposed before the outbreak of war in 1914 an inventory of fifty aircraft for 1915. In February 1914, Chief of the Admiralty Staff Admiral Hugo von Pohl was already asking for airplanes, not just as defensive weapons against enemy airships and airplanes, but also, more significantly, as offensive weapons for reconnaissance and attack in order to compensate for the German fleet's lack of cruisers.[7] The importance of naval aviation has been established.

In Bavaria the Inspectorate of the Engineers Corps, which would supervise Bavarian aviation under the Bavarian War Ministry's Army Department I, entered aeronautics by subsidizing the construction attempts of one of its officers, a Lieutenant Wildt, in the fall of 1910. It had promised earlier to help him if the Prussian Inspectorate of Transport Troops turned a deaf ear to his proposals, which the north German agency promptly did. The Bavarian Engineers would have done well to follow suit. Four times, from late 1910 through the summer of 1911, Wildt tried to build and fly his machines, and four times he failed miserably, all the while prolonging the agonizing strain on the Bavarian Army's limited aviation funds. Nevertheless, in July 1911 the Inspector of the Engineers Corps, General Karl von Brug, still recommended a subsidy of 20,000 marks for Wildt, and as late as October the

Engineers listed Wildt among their preferred producers.[8] Since the Engineers rejected several equally promising proposals from Bavarian citizens in 1911, Wildt's position as an officer seems to have been the most important criterion for acceptance of his design. Only pride, and the wild hope that success might give Bavaria a source of airplanes independent of Prussia, can explain the Engineers' stubborn catering to the fantasies of a fellow officer.

In any case, by 1911 the Bavarian Army had chosen to take a more reliable course in aviation, just as the Prussian Army had done when its efforts at airplane construction failed. When the Engineers decided to rely on private enterprise, the Prussian Army made its experience with and information on prospective military aircraft and aircraft manufacturers available through the Bavarian liaison officer at the Prussian Army's Research Unit and the Bavarian military plenipotentiary in Berlin.[9] The Engineers, however, deemed the extensive use of foreign (i.e., north German) aircraft companies for deliveries and pilot training unnecessary and undesirable, so they declined Albatros's offers in November to train Bavarian officer pilots and to deliver airplanes to Munich. Using a private flying school outside of Munich made it unnecessary for the airplane factories to train army pilots, which was the Prussian *modus operandi*.[10] When the need to expand Bavarian aviation in December forced the Engineers to purchase planes and to have pilots trained on the new machines, General von Brug used the Euler Firm, because Frankfort was closer than Berlin-Johannisthal[11] and perhaps because Euler, if not Bavarian, was at least not Prussian. On their limited aviation budget the Engineers bought only seven airplanes from Euler and one from Albatros, with the majority from one firm in order to ensure some standardization of their military machines. Their fondest hope—the growth of a Bavarian aviation industry that would relieve them of

*Table 8.* BAVARIAN ARMY AIRCRAFT PROCUREMENT, 1911–1913[*]

| Year | Data |
|------|------|
| 1911 | 1 Wildt monoplane, at 22,000 M. |
|      | 8 biplanes, at average prices of 20,000 M. |
|      |    1 Albatros |
|      |    7 Euler |
| 1912 | 23 biplanes, at prices from 9,000 M. to 22,000 M. |
|      |    17 Otto |
|      |    6 Euler |
| 1913 | 9 monoplanes, at average prices of 22,000 M. |
|      |    5 Albatros    1 Otto |
|      |    2 Etrich    1 Rumpler |
|      | 58 biplanes, at prices from 22,800 M. to 28,000 M. |
|      |    46 Otto |
|      |    12 LVG |

[*]KAdL, *Militaerluftfahrt*, III, 104. The KAdL chart incorrectly lists Euler as the manufacturer of all 23 airplanes delivered to the Bavarian Army in 1912.

the unwanted dependence on the Prussian Army and the north German aircraft industry—persisted. The distance from Munich to Frankfort or Johannisthal complicated procurement, repairs, and mobilization plans, a dilemma that could be solved if the Engineers successfully promoted a Bavarian aircraft industry.[12]

For these reasons Brug had enthusiastically greeted the founding of Bavaria's first aircraft firm, the Otto Works of Munich, which employed forty workers by the summer of 1911. Brug believed then that the company, though untested, was well-equipped and well-planned and showed great potential,[13] but the

Inspectorate of Engineers could not afford to become dependent on a single untested factory. In mid-January 1912, when the Otto company had produced a successful aircraft, Brug promptly decided to grant Gustav Otto most of Bavaria's airplane procurement and repair contracts because of its convenient location.[14] This decision would determine the course of the Bavarian Army's relationship with the German aircraft industry and with the Prussian Army's aviation agencies for the next two and one-half years.

The years from 1912 to August 1914 were a time of steady expansion for Bavaria's small airplane agencies, although they had only approximately one-fifteenth of the Prussian budgetary allotment for aviation.[15] The upper organizational reaches did not change: the Bavarian War Ministry, Army Department I under a Colonel Koeberle, at the top; next the Engineers Inspectorate under General von Brug; and then the Bavarian Inspectorate of Military Aviation and Motor Vehicles established in 1911. At the lower levels, however, a Flying Command instituted on 1 January 1912 had become a Flying Company by 1 April 1912 and an independent Battalion of the Aviation and Motor Vehicle Inspectorate by 1 October 1913. To train more flyers the army bought the private flying school and converted it into the Bavarian Military Flying School, making use of the Otto firm and, where necessary, the north German aircraft factories. In November 1912, Gustav Otto loaned the army a mechanic to train their military personnel; the same mechanic later became manager-engineer of the Army's Munich-Oberschleissheim Air Station in July 1913.

The Bavarian Army's partiality toward its hometown manufacturer caused friction between the Bavarian and Prussian armies over Otto's participation in the latter's military airplane competitions and disagreement within the Bavarian Army over the granting of permission to expanding north German firms to exploit the south German military market.

Gustav Otto asked the Prussian Army on 15 February 1912 to consider him for contracts for pilot training and airplane construction, and particularly for entry in its aircraft competition planned for the fall of 1912. The Prussian War Ministry originally opposed the idea, because it intended the contest only for manufacturers it would consider for contracts in a mobilization. The Otto Works, whose airplanes it considered inferior, was too far from Berlin. Nevertheless, transport department chief Colonel Schmiedecke later relented and informed the Bavarian War Ministry that Otto could participate on one condition: that the Bavarian Army give 60,000 marks to guarantee Otto a prize if he should place in the contest. The Bavarian Airship and Motor Vehicle Unit felt that the Otto firm's excellent workmanship, promptness of delivery, and importance to the Bavarian Army merited the 60,000 marks subsidy. General von Brug ascertained that the funds obligated the Prussian Army not only to let Otto enter the competition and receive a prize, but also to accept the Bavarian Army's claim on two of the prize-winning airplanes. Since Bavaria would thus enable Otto to participate and would secure two good airplanes for itself in the bargain, the Bavarian War Ministry granted the 60,000 marks. The Prussian War Ministry permitted Otto's entry on 25 May 1912.[16]

Meanwhile, in an attempt to circumvent the Prussian Army's objections, Otto founded the Ago Works in Johannisthal, which he empowered to handle all business—contracts, repairs, pilot training—with the Prussian Army.[17] Nevertheless, all the efforts of Otto and the Bavarian Army came to nought, because the Prussian General Inspectorate postponed the contest until early 1913 and later canceled it because of delays in aircraft motor production.[18]

On 10 February 1913 the General Inspectorate issued requirements for a transportable airplane complete with truck to the following eight firms: Bristol, Albatros, Rumpler, Fokker, DFW, Euler, Aviatik, and AEG. The victor in the contest would receive orders for twelve planes, and the runners-up might win consolation contracts. Because the north German firms already had a head start in developing transportable planes, Brug, without awaiting the consent of the Bavarian War Ministry, immediately informed Otto that his firm might be able to participate in the competition. To the Bavarian War Ministry he recommended that Otto be commissioned to build a transportable plane if he were not allowed to compete in the Prussian trials. Then the Bavarian military plenipotentiary in Berlin informed the Bavarian War Ministry that the General Inspectorate was sponsoring not a contest, but a trial for factories that had already delivered successful airplanes to the Prussian Army. Since the Ago Works had yet to present any airplanes for trials at Doeberitz, it, as well as AEG, had been stricken from the list of participants. Upon the General Inspectorate's confirmation of the plenipotentiary's report, Brug could only protest to the Bavarian War Ministry in April that the General Inspectorate had used the terms "contest" and "consolation prizes" in the original announcement. Nevertheless, the Bavarian authorities were once again powerless, and Otto was not included in the competition.

General von Brug surmised that the General Inspectorate's "regrettable" neglect of Otto for peacetime deliveries and competitions stemmed from the realization that Bavaria would claim all of Otto's wartime production. He argued, however, that Bavaria had no choice, since Prussia's monopolization of non-Bavarian firms would force it to do this. He insisted that the Bavarian firms had to be an integral part of the German airplane industry in peacetime in order to ensure some uniformity of performance of German military airplanes.[19]

Despite the validity of Brug's argument, Otto never presented an airplane to the Prussian Army. In October 1913, Otto did ask the Prussian War Ministry if he could demonstrate a plane at Doeberitz, since the Bavarian War Ministry had given several Johannisthal companies the opportunity to present their airplanes in Munich in the past year. But the General Inspectorate rejected his request, because it doubted that Otto was large enough to survive the competition. The Otto biplane had crashed repeatedly in the recent Prince Heinrich Flight and had given the impression of such faulty construction that the Prussian Inspectorate of Flying Troops had branded the Otto factory incapable of building a warplane.[20] Ironically, although the Ago Works became a leading prewar manufacturer of seaplanes for the German navy, it was never able to secure a contract from the Prussian Army.

While Gustav Otto attempted unsuccessfully to prove his firm to the Prussian Army, the expanding north German aircraft firms sought to enter the south German market by establishing branches in Bavaria. Their success depended largely on the Bavarian Army's assessment of the worth of the Otto Works. Not only had the Bavarian Army supported Otto's efforts to be included in the Prussian Army's contracts, it also gave the majority of its contracts to Otto. Of the twenty-three airplanes it purchased in fiscal year 1912 and the sixty-seven acquired in 1913, seventeen and forty-seven, respectively, were designed and manufactured by Gustav Otto, while the others came from north German firms. Would the Bavarian Army also protect the Otto factory from direct competition imported from outside Bavaria's borders?

In early August 1912 the *Waggonfabrik Jos. Rathgeber AG* (Rathgeber) of Moosach, near Munich, offered to begin licensed production of the Rumpler firm's successful monoplane, the Taube. Brug recommended to the Bavarian War Ministry that it dissuade Rathgeber from entering aircraft production, because substantial orders for monoplanes were unlikely, and the Bavarian Army could not support two firms with its contracts. Its first duty was to the Otto Works, which had offered to build a version of the Taube itself.[21] The Rathgeber company persisted and offered the Rumpler monoplane again on 22 October 1912. But this time Brug suggested that a definite decision should be postponed, because the speedy development of military aviation might permit orders to other factories, in particular branch factories, which would create competition without ruining Otto. His suggestion was rejected by the War Ministry, which considered that the circumstances since Rathgeber's first offer had not changed and that one factory sufficed to meet Bavaria's small needs in aircraft, accessories, and repairs.[22]

Coincident with Rathgeber's request, Albatros inquired if the number of Bavarian contracts warranted the founding of a branch factory in Bavaria. Brug's recommendation to the War Ministry in December 1912 repeated his advice concerning Rathgeber's second offer: Bavarian military aviation did not have to be based solely on the Otto firm, and the development of aviation might make a second firm a viable proposition. Nevertheless, the Bavarian War Ministry still refused to support a factory whose existence, in its opinion, depended on Berlin and not Munich.[23]

Brug's next opportunity to raise the question of competition for Otto arose when Aviatik recommended its new biplane on 25 March 1913. Although he had no intention of purchasing an Aviatik craft, he asserted that interfirm competition would raise the quality and lower the prices of aircraft. The Bavarian Army could procure single airplanes from outside firms and have them copied in Bavaria; however, in Brug's opinion Rathgeber's offer was better because it would create a stable aircraft company backed by a large firm. As usual, the Bavarian War Ministry opposed Rathgeber's entry into airplane production because of its belief that the army's contracts would not support two firms.[24]

After the failure of Rathgeber's negotiations with the Bavarian War Ministry, Rumpler decided to try himself. He informed the Inspectorate of Engineers that he was again in contact with Rathgeber and the *Lokomotivfabrik Krauss* about the establishment of a Rumpler branch in or near Munich. Once again, on 4 July 1913, Brug expounded his point of view to the War Ministry—this time at great length—using Rumpler's offer as the occasion. Although Otto's biplane had been among the best German aircraft the previous year, its performance had been surpassed by other German airplanes in the Prince Heinrich Flight of 1913, no doubt because the firm's lack of competition gave it no incentive to make improvements. The Taube was the best monoplane available, and the Prussian Army had decided recently to order only Taubes for its flying units. The Bavarian War Ministry itself had just assigned six officers to the Albatros and Rumpler factories for training on the monoplane.[25] Now Rumpler, the original German manufacturer of the design, was offering to build a factory in Bavaria. In Brug's opinion such a firm would be more stable than the Otto factory, yet it would not ruin Otto, who was already having difficulty fulfilling his repair contracts punctually. The dangers of strikes and fires, in addition to the commanding position vis-à-vis the army that a firm enjoying a monopoly would gain, were sufficient to make Brug realize that dependence on one company would be foolhardy. He recommended, there-

fore, that the Bavarian Army encourage Rumpler to establish a branch in Munich under the following conditions: the Bavarian Army would order twelve Taubes immediately to form a flying unit, further orders would depend on the satisfactory execution of the initial order, and the army would always be free to procure other aircraft.[26]

In the midst of the debate within the Bavarian Army over Rumpler's offer, Otto opportunely informed the War Ministry of his first monoplane's recent success in the Flight Round Berlin contest in August. In his opinion this triumph proved that his firm, the only south German entry in the contest, was at least as capable as the north German companies. Otto reminded the Bavarian Army of his "unselfish service," service which he believed his family's wealth would enable him to continue. Bavaria did not need Rumpler, who, in Otto's opinion, was "neither a designer nor a particularly cooperative supplier." Recalling his own difficulties in finding and training reliable workers in Munich, Otto warned that discussing the formation of a new firm in Munich was far easier than obtaining a reliable work force. As proof that a second factory would not survive, Otto cited the collapse earlier that year of the aspiring aircraft firm Germany, which never established itself firmly despite an outlay of some 800,000 marks.[27]

With information from Brug and Otto in hand, the Bavarian War Ministry decided on 18 September 1913 that to forsake the Otto Works after all its sacrifices would create unjustified hardships for the firm and make it move elsewhere ("elsewhere" was not specified) in the face of ruinous competition. Otto's aircraft,

✹ *Pusher biplane by the Otto Works of Munich, the only aircraft company in Bavaria until mid-1914. Courtesy of Peter Grosz.*

particularly earlier ones, had proved themselves, and the War Ministry attributed his failure at the Prince Heinrich Flight to the lack of preparation of the Bavarian flyers, not the airplane. Otto should have the opportunity to build a monoplane for evaluation before any commitment was made to Rumpler; it was known that the Rumpler Taube had operational shortcomings—it required a long takeoff and landing run and was not easily transportable or suited for observation duties. A second airplane manufacturer might be necessary in Bavaria only when the National Aviation Fund financed a flying school in Munich or when the army's needs expanded considerably, neither of which would occur for a few years.[28] The Bavarian War Ministry would make no commitments; the prospective manufacturer would have to bear the entire risk without any likelihood of commensurate profit.

When the Bavarian Inspectorate of Aviation and Motor Vehicles did deem it necessary to order Taubes from north German firms in October 1913, it hesitated to make any binding commitments on the numbers to be procured until Otto was included. In mid-November the Inspectorate ordered one Otto monoplane, one Taube from Rumpler, two from Etrich, and five from Albatros, the Albatros version being considered the most reliable of all.[29]

In the ongoing debate over new aircraft factories between Engineers Inspector General von Brug and the chief of Department I of the War Ministry, Colonel Koeberle, Brug's stand was more reasonable and flexible. Between the first and second Rathgeber offers in 1912, Brug had resolved that it was essential to create competition in the Bavarian aircraft industry, even if it meant relying on companies based in Prussia. By late 1912 the Bavarian Army's reliance on the Otto Works had pushed it into a technological backwater. While other German firms had turned to tractor aircraft, Otto still built only pusher planes, and the Bavarian War Ministry found exclusive dependence upon his firm less and less defensible.

The War Ministry's fear that a competing firm would have ruined Otto may be correct, even though calculations made by the Prussian Army in mid-1912 indicated that the Bavarian Army's orders for sixty-seven aircraft in 1913 would have been sufficient to support two firms. The War Ministry's intransigence sprang from one belief—that to preserve Otto as an independent manufacturer was to safeguard the autonomy of Bavarian military aviation. Yet the desired independence from Prussia could never be truly achieved, because Bavaria's aviation arm was too small and the autonomy of its entire military force nominal. Near total reliance on the Otto Works provided only a precarious measure of freedom from Prussia. Admittedly, the Prussian Army was pushing the Bavarian War Ministry toward this attitude by preventing Otto from participating in its competitions; but the Bavarian Army was in no position to retaliate by rejecting the attempts of capable north German firms to establish themselves in Bavaria. Yet the War Ministry, desperately trying to resist the encroachments of Prussian influence, unconditionally protected the Otto Works from outside competition. Even this policy, however, could not save the Otto firm.

Because of its failure to produce any new aircraft by early January 1914, the Otto Works, which was in severe difficulty, was involved in license negotiations with LVG in Johannisthal. Otto would have to release some of his workers if he received no contracts, so the Bavarian Inspectorate of Aviation and Motor Vehicles recommended that four of eight new biplanes which it intended to buy from LVG be procured from Otto.[30] Brug remarked that the Inspectorate's policy would solve nothing, since Otto could not close the negotiations and switch his factory to the production of LVG aircraft in time to meet the deadline. Despite substantial orders received in 1913, Otto remained on the brink of bankruptcy, a problem Brug realized was bound to recur, particularly during the winter, when flying activity was reduced and contracts declined. Brug therefore reiterated the absolute necessity of a stable, large aircraft firm in Bavaria.[31] Although he emphasized later that he did not want to prejudice the army against the Otto Works and that the army should always consider Otto first for all contracts,[32] Brug still maintained that Otto had reached an impasse in the development of his own airplanes and had become totally dependent on LVG, a situation that was inimical to the interests of the Bavarian Army.[33]

The Bavarian War Ministry overruled Brug's recommendation that it purchase all eight planes directly from LVG and in late January ordered twelve LVG biplanes—six from LVG and six from Otto.[34] Otto, however, as Brug had predicted, could not deliver his six airplanes on time and requested that he not be fined for breach of contract. The Bavarian Inspectorate of Aviation and Motor Vehicles refused to release him from the penalty, but now Brug interceded on Otto's behalf. He accepted Otto's excuses for his tardiness—errors in LVG drawings, LVG's delays in sending him the wing spars, a subcontractor's delay in finishing leather parts, and the unexpected length of time needed to make certain items—because the delivery schedules had been too tight to accommodate the unforeseen problems involved in initial orders of aircraft. The War Ministry, for once heeding Brug's recommendation, released Otto from payment of the fine.[35] Once again Brug had exhibited acuity and foresight where aircraft procurement was concerned. The War Ministry's policy of partiality toward Otto had failed, resulting in exactly the situation that it had sought to avoid—dependence on north German aircraft companies.

Although Gustav Otto informed the Bavarian War Ministry in July 1914 that he was prepared to build a branch factory close to any new air stations,[36] his factory was financially and technically incapable of expansion. For this reason Brug had welcomed an offer in June from Gotha to build a Bavarian branch of its aircraft department. In addition, Gotha's choice of Nuremberg-Fuerth coincided with the Engineers Inspectorate's plans to build a new air station there. Under these circumstances one might expect the War Ministry to have looked favorably on the north German factory's offer. Instead, the conditions set by the War Ministry were stringent: the army would dictate the type of aircraft and construction innovations to the firm, and it could also order the factory to copy other designs and to repair the aircraft of other companies. In return, the army guaranteed nothing. Gotha's reply was cordial, but noncommittal, and the Bavarian Army heard no more from it about a branch in Bavaria.[37]

The War Ministry's response to the Gotha's offer showed no change in attitude despite its willingness at least to propose conditions. The harshness of these requirements indicated the reluctance of the War Ministry to relinquish its opposition to "foreign" factories in Bavaria and to admit the errors of its previous policy toward outside firms. Undoubtedly, it had agreed to make the offer, all the while hoping that such harsh conditions would dissuade the railroad factory, only because events had vindicated Brug's judgment so often.

Meanwhile, the bulwark of the War Ministry's policy, the Otto Works, was experiencing no temporary setback. Otto's difficulties led to the financial collapse of his factory shortly after the war began. In July 1914, however, a new factory located at Speyer on the Rhine in the Bavarian Palatinate—the Pfalz Aircraft Works—announced its production of a light parasol airplane (a monoplane with wings positioned above the fuselage) for military use. Its location close to the western border and its financial and technical capabilities prompted the Engineers Inspectorate to request the presentation of a finished parasol for trials in late July 1914.[38] The relationship of Pfalz with the Bavarian Army is a matter of wartime history; suffice it to say that Pfalz and the successor to the Otto Works, the Bavarian Aircraft Works, continued the prewar tradition of the Otto Works by providing the Bavarian Army with aircraft factories based in Bavaria.

The problems between the Bavarian and Prussian armies over military aviation stemmed originally from the institutional split between the two within the German armed forces. In certain aspects of military aviation the Bavarian Army was subordinate to the Prussian Army: the Prussian War Ministry controlled its budget, the Prussian Research Unit set procurement guidelines and forwarded information about firms and planes, and Prussia ultimately controlled the mobilization and deployment of air forces. Sensitive about this dependence, the Bavarian Army attempted to establish its autonomy in the administration of military aviation through the procurement of military airplanes from a Bavarian manufacturer, the Otto Works.

The Prussian Army touched the raw nerve of Bavarian military inferiority when it excluded the Otto Works from its orders and military competitions, an action which further increased the Bavarian Army's desire for an independent aircraft industry. The Otto Works, as the sole Bavarian manufacturer, reaped the benefits, gaining the majority of Bavarian military contracts. In reality, there was no valid reason for the Prussian Army to reject the Otto and Ago companies out of hand. Objectively, the Bavarian War Ministry's reaction to the Prussian Army's rebuff of the Otto Works was senseless, and, in the long run, self-defeating. The policies of the two rival agencies and the consequent strife were a product of the same particularistic sentiment that had spawned

the inefficient division between Bavaria and Prussia in the Imperial German Army. However, in light of the aim of independence and not of efficiency or objectivity, the Bavarian War Ministry's support of the Otto Works was a qualified success, since it did maintain an independent source of airplanes from 1912 to 1914. However, the lack of competition was certainly the most important reason for the increasing backwardness of Bavarian military airplanes, and the demise of the Otto Works was the most conclusive proof of the precariousness of a program dependent on one firm.

The development of German naval and Bavarian military aviation, an aspect of the overall growth of German aviation and the aircraft industry, thus led to some differentiation between their own and the Prussian Army's aircraft manufacturers. The Bavarian Army's devotion to the Otto Works and the relatively small scale of its aviation forces prevented its becoming a substantial market for the rest of the industry. Meanwhile, the small size and experimental nature of the German Navy's aviation units and its concentration of seaplanes provided a market only for the few firms interested in (and capable of) devoting their talent to the complicated technical tasks of seaplane development and production. Although certain north German aircraft factories, like Albatros and Rumpler, did deliver airplanes to both the army and the navy, their production of floatplanes was clearly a secondary occupation; had it interfered with their production for the army, it would certainly have been dropped. The north German manufacturers viewed the need for additional markets basically in terms of the easiest and cheapest utilization of their surplus capacity. This meant the production either of more army airplanes or of sport airplanes, not of more complex naval seaplanes. Because of the special nature of Bavarian military and German naval aviation, the overall expansion of German aviation did not provide the north German airplane manufacturers, who formed practically the entire industry, with substantial new markets between 1912 and August 1914. Ironically, a new market for their exploitation came from an unexpected quarter.

✴ A French Morane Parasol monoplane, license-built by the Pfalz Aircraft Works, which was founded just before the war in the Bavarian Palatinate at Speyer on the Rhine. Courtesy of Peter Grosz.

### THE AUSTRO-HUNGARIAN ARMED FORCES

In Austria-Hungary, the General Staff assumed the initiative in expressing an interest in aviation. In 1907, mainly on the basis of foreign developments, the chief of the General Staff, General Franz Conrad von Hoetzendorff, was already pressing for aviation forces, although Austrian experimenters had yet to fly. Two noted Austrian aviation inventors of the early years, Igo Etrich and Franz Wels, were in the beginning stages of their endeavors, Wels having staged some successful powered glides in 1906 and 1907. Consequently, when Conrad made his initial recommendations, he could refer to no concrete domestic developments or successes. Nevertheless, one year later, in October 1908, Conrad advocated the support of any inventor who had a useful aircraft project, with specific reference to the continuing flight tests of Etrich and Wels.[39] Thus the General Staff under Conrad, like the German General Staff in imperial Germany, assumed the role of instigator in Austro-Hungarian military aviation.

By 1909 civilian interest in aircraft was increasingly evident. Civilian aviation groups like the Aero-Section of the Austrian Automobile Club and the Flying Machine Association banded together to form the Flight Technology Association. The pinnacle of the Austro-Hungarian Army, the Military Chancellery under Archduke Franz Ferdinand, participated in the formation of this group, an indication of the army's increasing interest in airplanes.[40]

Civilian interest was also manifest in the formation of the first official Austrian airfield. In October 1908 the Commander of the Transport Troops Brigade Command in the War Ministry, Major General von Schleyer, asked for Conrad's help in fulfilling a request from Etrich and Wels to use the city field in Wiener Neustadt. Victor Silberer, a member of both the Imperial Council and the Parliament of Lower Austria, also suggested the use of the Wiener Neustadt property as an air field in January 1909. In early May the commander of the Military Aeronautical Institute of the First Fortress Artillery Regiment, Captain Hinterstoisser, wrote the mayor and city council of Wiener Neustadt requesting use of the field for aviation. The city council at the urging of the mayor decided on 11 June to build and rent hangars on the land, and Igo Etrich promptly rented the first one. The army was thus spared the cost of building its own airfield, and in mid-August the Military Aeronautical Institute rented three hangars. By the end of 1909 the army was renting four of the seven hangars on the field. During the following year the runway was improved and reviewing stands and access ways built, all by private enterprise.[41]

Private initiative also deserves the credit for the Austrian Army's first airplanes, which were gifts from concerns or individuals. The military's first plane came from a syndicate led by theater director Carl Wallner, which presented a 1908 French Farman to the Military Aeronautical Institute for assembly in the spring of 1909 as a publicity scheme. The syndicate and the Institute agreed that the machine would serve simultaneously to train officer pilots and to stimulate public interest in military airplanes through public demonstrations. The War Ministry, which had the final say in such matters, consented to the Military Aeronautical Institute's construction of the plane, but warned that since their use of the military exercise field must not interfere with troop training, the public could not be admitted. In any case the plane, once assembled, did not fly, even after modification, and so it was given to the army museum. Count Clemens Maria von Radowitz, an Austrian resident of Paris, donated the army's second airplane, a French Blériot machine. The War Ministry accepted the gift in the fall of 1909, but refused to grant the funds to send an officer to Paris for training and to bring the airplane to Vienna. Radowitz finally had to send it at his own expense. Soon afterward, the industrialist Robert von Lieben donated the third airplane, a Wright biplane. Just as in imperial Germany, the early development of military aviation basically hinged on private initiative, from the creation of military airfields to the granting of planes to the army.[42] The significant difference was that the private grants of airplanes to the Austro-Hungarian military came from disinterested civilians, whereas in Germany such grants came from embryonic aircraft firms which would profit directly from military interest in aviation.

In the meantime, an aircraft industry had emerged in Austria-Hungary. The *Motorluftfahrzeuggesellschaft* (MLG) had been founded in Vienna on 23 April 1909 with 300,000 crowns capital by the Austro-American Rubber Company and the Daimler Motor Company. The guiding light of the undertaking was undoubtedly Camilio Castiglioni, the wealthy owner of the rubber factory; this was the start of his auspicious career as an aviation entrepreneur. The Jakob Lohner firm of Vienna, which built chassis, established an aircraft department in October 1909 under the direction of Ludwig Lohner, the owner's son, who had become increasingly interested in airplanes since his first exposure to them in 1906.[43] Chief of the General Staff Conrad, whose positive stance toward aviation was certainly no secret, is said to have encouraged some industrialists to found factories. Conrad understood the critical importance of the military-industrial relationship in the development of an aircraft industry, and he realized that military aid and contracts were absolutely necessary to the growth of an aircraft industry in the absence of a transportation or sport market. Consequently, he proposed the formation of an army flying company by the fall of 1909.[44]

Notwithstanding Conrad's positive attitude toward aircraft, the army's reluctance to invest money in flying machines and its willingness to rely completely on gifts and private initiative stemmed principally from the attitude of the War Ministry. The War Ministry hesitated to invest in an untested technological invention that might never prove to be militarily useful, so it preferred to withhold its financial support until private enterprise could develop a successful warplane.[45] The Austro-Hungarian War Ministry thus assumed basically the same attitude toward airplanes as its Prussian counterpart. According to Conrad, the minister of war, General Franz von Schoenaisch, regarded him as an "uncomfortable warner and instigator."[46] The war minister had to deal with two governments in getting budgetary credits accepted, and defense credits, after approval by the ministers of defense of Austria and Hungary, had to be accepted by the parliaments of both countries. The difficulties and complications inherent in this dual authorization system resulted in the increasing obsolescence of even basic armaments, in particular artillery, so that the war minister's reluctance to expend funds on an invention that might prove useless is understandable.

By 1910, however, the development of the airplane and the aircraft industry was beginning to draw a more positive response from the imperial army. On 29 November 1909, Etrich staged the first powered flight by an Austrian from the field at Wiener Neustadt, and by May 1910 his assistant Karl Illner had made the first Austrian overland flight with one passenger. The Transport Troops Brigade Command, following these events, declared in June 1910 to the War Ministry that the airplane could perform wartime reconnaissance tasks despite its shortcomings, which in any case would soon be solved by the extraordinarily fast development of aircraft technology. The command consequently resolved to purchase the Etrich monoplane and three relatively untested types, the Pischoff monoplane and the Pfleiderer and Warchalowski biplanes.[47] The latter two types were under construction at the Austro-Hungarian Auto-plane Works, a company founded in June 1910 in Vienna and Budapest with a capital of one million crowns by four metal and machine factories. The company promptly requested the army's full support in the production of military airplanes.[48]

An army Military Technical Committee, which observed the Budapest Air Week in June, reached a conclusion similar to that of the Prussian Army's Research Unit (headed by Captain de le Roi) in March 1910 when it strongly recommended that the army involve itself in the development of airplanes in order to ensure that constructors followed military and not sporting needs. In order to avoid falling behind other countries, the committee advised that the army should buy the best domestic airplanes—the Etrich, Pischoff, and Warchalowski craft—in order to examine the possible usefulness of the airplane and to promote a domestic industry.[49] In response to this suggestion, the War Ministry bought only a Blériot monoplane from an Austrian army officer at a price of 12,000 crowns, preferring to postpone the acquisition of a "worthy" domestic airplane until later. It did offer to consider buying Etrich's aircraft if he lowered the price from 25,000 crowns to 10,000 crowns, but simultaneously declared its intent to consider other domestic firms, in particular the Auto-plane Works, for contracts.[50] Thus the War Ministry, ignoring the suggestion of the Technical Committee, preferred to offer practically the same price for a new Etrich Taube as for a used and outdated Blériot.

At the Wiener Neustadt Flying-meeting in September 1910, Emperor Franz Joseph offered his blessing to the new endeavor by personally wishing Igo Etrich luck, and Conrad flew for the first time during the air show. This experience served to convince the chief of the General Staff even more firmly of the military importance of aircraft, and he promptly recommended the procurement of 200 airplanes for forty flying companies at a cost of approximately four million crowns. According to Conrad's plan, the army would possess 250 warplanes and 250 training planes by 1915. There was no chance, however, that he would receive such a large sum; nevertheless, in an audience with Emperor Franz Joseph on 12 November 1910, Conrad emphasized the urgency of aircraft procurement and pilot training. He then requested less, 300,000 crowns, for initial expenses. But less was still too much, as war minister Schoenaisch and Austrian finance minister Aehrenthal opposed the plans.[51] One must grant, however, that Conrad's initial plans probably could not have been carried out—not only for financial reasons, but also because of the embryonic nature of the aircraft industry and its designs.

At least by November the War Ministry had accepted the Transport Troops Brigade Command's recommendation to buy the Etrich monoplane for 25,000 crowns if the plane passed the army's minimum performance standards for airplanes—capability for a two-hour flight, easy assembly, a minimum speed of forty-five miles per hour, and a payload of 300 pounds. Since the Command preferred monoplanes to biplanes because the former were easier to assemble, the Etrich monoplane had the

*Table 9.* ORGANIZATION OF THE AUSTRO-HUNGARIAN FLYING TROOPS, 1911[1]

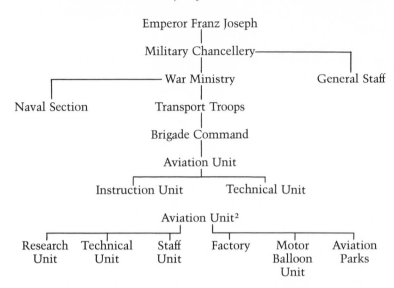

[1]Klaus Peters, "Zur Entwicklung der Oesterreichisch-Ungarischen Militaerluftfahrt von den Anfaengen bis 1915," pp. 246–47. Ph.D. diss., Univ. of Vienna, 1971.
[2]After 1913.

best prospects for success. Nevertheless, the Transport Troops Brigade Command also intended to create competition among its manufacturers, so it still investigated other domestic prospects.[52]

The Etrich Taube was the only aircraft to pass the army's trials in March 1911, and by June 1911 the Transport Troops Brigade Command, with the War Ministry's permission, had ordered seven more at a price of 25,000 crowns apiece. The planes were delivered by the MLG, to which Etrich had sold the Austrian production rights in June 1910, but were constructed at the Lohner factory because the MLG served only as a middleman. Despite requests for support and offers of airplanes from other firms, the Command refused to deal with other companies unless their airplanes equaled or surpassed the performance of the Etrich monoplane. Thus when even the War Ministry relented and proposed to buy a new Lohner biplane in order to compensate the firm for its expenses before the limited budgetary allocation expired in November, the Command demurred because the biplane did not meet the standards.[53]

The Transport Troops Brigade Command considered itself lenient in accepting even the Etrich monoplanes, since they had not met its demands for operability from rough terrain. The Command consequently made certain that the MLG met its contract requirements. It penalized the firm 9,800 crowns for tardiness in its deliveries in November 1911, a sizable sum considering the fledgling nature of the enterprise. The army then demanded a radically modified Etrich type, with side-by-side as opposed to tandem seating for pilot training, within twelve weeks. MLG declared that such modifications were impossible in so short a time and suggested that the army take a safer path and buy five more of the old type.[54] The Transport Troops Brigade Command was clearly determined to improve the performance, safety, and usefulness of its aircraft. Its performance standards rose at the end of 1911 to fifty miles per hour and a climb rate of 1,000 meters in fifteen minutes, and its requirements for landing and takeoff capability exceeded those of any other European army. Although the Command's demand for the prompt fulfillment speed of the major modification of the Taube was extravagant, the army felt that MLG's reply showed a reluctance to

improve its aircraft to suit the army's technical demands. In any case, MLG had no choice but to accept the new seating arrangement in order to gain the contracts; however, it would have cause to regret this in the future.

The Transport Troops Brigade Command concluded from this episode that the army had to be independent of its manufacturers and immediately recommended to the War Ministry that the army begin production of its own aircraft after buying the four Taubes from MLG. The Command also suggested that, since there was no patent on the Etrich monoplane in Hungary, the army could produce it there without infringing upon MLG's rights and pay Etrich a license fee. The War Ministry agreed that the army should prepare immediately to produce its own airplanes but sensibly questioned whether the acquisition of patent rights to the Taube was wise since it would probably be obsolete in the near future.[55]

By the fall of 1911 the relationship between the Austro-Hungarian Army and the aircraft industry was clearly established, though on uncertain footing. The General Staff under Conrad von Hoetzendorff was enthusiastically pressing for more airplanes, while the War Ministry and the Transport Troops Brigade Command, though interested in promoting technological development, were far more reluctant and harsher about standards for the imperial army's airplanes. The War Ministry and Transport Troops Brigade Command intended to maintain their independence of the only truly successful Austrian airplane company, the MLG-Lohner combination, to the extent that they contemplated building their own airplanes in 1911. The Austro-Hungarian military arsenals had long constructed much of the armed forces' weaponry, although adherence to this precedent would probably mean the crippling of the airplane industry. Meanwhile, the tiny industry grew, but it faced the problems of far too few military airplane contracts and the military's neglect of its facilities in training army pilots. In Germany the army's desire for independence from the aviation industry was tempered by practical considerations. The Austro-Hungarian Army's refusal to allow the industry to train pilots was dysfunctional, since it did not have the facilities to train sufficient personnel itself.

At least in Austria-Hungary the airplane did not have to compete with the airship for military funds. The prohibitive cost of building an airship fleet large enough to be effective, the danger of fire, and the large number of personnel required—all led to the refusal of the army to invest in airships. By 1911 the imperial army had one airship, which was destined to crash on 20 June 1914, taking the army's minuscule airship force with it.[56]

A number of organizational changes affecting military aviation occurred in the fall of 1911. Schoenaish stepped down as war minister on 20 September 1911 and was replaced by General Moritz von Auffenberg-Komarow, who considered aviation necessary for a modern army. Consequently, in October an Aviation Unit was established as a subordinate agency of the Transport Troops Brigade Command for the study, testing, procurement, production, and repair of aviation materials. The commandant of the Aviation Unit, appointed in April 1912, was Lieutenant Colonel Emil Uzelac, an untiring advocate of airplanes who learned to fly at forty-five years of age.[57] Such changes heralded the expansion of Austro-Hungarian military aviation.

When Uzelac assumed command the Aviation Unit had only twelve airplanes at its disposal. Eighty airplanes were procured in 1912, the majority of which were not MLG-Lohner Taubes but the recently developed Lohner biplane, the Pfeilflieger, much improved since its failure to meet the army's standards in 1911. The Hungarian Airship and Flying Machine Company, a firm founded in Budapest in November 1912 by Camilio Castiglioni, the owner of MLG, received twenty orders for its new biplane at the end of 1912.[58] The Taube, and MLG with it, had not kept pace with the army's demands.

MLG was in serious difficulties with the army over the four modified Etrich trainers the Transport Troops Brigade Command had decided to buy in November 1911. The planes with side-by-side seating were supposed to be ready in May or June 1912. When it became clear to MLG that this completion date was impossible, they assured the army that they were working as hard as they could to complete the planes and asked that the usual penalty for tardiness be dropped. The matter was unresolved at the end of 1912, since the planes were still not finished.[59]

A campaign in the summer of 1912, so similar to Germany's that imitation seems probable, marked the entry of the general public into the military-industrial relationship in an Austrian Air Fleet Fund. The similarity, however, stopped there. Although the Austrian venture had the support of the army and was allowed to use the imperial eagle as an insignia, the government and the army did not participate directly in the fund. The campaign raised only 1,162,000 crowns by 30 September 1913 and 1.5 million crowns by 1914. The committee later implied that only the German citizens of the Austro-Hungarian empire had contributed to the Fund. Although there are no documents confirming this assertion, if it is correct, it demonstrates that the Air Fleet Fund may have been the victim of the national divisions in the Austro-Hungarian monarchy. The Fund committee presented the money to the army on 30 July 1914 and recommended that it not be given directly to the industry but rather be used entirely for military aviation, such as in the construction of military air parks. The distrust and distaste for the industry manifested by the army were also evident among the members of the civilian Fund committee.[60]

The Austro-Hungarian Army also failed to use the civilian air shows and flight contests in the empire to the advantage of military aviation. The Austrian Aero-Club desired to stage an overland flight in September 1913 as national propaganda for an Austrian air fleet and as maneuvers to help the army select its airplanes, and so it asked whether army pilots and observers could participate in order to increase the number of experienced contestants.[61] The War Ministry refused, with the feeble explanation that the army had to concentrate on military training. Later, the War Ministry would excuse its nonparticipation on the dubious and even absurd grounds that it was acceding to the wishes of civilian pilots for the exclusion of army flyers and that the competition of officers with civilian pilots, most of whom were their social inferiors, was not advisable.[62] Perhaps the War Ministry feared the defeat of its aristocratic officer pilots by their social inferiors, just as the Prussian Army did. However, rather than follow the Prussian example and aggressively bend the civilian endeavors to its will, the Austro-Hungarian War Ministry preferred to retreat into isolation. Unlike the Prussian Army, the Austro-Hungarian military made little use of the opportunities offered by civilian aviation groups to foster military aviation.

Aircraft procurement policies were largely unchanged. In 1913 the army continued its preference for the Lohner biplane. Lohner became the only manufacturer delivering to the Austro-Hungarian Army, thus confronting the army's consumer monopoly with a producer monopoly. Ironically, the army itself was partially at fault for the creation of the monopoly it abhorred; its performance requirements were quite high, in some cases higher than those of the German Army, thus eliminating many planes from consideration, while its policies of contract awards to the aircraft industry were less encouraging.[63] Its relationship with the MLG provides a case in point.

In February 1913, when the four modified Etrich monoplanes were finally nearing completion, MLG asked the army to accept them; the delays, it insisted, had resulted from the unattainable nature of the army's demands given the present state of aviation technology.[64] The Aviation Unit refused to accept the planes regardless of whether they met the requirements, since the funds originally allotted for them had been stricken by the War Ministry. Although the Aviation Unit told MLG that it could appeal the decision to the War Ministry, it informed the War Ministry that the planes should be rejected, since they would soon be obsolete. If MLG insisted on their acceptance, the possible penalty for late delivery amounted to twice the original cost of the four planes. In any case, the Aviation Unit offered to manufacture the planes itself if necessary. If the War Ministry had to have the Etrich training planes, the Unit suggested that it should buy them for 15,00 to 17,000 crowns apiece—10,000 crowns less than the original price.[65]

Although the Transport Troops Brigade Command wondered why the Aviation Unit had not reached some agreement with MLG in 1912, when it was obvious that the planes would not be ready punctually, it concluded that the penalty for tardy delivery enabled the army to control the situation and dictate terms to the firm. In the Command's opinion, the dissolution of MLG would really be in the army's interest, since the company was only a middleman and had made no technical strides after assuming control of Taube sales in 1910. MLG was reduced to appealing to the Aviation Unit's sense of justice and good will. The War Ministry's decision was an equitable one: it would buy the first trainer at a small penalty and give the firm until the beginning of May to deliver the other three, after which time the army would consider the contract null and void. Nevertheless, that was the last contract to MLG. When the time came to award a contract for

an experimental monoplane in November 1913, the Unit recommended that the army build the plane rather than grant the order to MLG.[66]

Now the army had to extricate itself from its total dependence on Lohner. In February 1913 the War Ministry bought a German DFW biplane in order to encourage domestic manufacturers to develop better airplanes.[67] Already in January 1913 the German firm Aviatik had informed the Hungarian Ministry of Commerce of its intention to establish an aircraft factory in Hungary employing 100 workers for the production of two planes weekly. In return, it asked the government to grant it a fifteen-year tax exemption, lower freight taxes, the free use of Hungarian military airfields, and the assurance that the army would buy the planes. The Hungarian Ministry of Commerce informed the War Ministry that it supported the Aviatik proposal, since it had good reports about the firm. At the advice of the Aviation Unit, the War Ministry decided in April to approve the enterprise in order to create competition among planes and factories. However, the stipulations were strict: the firm would have to be smaller than described because of the limited number of airplanes the War Ministry would buy from Hungary; there could be no assurance of contracts, since this would injure competition; to ensure the firm's independence, licensed production of planes made in Germany was forbidden; and the company could not use military airfields. Aviatik naturally shied away from such harsh terms, but the War Ministry stood firm because it clung to the belief that it could buy any license to copy a plane at one-half the usual price and produce the plane more cheaply in its own workshops.[68]

✠ *An Albatros twin-float monoplane at the seaplane competition on Lake Constance from 6 June to 5 July 1913. Courtesy of Peter Grosz.*

Initial feelers from the German aircraft industry were thus abortive.

Despite the unfortunate state of the Austro-Hungarian aircraft industry, military aviation grew in 1913 and 1914, as the small aviation budget proved adequate for some expansion of the Aviation Unit and flying troops. The army had procured only sixteen airplanes in the years 1909–1912, but by the outbreak of the war it had seventy-seven airplanes, with forty-nine more on order in the next three months. The aviation budget rose from 90,000 crowns in 1909 to 800,000 crowns in 1914, a significant increase, though minuscule in absolute terms in comparison with the German budget for military aviation.[69] The bulk of these budgetary allocations had obviously been spent in late 1912–1913 when the army began its expansion of military aviation. In the absence of concrete information on budgetary allocations between 1909 and 1914, it seems that the allocation in 1912–1913 was probably larger than 800,000 marks, judging by the large numbers of airplanes ordered. The funds probably decreased after disappointing failures of the army's aircraft in early 1914. Early in 1914 the War Ministry had optimistically promised Conrad von Hoetzendorff eight flying companies by the fall of 1914 and forty companies with 240 planes by early 1916. Evidence of the insufficiency of funds was the War Ministry's acknowledgment on 22 July 1914 that it had equipment totaling only 750,000 crowns (the equivalent of one and two-thirds flying companies, when it expected to provide for fifteen companies by 30 June 1916, a drastic reduction of the earlier proposal of forty companies by this date. It also had to admit that this goal would be possible only if it drew 1,550,000 crowns from the budget for the following year 1916–1917.[70]

An unexpected setback in March 1914 was a major factor in the army's inability to fulfill these plans. The War Ministry permitted army pilots to test fly Lohner aircraft since the firm did not have sufficient pilots, a situation that was owing in part to the army's refusal to permit airplane factories to train army pilots. In March 1914 the fatal crash of a Lieutenant Elsner in a Lohner Pfeilflieger forced the army to ban flying in those planes until they could be examined and strengthened. This measure was normal procedure in all countries, as the War Ministry pointed out when it came under attack in newspaper articles in June deploring the state of Austro-Hungarian military aviation.[71] However, other large states, unlike Austria, had more than one type of military airplane.

The Austrian press openly criticized the depressed state of Austro-Hungarian military aviation in early June 1914, blaming even the highest level of government officials in veiled references. Austrian aviation had reached a dead end, just when neighboring states were introducing more airplanes into their armed forces. In the opinion of the press, the Austrian military had so ruined its domestic producers that it was now forced to rely on foreign manufacturers. The German airplane industry had quickly seized upon this favorable opportunity; the papers noted the large number of German officers and planes visiting Vienna and Budapest during the summer to show the capability of the German aircraft factories. Ironically, after all the years of the army's protests of lack of money for aviation, the funds for airplanes which the recent budget had granted were all flowing to foreign factories. The army had dictated impossible demands to the domestic industry; now foreign companies would dictate to the Austro-Hungarian military. As the key sponsor of Austrian aviation, the Austro-Hungarian Army had failed miserably.[72]

Unfortunately for the War Ministry, these reports came to the attention of Archduke Franz Ferdinand in the military chancel-lery, who promptly demanded an explanation. In a detailed memorandum, the War Ministry explained that bans on airplanes occurred frequently in other states.[73] It attributed the relatively small size of the Austrian airplane forces to the lack of funds and to the embryonic state of the empire's airplane industry. Nevertheless, the army had seventy-seven airplanes, would receive forty-nine more by September, and planned to order 100 airplanes with the budget for 1914. The War Ministry excused the absence of competitive production by saying that its efforts to foster competition had failed until 1914 because nobody in Austria-Hungary was interested and foreign companies demanded too many guarantees. Only after the formation of a branch of DFW in Hungary in January under the Austrian designer Adolf Bier did other German firms like Albatros, LVG, and Aviatik begin actively to establish planes in Austria or Hungary. The War Ministry intended to restore domestic competition and cover any wartime needs with these firms. To give these planned branches a sound financial and technical basis, it would order a small number of airplanes directly from the German mother companies, but after these initial orders all further deliveries would be manufactured domestically. The War Ministry attributed the shortage of pilots and Austria-Hungary's backwardness in aviation mostly to the fact that preliminary work on the army bills was done from one to two years ahead of time, too soon to foresee the speedy development of aviation.

Archduke Franz Ferdinand never saw the War Ministry's attempt to explain and excuse the bleak situation in military aviation because the report did not reach his desk until after his assassination at Sarajevo. Chief of the General Staff Conrad von Hoetzendorff commented, however, that if the press had been too severe in its criticisms, the War Ministry had certainly painted too optimistic a picture of the condition of the air forces and aircraft industry, since the army was falling farther and farther behind in its aircraft building program.[74]

As both the War Ministry and the press explained, the German aircraft industry was to pull the Austro-Hungarian chestnuts out of the fire. The first fruitful proposal from the German aircraft industry came from DFW in early 1914. The Leipzig firm had contracted with the Hungarian Ministry of Justice to build airplanes in Hungarian state workshops as soon as the War Ministry assured them of a yearly acceptance quota of twenty airplanes for ten years, the minimum necessary for the company's survival. In time of mobilization, DFW would let the army direct their factory, which had the potential to increase its annual production to 150 or 200 airplanes with 400 workers. After twenty years, the army could even buy the factory from DFW for the worth of its investment. The War Ministry and the Aviation Unit estimated that the army would need 80 to 100 airplanes annually for the next five years, at which rate it could support three new factories, one in Hungary and two in Austria, if they could survive on twenty contracts annually. Although the War Ministry welcomed the competition, it could not promise DFW any orders in advance. Nevertheless, since it was clear that the army needed more airplanes despite the lack of contract guarantees, DFW founded the Hungarian Lloyd Aircraft and Motor Factory in Budapest-Aszod with 500,000 crowns capital and began production in the state workshops there in May. The War Ministry bought thirteen DFW airplanes from the German firm on 30 July in order to get Hungarian production under way. Also in May, Albatros founded the Austro-Hungarian Albatros Works in Vienna with 100,000 crowns capital.[75]

The Austro-Hungarian Army bought six biplanes from the German firm Aviatik in June, with the proviso that it would buy even more if the planes' performance was acceptable. Although Aviatik permitted the army to encourage the licensed production of the planes in Austria, the urgency of the international situation at the end of July forced the army to order thirty-three more biplanes from Aviatik in Mulhausen. In August, Aviatik decided to establish a branch in Austria-Hungary headed by Karl Illner, formerly with Igo Etrich and then MLG, with 100,000 crowns capital.[76] After a visit to Johannisthal by an Austrian military airplane commission, the chairman of the board of LVG, Georg Maschke, offered to found an independent company in Austria to produce LVG planes under license and any other aircraft desired by the Austrian War Ministry, if the War Ministry would grant him a contract for twenty-five airplanes. The War Ministry was willing to discuss the matter with him so long as it was understood that any orders would have to suit the budget.[77]

The German aircraft industry was firmly established in Austria-Hungary, reversing to some extent the earlier emigration of Austrian aeronautical engineers and businessmen to Germany when the Austro-Hungarian Army was awarding so few contracts for airplanes.[78] But the German firms had come too late to prepare the military and the industry for mobilization. By the end of July 1914 the army had at its disposal only forty field airplanes and eighty-five completely trained field pilots, since final training had been delayed by the ban on Lohner airplanes. The War Ministry's mobilization plans entailed no exemptions for draftees in the airplane industry, so on 1 August 1914, at the last minute, it had to decree that the managers and workers in the Lohner company, the Austrian branch of Aviatik, DFW's Hungarian Lloyd, and the Hungarian Airship and Flying Machine Factory companies would be released from service.[79] The Austro-

Hungarian military aviation forces and the aircraft industry were clearly not ready for war of any kind, as Conrad von Hoetzendorff had feared years before.

Between the turn of the century and the First World War, the Imperial Austro-Hungarian Navy received considerable budgetary attention as it attempted to develop not only its coastal defense system but also its high-seas fleet. The navy showed an interest in airplanes relatively early, when it sent several officers to England and France in 1909 for flight lessons. Later, naval pilot-training was conducted by the aircraft industry, then the army aviation school, and by 1914 by the navy itself at the naval station at Pola.[80]

The Naval Technical Committee of the War Ministry's Naval Section failed in an early attempt to build its own airplane, and so it turned to private enterprise, specifically MLG-Lohner, for the development of a seaplane. The Naval Section received its first Lohner Pfeilflieger with floats in December 1911, and in Sep-tember 1912 the Austrian Navy League donated another Lohner biplane to the navy. By August 1914, Lohner had delivered thirteen Pfeilfliegers to the navy, some of them through MLG and others directly to the naval base at Pola.[81]

In 1913, however, the Naval Section decided to concentrate on the flying boat, which was more feasible for operations in the Adriatic than the Germans had found it to be in the North Sea. The navy consequently bought four French and two American Glenn Curtiss flying boats to use as models for the construction of two flying boats in its naval arsenal and then to place at the disposal of Austrian firms for their construction attempts. In early June the Lohner firm delivered its first flying boat, and by August it had delivered eleven to the navy through MLG. By the beginning of the war the navy possessed thirty airplanes, sixteen of which it considered usable in case of war.[82] Thus Austrian naval aviation, like its German counterpart, was still in an embryonic state in August 1914.

# V. CONCLUSION

The Prussian Army's aviation forces and the north German aircraft industry were not only prepared in August 1914 for the short war that most people expected, but they were also capable of substantial expansion and independent technical advancement. Military aviation in both Bavaria and the Austro-Hungarian empire suffered because of dependence on single factories, and naval aviation in both empires had not yet advanced beyond the experimental stage. A summary analysis of the development of military and naval aviation in the German and Austro-Hungarian empires provides the basis for a general interpretation of the relationship between the armed forces and the aircraft industry in Central Europe before World War I.

Because of technological difficulties and relatively small budgets, naval aviation, especially the development of seaplanes, in all countries was at best rudimentary in 1914, although noticeable advancement was being made, particularly in England. Thus the primitive state of naval aviation in Germany and Austria-Hungary was little cause for alarm, especially in the latter, which had only a limited coast on the Adriatic. During the prewar years naval aviation developed independently in Germany, where the floatplane was adopted because of its stability in the heavy seas of the north Atlantic and Baltic, and in Austria-Hungary, where the flying boat was preferred in the calmer Adriatic. This independent development was thus the natural result of the very real differences in the maritime conditions of the two empires. The funds allocated to the Austro-Hungarian Navy for aviation (e.g., 670,000 crowns in 1913) compared far more favorably with those allotted for German naval aviation (approximately 6,000,000 marks for airplanes and airships) than did the budgetary allocation for aviation of the Austro-Hungarian Army with that of the German Army.[1] At the same time, the aviation demands of the Austro-Hungarian Army and Navy were so small that they could be met by one firm, Lohner; there was no need for differentiation of producers before the war, such as had occurred in Germany.

There is no simple answer to the question of the effect of bureaucratic schisms within the respective armies on the course of military aviation. The Prussian, Bavarian, and Austro-Hungarian armies were not monolithic in their attitudes toward the airplane. The general staffs in Germany and Austria-Hungary pressed constantly for support of military aviation, encouraged by their realization that the airplane would be useful for reconnaissance, communications, and possibly for the bombing of ground targets or air combat against airships. While the field commanders, desirous of having this potential weapon available for future conflict, advocated the expansion of aviation and air forces, the war ministries in both countries withheld their full support from airplanes. The third agency involved in aeronautical matters, the transport troops in Prussia and Austria-Hungary and the engineers in Bavaria, were pragmatic and cautious in their approach toward the development of the airplane. Meanwhile, those closest to the airplane and daily operations, men like Wolfram de le Roi of the Prussian Research Unit, Emil Uzelac of the Austro-Hungarian Aviation Unit, and Wilhelm Siegert of the Prussian Inspection of Flying Troops, were absolutely convinced of the airplane's capabilities and were staunch supporters of military aviation.

Nevertheless, the war ministries, because of their control of the budget, were the critical agencies. The Prussian War Ministry in particular has been subjected to much criticism for its conservatism toward technology in general and the airplane in particular. Both the Austro-Hungarian and the Prussian war ministries openly admitted their aversion to spending money on untested machines that might prove militarily worthless. Such a stance had much merit in the early days of the airplane: it avoided wasting funds and, in the case of Prussia, diverting them from tried (and supposedly truer) aeronautical devices like the airship. Such a stance, however, was no longer justifiable after 1910 because of the rapid development of the airplane, a fact acknowledged by the Cologne Commission in Prussia. The war ministries' reaction to these circumstances after 1910 is a more accurate indication of whether their attitude toward the airplane was too conservative.

The Prussian War Ministry, despite its caution, did initiate contact with airplane inventors and was willing to finance and help the early aircraft manufacturers within well-defined limits—airfield subsidies, pilot-training contracts, contest awards,

and even a few airplane contracts—and with the attitude that it was up to the industry to develop the planes. It thus assumed an essentially passive though supportive stance. Had the Hoffman project succeeded in its attempt to build the army's own plane, perhaps the War Ministry would have become quite active in early aircraft construction and technology. Nevertheless, while its participation before 1912 was limited, its stance changed in late 1911 and early 1912. Probably under the pressures of the Moroccan crisis of 1911 and the Balkan crisis beginning in 1912, the Prussian War Ministry had decided by March 1912, before the proclamation of the National Aviation Fund, to increase its airplane orders substantially. The War Ministry then began to play a more active role in airplane development through the transport troops and its own agencies, directing and controlling the allocation of the National Aviation Fund, applying more defense funds to the task, using the technological and scientific resources at its command, and applying additional technical standards and economic controls to the industry in order to focus its production upon military goals. This approach was sensible and pragmatic: it avoided waste before 1912, and afterwards cautiously channeled the production of the industry toward the development of standard types of reconnaissance and communications airplanes. It is unquestionable that the Prussian War Ministry manifested a clear and increasingly firm commitment to military aviation; the only problem was the division of its resources between the airplane and the airship.

An examination of the developments in Austria-Hungary, however, seems to indicate the absence of a basic commitment to aviation and an inability to raise adequate funds for aviation on the part of the War Ministry, a conclusion corroborated by the irate Viennese press in June 1914. The excuses of division of resources did not exist in Austria-Hungary, since the airship, because of its expense, had receded from the picture by 1912. Admittedly the empire, plagued by national divisions, demanded less of its subjects for defense budgets and consequently spent proportionately less in all areas of armaments. Nevertheless, the Austro-Hungarian military aviation budget of less than one million crowns in 1914 was pitifully small in comparison with the German allocation of over twenty-five million marks for airplanes alone, excluding airships. The imperial Austro-Hungarian eagle was to be defended in the air by a gnat. The absence of this basic commitment led to the crisis in Austro-Hungarian military aviation before World War I.

The Austro-Hungarian War Ministry and its subordinate agencies set comparatively high standards and so awarded few contracts to the aircraft industry; a situation resulted analogous to that faced by the German Navy in 1912—many firms could not meet the requirements. In Germany this situation never threatened the viability of the aircraft industry, as the firms simply avoided seaplane production and continued to produce for the Prussian Army. In Austria-Hungary, however, the insistence of the principal consumer, the War Ministry, on unrealistically high standards contributed directly to the collapse of the Austro-Hungarian aviation industry. The snobbery displayed by the Austro-Hungarian Army with regard to acceptable airplanes, as compared with the Prussian Army, is clearly evident in the case of the Taube. Originally an Austrian design, it was used in Germany as a first-line airplane through 1914 and even served in isolated instances during the early days of the World War. Yet in Austria-Hungary the Taube was, by 1912, acceptable to the army only as a training airplane; and even in that capacity it was so severely modified to meet military demands that it soon became useless.

The Austro-Hungarian War Ministry and its agencies also suf-fered from the belief that, if necessary, they could always build their own plane, although they never attempted the venture and never threatened the airplane manufacturers with the prospect. Had they noted the failure of the Prussian and Bavarian armies, and, closer to home, the Austro-Hungarian Navy, and drawn the conclusion that it was safer and more productive to rely completely on private enterprise without military construction, they might have done more to encourage the domestic airplane industry. However, because of these strong reservations, the Austro-Hungarian Army found itself in 1914 with no reliable airplanes.

The German and Austro-Hungarian armies also pursued dissimilar policies in regard to civilian participation in the development of military aviation. The Prussian Army and the German armed forces in general were not averse to employing public fund-raising campaigns and civilian aviation groups. They actively supported and encouraged these efforts, channeling them to their own ends, as their participation in the National Aviation Fund and their relationship with the German Aviators Association demonstrated. The civilian agencies of the German government, particularly the Imperial Office of the Interior, gladly aided military aviation when the opportunity arose. Even Emperor Wilhelm and Prince Heinrich of Prussia took sufficient interest to play a positive role in the promotion of military aviation. The Prussian Army did not hesitate to enlist their aid and to use its influence to ensure that all civilian efforts in Germany directly helped the cause of military aviation.

The situation in Austria-Hungary was different. Despite the recommendation of Chief of the General Staff Conrad von Hoetzendorff that the imperial army involve itself in similar fashion in civilian aviation, the Austro-Hungarian War Ministry preferred not to do so. Neither it nor the civilian government participated actively in the Austrian Air Fleet Fund in 1912, and the War

Ministry even rejected civilian attempts in 1913 to aid the cause of military aviation. This reluctance to use civilian means to sponsor military aviation may have been a function of a basically different attitude on the part of the Austro-Hungarian Army toward civilian life. The Prussian Army, in its supreme social and political position in German life, interfered in civilian affairs and employed tractable civilians for its own ends with impunity. The Austro-Hungarian Army manifested a definite reluctance to intrude upon civilian life. The army in Austria-Hungary was simply not the powerful institution that the Prussian Army was. Although it remained a vital cornerstone of the Hapsburg empire, the per capita military expenditures were low, and the consequent severe difficulties in maintaining a strong, modern, and well-equipped army were certainly reflected in the lack of adequate military aviation forces.

These basic differences demonstrate that one must beware of regarding Austria-Hungary as a carbon copy of its northern neighbor and ally. The civilian response to the Austrian aviation fund gives further proof. If the fund committee was correct in stating that only Germans contributed to the fund in Austria-Hungary, then the appeal to national danger affected only German-dominated Austria. If one compares the relative figures of German population in Austria-Hungary and Germany (approximately 13 million in Austria-Hungary to 65 million in Germany), then the 1.5 million crowns contributed in Austria-Hungary compares favorably with the 7 million marks contributed in Germany. The Austrian fund's failure may be just one

✳ *A Lohner Aspern biplane of the Austro-Hungarian Army. A Lohner Aspern biplane, second version (inset), of the Austro-Hungarian Army. Courtesy of Peter Grosz.*

more symptom of the inability of a multinational empire to survive in an era of ardent nationalism.

Ironically, the size and the budget of the Austro-Hungarian military aviation force in 1914 are more comparable with those of Bavaria than they are with those of the German Empire, or even with those of Prussia. The circumstances in Austria-Hungary and Bavaria—the existence of an aircraft industry based on a single firm and the failure in 1914 of either the firm or its aircraft—are too similar to be ignored. Austria-Hungary's great power status was certainly not reflected in its aviation forces.

Austro-Hungarian military aviation could not overcome its prewar deficiencies when faced with the challenge of World War I. The small aircraft industry delivered only some 5,400 aircraft during the conflict, while the powerful German firms delivered over 48,000 planes to the armed forces. There is no better indicator of the critical effect of the prewar years on wartime aviation.

What general conclusions can be drawn about the nature of the relationship between the armed forces and the aircraft industry? Most basically the relationship was a symbiotic one: the armed forces needed aviation, the industry needed contracts, and to these ends both were interested in the development of better airplanes. These interdependent needs had driven the industry toward the military and made the military receptive to its advances from the very beginning, when the airplane was not feasible for commercial use or sport. There was room in this relationship, however, for disagreement—on prices, the number of contracts, the quality of airplanes, on the very worth of military aviation—and the firms and the armed forces attempted to obtain the best bargain from one another.

The war ministries generally valued the importance of the airplane and military aviation less than did the industry, and the industry consequently lost the leverage that a highly valued product brings in bargaining. The firms sought to encourage the army to purchase more aircraft and thus to increase the size of the air forces at a faster rate. Within the military establishment the general staffs, watching the progress of other European powers, especially France, pressed the war ministries to incorporate aviation forces into the armies at a much faster rate. The war ministries, however, preferred a slower, more cautious, more structured program for organizational and technological reasons. In Prussia the possession of another aerial weapon, the airship, also increased the military authorities' reserve toward the airplane. Because the actual military worth of the airplane was largely a matter of conjecture and because the military enjoyed the status of monopoly consumer, the armed forces had the advantage in their dealings with the industry.

That the upper levels of industry and the state in modern times are intertwined through personal and financial connections has become a common assertion. In the case of imperial Germany, research has shown the existence of such tangible connections between the state government and industry that the East German historian Walter Bartel has termed the state government the "instrument of the Junkers and the business lords."[2] Large international industrialists like Krupp used governments for their own profit. The Krupp firm, which dominated the domestic armaments market, had no competition in its production of nickel-steel armor plate and certain sizes of large cannon. This commanding position enabled it to charge the German military exorbitant prices, far higher than its prices in more competitive foreign markets. The armed forces undoubtedly detested this situation as much as their fervent adversaries the Social Democrats, because the scandals about Krupp profits made the military look like the foolish pawn of the capitalists. The navy was constantly preoccupied with the creation of competition for Krupp in

order to release it from dependence on the firm and to lower Krupp's prices.[3] In peacetime, governments were almost powerless to control the larger firms of the armaments industry, which formed an international establishment obeying its own laws and agreements. The experience of being faced with Krupp's virtual monopoly in certain areas of the armaments market had undoubtedly encouraged the army and navy in Germany to promote competition among their other producers. The position of the Skoda works in Austria-Hungary might also have encouraged the promotion of competition among the other producers for the Austro-Hungarian armed forces.

The aircraft industry's relationship with the imperial German and Austro-Hungarian armed forces indicates that the aircraft manufacturers lacked the power to dictate terms to the military establishment. The industry, because of its small size, the only-partially-recognized importance of its product to the military, and the lack of foreign markets and of personal and financial connections in high places, found itself subordinate to and regulated by the military. As international armaments manufacturers used the state government, so the aircraft industry between 1909 and 1914 was the instrument of the military.

The military's control of the market, as virtually the only consumer, remained undiminished throughout the prewar years in both empires, thus enabling it to preserve its grip on the maturing aircraft industry. With this business advantage, the military guided the industry in technological matters and sought to preserve an industry composed of competing firms and to prevent a cartelized or monopolized industry.

Competition in the Austro-Hungarian aircraft industry disappeared, ironically enough, because the army was shortsighted in using its control: it set high standards for planes yet was reluctant to offer sufficient contracts to make competition attractive. Ultimately, the only way out of this dependence on one firm was to allow, and even encourage, German firms to enter the Austro-Hungarian market, although reliance on foreign businesses was almost as repugnant as reliance on one domestic supplier. In contrast, the Prussian War Ministry had first encouraged a competitive industry with minimal investment; then, as the airplane became more valuable, it had ordered more. Although as individual firms excelled in their production, the army's leverage might decrease, it would remain sufficiently strong so long as the War Ministry preserved competition among its manufacturers. Of course, this presumed an investment of funds that the Austro-Hungarian military could not allocate to the task.

The armed forces were definitely the dominant partner in the military-industrial relationship. Their contracts were the airplane industry's life blood, and an airplane firm could survive only by meeting their demands. The industry was the source of technological progress, the innovative force; the task of the military was to shape this creative talent for its own ends. Although it set standards from the beginning, the military increased its control of production in the airplane industry after 1912. As the military gained more technological expertise, it interfered more frequently in the technology and construction of military airplanes. The military became more active in all stages of the production cycle—setting requirements, controlling construction, taking delivery, running military trials, accepting the aircraft, and writing new requirements—and the industry became more passive, seeking simply to meet the army's demands. The firms' weak positions vis-à-vis the military forced them to approach it with circumspection, always avoiding a direct confrontation with the military authorities.

As the armed forces controlled the rate of development of their aviation branches, they were able to determine not only the effects of these new organizations on the military but also, to a great extent, the development of the aircraft industry. The effects of the relationship on the military are obvious. Every branch of the imperial German and Austro-Hungarian armed forces had an air arm, however small. As these air forces grew, so too did the business of the military with private industry and the military technical apparatus for examining and accepting the industry's products. The potential socioideological effects of the expansion of technical forces, which the Prussian War Ministry so feared, did not occur in the expansion of the aviation branch, because it remained too small before 1914 to have brought about an unassimilable influx of bourgeois officers.

The military, as the sole profitable market of the airplane industry, determined the rate of the industry's expansion. The airplane companies had been founded on the expectation of forthcoming military demands, and their survival depended on their ability to secure aircraft construction and, in the case of Prussia, pilot training contracts from the armed forces. The successful factories sold practically their entire output to the armed forces; the unsuccessful ones went bankrupt because of their inability to do so. The prospects of increasing military contracts erased the initial hesitation of private capital to enter aircraft production, and the ranks of airplane manufacturers swelled, as smaller firms grew and as large industrial concerns, electric and locomotive companies, entered competition.

The increasing number of larger firms in the industry forced small enterprises to grow in order to remain competitive and solvent. More skilled engineers, designers, and business managers were needed to manage increasingly complicated technical and financial affairs. As the firms expanded, many of the industry's entrepreneurs, who were technicians and inventors, could no longer direct personally the details of production and had to become businessmen or hire business managers. Those who were unable to adjust to the demands of larger scale production generally lost their own firms and went to work for larger factories or for the military's growing technical apparatus. Only a few, such as Rumpler, Fokker, and Heinkel, successfully made the difficult transition from small entrepreneur to business director of a large firm. Even the Convention of Aircraft Industrialists in Germany could not prevent the domination of the industry by the large firms preserve the small firms as viable competitors for military contracts. The need for funds for experimentation and expansion dictated the formation of joint stock companies (AG or *Aktiengesellschaften*) or limited liability companies (GmbH or *Gesellschaften mit beschraenkter Haftung*), since the future belonged to the airplane manufacturers with the capital to innovate and expand. Although the aircraft firms were scarcely large-scale concerns like Krupp, which employed some 70,000 workers in Essen in 1914, the aircraft industry's successful manufacturers had assumed the production and business methods of large firms.

The airplane industry's mode of production and development thus conformed to the evolutionary pattern of German industry in particular and of the assembling industries in general.[4] The relationship between the armed forces and the aircraft industry thus condensed into a matter of years an evolution of the industry that might have taken decades.

According to the Military Science Department of the German Air Force, the development of military airplanes in these early years was synonymous with the development of the airplane itself, because the demands placed upon military airplanes— speed, rate of climb, payload, range, light weight, and strength— applied to all types of airplanes.[5] This is largely true. A substantial sport market did not develop in the years prior to World War I, partly for reasons of expense and risk. Nor was the airplane commercially feasible for transportation. And it is undeniable that the military, and only the military, made possible the development of the airplane industry in the prewar years. Nevertheless, when the Prussian Army's Research Unit and the Austro-Hungarian Army's Transport Troops Brigade Command decided, quite early, to channel the industry's production toward developing airplanes to the army's specifications, they clearly recognized a difference in the requirements of sport and military aviation. In addition, the Prussian General Inspectorate's negative response to the industry's attempt in 1913–1914 to promote a sport aviation market of light, fast private aircraft indicated its conviction that the construction of one type—the military airplane— precluded the development of all others.

The military's negative attitude toward sport aviation in imperial Germany seems to conflict directly with its promotion of sport flying during the Weimar Republic and the Nazi regime. In reality, the different policies show that the military wisely accommodated its continuing interest in the development of military aviation to new political and technological circumstances. In the Weimar and Nazi periods, to circumvent the provisions of the Versailles Treaty banning military aviation in Germany, gliders and light airplanes were used quite successfully as inexpensive means of creating widespread interest in flying and of training pilots. Also, by the 1930s the airplane had developed sufficiently so that military (and commercial) airplanes were far more sophisticated and expensive than lightweight sport craft. These circumstances encouraged the use of inexpensive planes for rudimentary flight training, and if independent civilians conducted the "sport," all the better for the German military financially as well as politically.

During the imperial era the military, especially in Prussia, could count on the unquestioning support of civilian groups for military aviation itself; and there was no need to encourage the development of sport aviation. The continued monopolization of the consumer market by the armed forces, even after the industry had excess resources, stemmed as much from the attitudes of civilian aviation organizations which catered to the military as it did from the military itself. One can only conclude that while this total concentration of the industry on military production may have distorted the development of airplanes, there simply was no real alternative to the military market. When the armed forces provided insufficient contracts and pursued ill-advised policies, the industry suffered, and in the case of Austria-Hungary, nearly disappeared. When the military pursued positive policies, the industry thrived.

In conclusion, three general points merit emphasis. First, the best policy that the military could pursue, both for itself and for the airplane industry, was the promotion of competition in order to secure the best airplanes at the lowest prices possible. Second, the military could not be expected to be innovative in a scientific sense, that is, to develop the airplane simply because it was a new invention. Instead, it was innovative within the narrower limits of applying the new technology to military ends. Consequently, the military has been not only a prime force of modernization in developing nations in the twentieth century, but also an important source of funds and technological expertise in highly developed, industrialized societies. Finally, like nuclear power, the airplane belongs to that select group of inventions and discoveries that, once discovered by civilians, lay fallow until the military saw fit to sponsor their development for military ends. Only later was their potential for civilian purposes fulfilled. This sequence of events provides an interesting and instructive comment on man's priorities.

# ABBREVIATIONS

AD     *Allgemeine Kriegsdepartement.* War Department (Prussian); A7, Transport Department; A7L, Aviation Department.

a.D.     *ausser Dienst.* Retired.

AG     *Aktiengesellschaft.* Joint stock company.

AM     *Archiv der Marine.* Naval Archive.

BA     *Bundesarchiv.* Federal Archive.

BKA     *Bayerisches Kriegsarchiv.* Bavarian War Archive.

CDFI     *Convention der Flugzeugindustrieller.* Convention of Aircraft Industrialists (or Manufacturers).

DLV     *Deutscher Luftfahrerverband.* German Aviators Association.

DM     *Deutsches Museum.* German Museum.

DN     *Nachlass Hermann Dorner.* Herman Dorner Collection.

EN     *Nachlass August Euler.* August Euler Collection.

Fl. Bat.     *Flieger Bataillon.* Flyers Battalion.

GG     *Grosser Generalstab.* General Staff (Germany).

GIdMV     *General Inspektion des Militaerverkehrswesens.* General Inspectorate of Military Transportation.

GmbH     *Gesellschaft mit beschraenkter Haftung.* Limited liability company.

GSC     *Generalstabschef.* Chief of the General Staff (Austria-Hungary).

Hptm.     *Hauptmann.* Captain.

IdFlieg     *Inspektion der Fliegertruppen.* Inspectorate of Flying Troops.

IdV     *Inspektion der Verkehrstruppen.* Inspectorate of Transport Troops.

II     *Inspektion der Ingenieurkorps.* Inspectorate of the Corps of Engineers.

ILuK     *Inspektion des Militaer-Luft- und Kraftfahrwesens.* Inspectorate of Military Aviation and Motor Vehicles.

KAdL     *Kriegswissenschaftliche Abteilung der Luftwaffe.* Military Science Department of the German Air Force.

KILuK     *Koeniglich Inspektion des Militaer-Luft- und Kraftfahrwesens.* Inspectorate of Military Aviation and Motor Vehicles (Bavaria).

KKM     *Koeniglich Kriegsministerium.* War Ministry (Bavaria).

KM     *Kriegsministerium.* War Ministry (either Prussian or Austro-Hungarian).

LA     *Luftfahrtarchiv.* Aviation Archive.

Lsa    *Luftschiffer Abteilung.* Aviation Unit.

LuVA    *Lehr und Versuchsanstalt fuer dar Militaerflugwesen.* Instruction and Research Institute for Military Aviation.

MA    *Bundesarchiv.* Federal Archive.

Maa    *Militaeraeronautisches Anstalt.* Military Aeronautical Institute.

Oberlt    *Oberleutnant.* First Lieutenant.

OK    *Oesterreichisches Kriegsarchiv.* Austrian War Archive.

RA    *Reichsarchiv.* Imperial Archive.

RdI    *Reichsamt des Innern.* Imperial Office of the Interior.

SS    *Staatssekretaer.* State Secretary.

SSdI    *Staatssekretaer des Innern.* State Secretary of the Interior.

VAdV    *Versuchsabteilung der Verkehrstruppen.* Research Unit of the Transport Troops.

Vdmi    *Verein deutscher Motorfahrzeugindustrieller.* Association of German Motor Vehicle Industrialists.

Vpk    *Verkehrstechnische Pruefungskommission.* Transport Technology Test Commisson.

Vtbk    *Verkehrstruppen Brigade Kommando.* Transport Troops Brigade Command.

# NOTES

1. Walter Goerlitz, *History of the German General Staff, 1657–1945*, trans. Brian Battershaw (New York: Praeger, 1953), 141–56.

2. Fritz Fischer, *Germany's Aims in the First World War* (New York: Norton, 1967), 19–20 n.

3. Hptm. a.D. Hans Ritter, *Der Luftkrieg* (Berlin and Leipzig: Verlag von K. F. Koehler, 1926), 25.

4. Maj. a.D. Hilmer Freiherr von Buelow, *Geschichte der Luftwaffe: Eine kurze Darstellung der Entwicklung der fuenften Waffe* (Frankfort on the Main: Verlag Moritz Diensterweg, 1934), 3.

5. Hans Herzfeld, *Die Deutsche Ruestungspolitik vor dem Weltkriege* (Bonn and Leipzig: Kurt Schroeder Verlag, 1923), 153–57.

6. Gordon A. Craig, *The Politics of the Prussian Army, 1640–1945* (New York: Oxford Univ. Press, 1955, 1964), 217–54.

7. *Ibid.*, 235–37.

8. D. J. Goodspeed, *Ludendorff. Genius of World War I* (Boston: Houghton, 1966), 1–22.

9. *Ibid.* See also Fritz Fischer, *Krieg der Illusionen. Die deutsche Politik von 1911 bis 1914* (Dusseldorf: Droste Verlag, 1969), 251–57.

10. Jonathan Steinberg, *Yesterday's Deterrent: Tirpitz and the Birth of the German Battle Fleet* (New York: Macmillan, 1965), *passim.*

11. RA, *Kriegsruestung und Kriegswirtschaft*, 2 vols. (Berlin: E. S. Mittler und Sohn, 1930), II, 530, Table 21.

12. Gerald D. Feldman, in his examination of the relationship among army, industry, and labor as a function of interest-group politics during World War I, concluded that German mobilization was determined partially by conflicts within the ruling military-bureaucratic elite in Prussia. Feldman, *Army, Industry, and Labor in Germany, 1914–1918* (Princeton: Princeton Univ. Press, 1966), *passim.*

13. David S. Landes, *The Unbound Prometheus. Technological change and industrial development in Western Europe from 1750 to the present* (Cambridge: Cambridge Univ. Press, 1969), 300.

14. Fischer, *Illusionen*, 516–27.

15. Kurt Stenkewitz, *Gegen Bajonett und Dividende: die politische Krise in Deutschland am Vorabend des ersten Weltkrieges*, Schriftenreihe des Instituts fuer deutsche Geschichte an der Karl-Marx-Ueniversitaet Leipzig (Berlin: Ruetten & Loening, 1960), 149.

16. Eckart Kehr, "Soziale und finanzielle Grundlagen der Tirpitzchen Flottenpropaganda," *Moderne deutsche Sozialgeschichte*, ed. Hans Ulrich Wehler (Cologne, Berlin: Kiepenheuer & Witsch, 1968), 393.

17. Cf. Steinberg, *Deterrent, passim*; Fischer, *Germany's Aims*, 18; Kehr, "Flottenpropaganda," *passim*.

18. Fischer, *Illusionen*, 159–63; Stenkewitz, *Krise*, 74.

19. Robert A. Kann, *The Habsburg Empire. A Study in Integration and Disintegration* (New York: Praeger, 1957), 61–63.

20. One mark = 1.18 crowns, or 0.85 marks = 1 crown.

21. Oskar Regele, *Feldmarschall Conrad. Auftrag und Erfuellung 1906–1918* (Vienna, Munich: Verlag Herold, 1955), 61–63.

22. Arthur J. May, *The Habsburg Monarchy, 1867–1914* (New York: Norton, 1951, 1968), 491. Kann, *Habsburg Empire*, 9, 187, 109 n. 7.

23. Z. A. B. Zeman, *Twilight of the Habsburgs. The Collapse of the Austro-Hungarian Empire* (New York: American Heritage Press, 1971), 18.

24. Gerard E. Silberstein, *The Troubled Alliance: German-Austrian Relations 1914–1917* (Lexington, Ky.: Univ. Press of Kentucky, 1970), 65.

## CHAPTER II. THE PRUSSIAN ARMY AND THE NORTH GERMAN AIRCRAFT INDUSTRY, 1908–1911

1. The preceding discussion of the early development of Prussian military aviation is based on information in: KAdL, *Militaerluftfahrt* I, 1–73; II, 107–109, Doc. No. 56.

2. Michael Balfour, *The Kaiser and His Times* (New York: Norton, 1964, 1972), 290.

3. Buelow, *Luftwaffe*, 3.

4. KAdL, *Militaerluftfahrt* II, 109–13, Doc. No. 58.

5. *Ibid.*, 114–16, Doc. No. 59.

6. "Bericht ueber den Stand der Flugmaschinenfrage und die Stellung der Militaerbehoerden verschiedener Kulturstaaten zu ihr," Stock No. IL 26/2, MA.

7. "Jahresbericht ueber die Taetigkeit des Deutschen Luftflottenvereins im Jahre 1909," *Die Luftflotte* II, No. 5 (May 1910), 4–5.

8. DLV, memorandum in 1919 on "Die Foerderung der Luftfahrt vor dem Kriege innerhalb des Rahmens der Betaetigung des Deutschen Luftfahrer-Verbandes," Stock No. IL 2/45, MA.

9. KAdL, *Militaerluftfahrt* I, 117; III, 18–19; Peter Supf, *Das Buch der deutschen Fluggeschichte*, 2 vols., 2d ed. (Stuttgart: Drei Brunnen Verlag, 1956–58), I, 266.

10. KAdL, *Militaerluftfahrt* I, 117.

11. *Ibid.*

12. IdV Sec. IIc No. 549.09, 26 Jan. 1909, Stock No. IL 26/6, MA.

13. KAdL, *Militaerluftfahrt* I, 117.

14. IdV Sec. IIc No. 549.09, 26 Jan. 1909, Stock No. IL 26/6, MA. The Research Unit had estimated the cost at 42,000 M.—30,000 M. for the plane, 2,000 M. for the use of the workshop, and 10,000 M. for incidentals. This estimate did not include 12,000 M. proposed for Hoffman himself, which the Inspectorate of

Transport Troops refused. Nevertheless, the original cost estimate was "substantially exceeded." (KAdL, *Militaerluftfahrt* III, 20 n. 2.) Peter Supf estimated that 50,000 M. were spent. (Supf, *Fluggeschichte* I, 363.)

15. The Hoffman project was also accused of stifling private initiative, but this allegation has never been proven. Hermann Thomsen, "Die Luftwaffe vor und im Weltkriege," 487–527, *Die Deutsche Wehrmacht 1914–1939* (Berlin: Mittler und Sohn, 1939), 495.

16. Dr. G. Philipp, "Deutschlands Flugzeugfuehrer Nr. 1 zum 70. Geburtstag," *Deutsche Luftwacht*, Issue *Luft-Welt* V, No. 12 (Dec. 1938), 407.

17. Euler to KM, 2 Oct. 1911, Stock No. IL 25/35, MA. Euler to Eichhorn, 14 Dec. 1908; KM, Sec. Ia No. 615/12.08.135 to Eichhorn, 4 Jan. 1909; Eichhorn to Euler, 22 Jan. 1909; contract between Euler and the Military Treasury, 30 Jan. 1909; vol. CCXXXVIII, EN, BA.

18. Euler to Major Mueller of the Nassau Pioneer Battalion, 15 Feb. 1909; contract between Euler and the Battalion; vol. CCXXXVIII, EN, BA.

19. In Supf, *Fluggeschichte* I, 277–78.

20. *Flugsport* I, No. 11 (21 May 1909), 316–17. KAdL, *Militaerluftfahrt* III, 168 n. 1. Arthur Mueller, *Thersites, nicht Gracchus* (brochure), 20 July 1913, Stock No. IL 2/26, MA.

21. A. R. Weyl, *Fokker: The Creative Years*, ed. J. M. Bruce (London: Putnam, 1965), 28–29.

22. KAdL, *Militaerluftfahrt* II, 125–35, Doc. No. 62.

23. Georg von Tschudi, *Aus 34 Jahren Luftfahrt. Persoenliche Erinnerungen* (Berlin: Verlag von Reimar Hobbing, 1928), 106–10.

24. Robert Kaunders, "Zehn Jahre Flugplatz Johannisthal," *Illustrierte Flug-Welt* I (24 Sept. 1919), 196. Tschudi, *Erinnerungen*, 110.

25. Tschudi No. 7595 to RdI; VDMI to RdI, 26 Jan. 1912; Tschudi to SSdI, 27 Jan. 1912; KMAD No. 710.2.12.A7 to SSdI, 22 Mar. 1912, SSdI No. IA 836.12.10008 to KM, 24 Feb. 1913; Stock No. IL 2/26, MA.

26. Karl G. Kuhne, "Zehn Jahre deutscher Flugzeugbau," *Illustrierte Flug-Woche* I, No. 3 (30 July 1919), 75–76.

27. Supf, *Fluggeschichte* I, 368–69; KAdL, *Militaerluftfahrt* I, 120–21.

28. KAdL, *Militaerluftfahrt* II, 118–25, Doc. No. 61.

29. Supf, *Fluggeschichte* I, 368–69.

30. KAdL, *Militaerluftfahrt* I, 121.

31. "Nachweisung der im Rechnungsjahr 1910 (1 Apr. 1910–31 Mar. 1911) beschafften Flugzeuge," Stock No. IL 26/7, MA.

32. Albatros to KM, 25 Oct. 1910; VAdV Sec. IIa No. 10672.10; Stock No. IL 25/32, MA.

33. KAdL, *Militaerluftfahrt* I, 121.

34. Supf, *Fluggeschichte* I, 215.

35. "Nachweisung der im Rechnungsjahr 1910 Beschafften Flugzeuge," Stock No. IL 26/7, MA.

36. Kuhne, "Flugzeugbau," 77.

37. Albatros to the VAdV-LA, 3 Dec. 1910, Stock No. IL 34/15, MA.

38. KAdL, *Militaerluftfahrt* III, 22, 28.

39. Buelow, *Luftwaffe*, 8.

40. KAdL, *Militaerluftfahrt* II, 118–25, Doc. No. 61.

41. Military Attaché Major von Winterfeldt No. 277.10 to KM, 3 Dec. 1910; KMAD No. 132.12.10.A7 to IdV, 7 Dec. 1910; VAdV Sec. 2a No. 351.10 to KM, 10 Dec. 1910; IdV No. 11793.10; Stock No. IL 25/32, MA.

42. KAdL, *Militaerluftfahrt* III, 23, 31; II, 116–18, Doc. No. 60.

43. *Ibid.*, I, 122.

44. *Ibid.*, II, 125–35, Doc. No. 62.

45. *Ibid.*, II, Chart No. 54. RA, *Kriegsruestung* II, 530, Table 21.

46. KAdL, *Militaerluftfahrt* I, 125–26.

47. ILuK Sec. IIc No. 2283.11 to GIdMV, 23 June 1911, Stock No. IL 25/35, MA.

48. Mueller, *Thersites*, Stock No. IL 2/26, MA. Albatros to KM, 27 Mar. 1911; VAdV memorandum on Albatros subsidy, 20 Apr. 1911; ILuK Sec. IIc No. 137.11 to GIdMV, 27 Apr. 1911; GIdMV Sec. IIc No. 3323.11, 6 May 1911; Stock No. IL 27/11, MA. Albatros-LVG contract, 27 Apr. 1911, App. No. 3 of ILuK Sec. IIc No. 2883.11 to GIdMV, 23 June 1911; Albatros to ILuK, 14 June 1911, App. No. 4 of ILuK Sec. IIc No. 2883.11 to GIdMV, 23 June 1911; LVG to KMAD, 30 June 1911; KMAD No. 33/7.11.A7 to GIdMV, 25 July 1911; Stock No. IL 25/35, MA.

49. GIdMV Sec. IIc No. 8701.11 to KMAD, 9 Sept. 1911; KMAD No. 148/9.11.A7 to GIdMV, 15 Sept. 1911; ILuK Sec. IIc No. 5557.11 to GIdMV, 29 Sept. 1911; GIdMV Sec. IIc No. 9903.11 to KMAD, 4 Oct. 1911; Stock No. IL 25/35, MA. ILuK Sec. IIc No. 3070.12 to GIdMV, 30 Mar. 1912, Stock No. IL 26/19, MA.

50. DFW and Rumpler to Wiener, 24 Jan. 1912, Stock No. IL 26/11, MA.

51. Albatros to the KMAD, 20 Jan. 1912, Stock No. IL 26/16, MA.

52. GIdMV Sec. IIc No. 1414.12 to KMAD, 20 Feb. 1912, Stock No. IL 26/16, MA.

53. KMAD No. 299/12.g.A7 to GIdMV, 4 Mar. 1912, Stock No. IL 26/16, MA.

54. ILuK Sec. IIc No. 2309.12 to GIdMV, 13 Mar. 1912, Stock No. IL 26/16, MA.

55. GIdMV Sec. IIc No. 1578.12 to KMAD, 22 Feb. 1912, Stock No. IL 26/11, MA. KM No. 167/3.12.A7 to GIdMV, 9 Mar. 1912; GIdMV Sec. IIc No. 3148.12 to KM, 25 Mar. 1912; Stock No. IL 26/19, MA.

56. *Flugsport* III, No. 7 (29 Mar. 1911), 241; No. 18 (8 Aug. 1911), 624–25. Willi Hackenberger, *Die Alten Adler: Pioniere der deutschen Luftfahrt* (Munich: J. R. Lehmanns Verlag, 1960), 63. Philipp, "Flugzeugfuehrer," 409. "Maenner der Luftfahrt," *Illustrierte Flug-Welt* II, No. 7 (31 Mar. 1920), 196.

57. Karl Erich Born, "Einfuehrung des Herausgebers," *Sozialgeschichte*, 19.

58. On the reasons for the Convention's formation, see: *Flugsport* III, No. 7 (29 Mar. 1911), 241. Albatros to ILuK, 27 Jan. 1912; Dorner to ILuK, 31 Jan. 1912; Rumpler to ILuK, 31 Jan. 1912; Wright to ILuK, 1 Feb. 1912; Euler to ILuK, 5 Feb. 1912; Stock No. IL 27/11, MA.

59. VDMI General Secretary Sperling to GIdMV, 14 Sept. 1911, Stock No. IL 25/35, MA.

60. VDMI No. 113 to ILuK, 24 Oct. 1911, Stock No. IL 27/11, MA; ILuK Sec. IIc No. 6044.11 to GIdMV, 14 Oct. 1911, Stock No. IL 25/35, MA.

61. LVG to ILuK, 18 Jan. 1912, Stock No. IL 27/11, MA.

62. ILuK Sec. IIc No. 711–717.12 to Albatros, Rumpler, Aviatik, Euler, Dorner, Harlan, Wright, 26 Jan. 1912, Stock No. IL 27/11, MA.

63. Albatros to ILuK, 27 Jan. 1912; Dorner to ILuK, 31 Jan. 1912; Rumpler to ILuK, 31 Jan. 1912; Harlan to ILuK, 30 Jan. 1912; Wright to ILuK, 1 Feb. 1912; Euler to ILuK, 5 Feb. 1912; Aviatik to ILuK, 1 Feb. 1912; Stock No. IL 27/11, MA.

64. On pilot training, see: KAdL, *Militaerluftfahrt* I, 132. ILuK Sec. IIc No. 7114.11 to GIdMV, 16 Nov. 1911; KMAD No. 496/

1.12.A7 to GIdMV, 20 Jan. 1912; Albatros to ILuK, 7 Mar. 1912; Stock No. IL 26/11, MA.

65. ILuK Sec. IIc No. 7114.11 to GIdMV, 16 Nov. 1911, Stock No. IL 26/11.

66. Hackenberger, *Pioniere*, 73.

67. ILuK Sec. IIc No. 7114.11 to GIdMV, 16 Nov. 1911; ILuK Sec. IIc No. 7178.11 to GIdMV, 12 Dec. 1911; Stock No. IL 26/11, MA.

68. II No. 258 to KKM, 18 Jan. 1912, Stock No. M Kr 1360, BKA.

69. ILuK No. 2447.11 to GIdMV, 28 June 1911, Stock No. IL 76/11, MA.

70. KMAD No. 348/8.11.A7 to GIdMV, 6 Sept. 1911, Stock No. IL 27/2, MA.

71. KMAD No. 776/11/g/A7 to GIdMV, 26 Oct. 1911; GIdMV Sec. IIc No. 11377.11 to KMAD, 3 Nov. 1911; GIdMV Sec. IIc No. 5970.11 to KMAD, 11 Nov. 1911, Stock No. IL 25/35, MA.

72. ILuK Sec. IIc No. 7165.11 to GIdMV, 18 Nov. 1911; ILuK Sec. IIc No. 2352.12, 15 Mar. 1912; Stock No. IL 26/11, MA.

73. AEG's entry is discussed in the following documents: KMAD No. 148/12.geh.A7 to GIdMV, 29 Jan. 1912; GIdMV Sec. IIc No. 1015.12 to KMAD, 5 Feb. 1912; ILuK Sec. IIc No. 2041.12 to GIdMV, 16 Mar. 1912; Stock No. IL 26/11, MA.

74. Albatros to ILuK, 2 Mar. 1912; Rumpler to ILuK, 2 Mar. 1912; Stock No. IL 26/11, MA.

75. Adolf Borchardt to KMAD, 21 Feb. 1912, Stock No. IL 26/11, MA.

76. Supf, *Fluggeschichte* I, 278.

77. Rumpler to KM, 4 Dec. 1911, Stock No. IL 26/11, MA.

78. "Nachweisung der im Rechnungsjahre 1911 beschafften Flugzeuge," Stock No. IL 26/7, MA. KAdL, *Militaerluftfahrt* I, 141; III, 38.

79. Ritter, *Luftkrieg*, 26–30.

80. Buelow, *Luftwaffe*, 12. KAdL, *Militaerluftfahrt* I, 130–32; II, 73–76, Doc. No. 37; III, 37.

81. KAdL, *Militaerluftfahrt* I, 141; II, 141–45, Doc. No. 66.

82. ILuK Sec. IIc No. 504.12 to GIdMV, 23 Jan. 1912, Stock No. IL 26/11, MA. GIdMV, 7 Sept. 1911; GG No. II JN 59.1/11. I to GIdMV, 11 Nov. 1911; GG No. 12339.I to GIdMV, 11 Oct. 1911; GIdMV Sec. Ib No. 540 M12/13 to *Koenigliche Kommandos* (except Bavaria), 23 Jan. 1912; Stock No. IL 26/9, MA.

83. ILuK Sec. IIc No. 504.12 to GIdMV, 23 Jan. 1912, Stock No. IL 26/11, MA.

84. Dorner to Kommerzienrat Karl Lanz, 20 Nov. 1911; Business Report No. 2 of the Dorner Co., Aug. 1912; DN, DM; Dorner to ILuK, 6 Sept. 1912, Stock No. IL 26/16, MA.

85. K. D. Seifert, "Das grosse Geschaeft. Anfang und Weg der imperialistischen deutschen Flugzeugindustrie," *Fluegel der Heimat* III, No. 11 (Nov. 1958), 25.

86. Wright Co. to KM, 12 Jan. 1912; ILuK Sec. IIc No. 504.12 to GIdMV, 23 Jan. 1912; Stock No. IL 26/11, MA. Professor August von Parseval, "Die Bedeutung der deutschen flugtechnischen Industrie," *Die Luftflotte* IV, No. 5 (May 1912), 74–75.

87. ILuK Sec. IIc No. 7543.11 to GIdMV, 2 Dec. 1911, Stock No. IL 26/11, MA.

88. Supf. *Fluggeschichte* I, 378.

89. *Ibid.*

90. Georg Paul Neumann, *Die deutschen Luftstreitkraefte im Weltkriege* (Berlin: Mittler und Sohn, 1920), 59.

91. *Die Luftflotte*, vols. 3 and 4 (1911, 1912), *Jahrbuch des Deutschen Luftschifferverbandes 1911*.

92. One mark = 1.25 francs, or 1 franc = 0.80 mark.

93. Karl Dieter Seifert, *Geschaeft mit dem Flugzeug: vom Weg*

*der deutschen Luftfahrt* (Berlin: VEB Verlag fuer Verkehrswesen, 1960), 20; KAdL, *Militaerluftfahrt* II, Chart No. 106.

94. Buelow, *Luftwaffe*, 14.

## CHAPTER III. THE GROWTH AND MOBILIZATION OF NORTH GERMAN MILITARY AVIATION, 1912–1914

1. KAdL, *Militaerluftfahrt* II, 143, Doc. No. 66.

2. Report of Conference, 18 Apr. 1912; KMAD No. 925/4.12.A7 to CDFI, 6 May 1912; Stock No. IL 27/40, MA.

3. *Deutsche Luftfahrer Zeitschrift* XVI, No. 11 (29 May 1912), 284.

4. Supf, *Fluggeschichte* II, 497.

5. Hptm. a.D. Alfred Hildebrandt, "Die Notlage der deutschen Flugzeugindustrie," *Deutsche Luftfahrer Zeitschrift* XVI, No. 13 (26 June 1912), 313–14; *Flugsport* IV No. 20 (25 Sept. 1912), 741–42; Oberlt. E. Mickel-Coeln, "Die Verwendung der Nationalflugspende in Deutschland," *Deutsche Luftfahrer Zeitschrift* XVII (19 Mar. 1913), 129–52.

6. KAdL, *Militaerluftfahrt* II, 152–58, Docs. 71 and 72.

7. See pp. 8–10.

8. KAdL, *Militaerluftfahrt* I, 140.

9. A. H. G. Fokker and Bruce Gould, *Der Fliegende Hollaender. Das Leben des Fliegers and Flugzeugkonstrukteurs A. H. G. Fokker*, trans. Dr. Carl Hans Pollog (Leipzig, Stuttgart, and Zurich: Rascher & Cie., A. G., 1933), 134–35.

10. KAdL, *Militaerluftfahrt* II, 180, Doc. 80.

11. *Ibid.*, 152–58, Docs. 71 and 72.

12. *Ibid.*

13. GIdMV Sec. IId No. 17235 KMAD, 14 Dec. 1912, Stock No. IL 27/37, MA.

14. IdFlieg Sec. IIb No. 1871.13 to ILuK, 15 Nov. 1913, Stock No. IL 26/94, MA.

15. Rumpler to KM, 24 Oct. 1912, Stock No. IL 26/16, MA. Rumpler to GIdMV, 10 Feb. 1914, Stock No. IL 26/94, MA.

16. KAdL, *Militaerluftfahrt* III, 318–20, App. 71.

17. Fliegertruppe No. 4008.13, 6 June 1913, Stock No. IL 26/68, MA.

18. Gotha to KM, 3 Feb. 1913, Stock No. IL 26/65, MA. GIdMV No. 1213.13, 13 Feb. 1913, Stock No. IL 26/64, MA. GIdMV Sec. IId No. 1985.13 to KMAD, 13 Feb. 1913, Stock No. IL $6/85, MA. Gotha Dept. II Aircraft Works to GIdMV, 21 Oct. 1913, Stock No. IL 26/94, MA. Gotha to GIdMV, 31 Nov. 1913, Stock No. IL 26/85, MA.

19. KAdL, *Militaerluftfahrt* III, 318–20, App. 71.

20. Stock No. IL 26/118, MA.

21. ILuK Sec. IIc No. 4100.14 to GIdMV, 7 Apr. 1914, Stock No. IL 26/118, MA.

22. KMAD No. 805/4.14.A7 to VDMI, 8 May 1914, Stock No. IL 26/118, MA.

23. GIdMV Sec. IId No. 10385.13 to ILuK, 20 June 1913; ILuK Sec. IIc No. 7743.13 to GIdMV, 4 July 1913; Stock No. IL 27/71, MA.

24. Reichstag, *Stenographische Berichte* CCXC, 5422A–5423D.

25. F. Berg to IdFlieg; Fl. Bat. No. 4 Sec. I No. 430, 4 July 1914; Stock No. IL 97/20, MA.

26. "Ein Treuer Patriot" to KM, 23 Jan. 1913; KMAD No. 873/2.13.A7 to GIdMV, 4 Mar. 1913; Stock No. IL 26/68, MA.

27. Wright to GIdMV, 12 Dec. 1912; ILuK Sec. IIc No. 12127.12 to GIdMV, 7 Dec. 1912; GIdMV Sec. IId No. 17235 to

KMAD, 14 Dec. 1912; GIdMV Sec. IId No. 17509.12 to KMAD, 30 Dec. 1912; Stock No. IL 27/37, MA.

28. Aviatik to GIdMV, 5 Feb. 1914; ILuK Sec. IIc No. 1157.14 to Aviatik, 16 Feb. 1914; Aviatik to ILuK, 24 Feb. 1914; DFW to GIdMV, 24 May 1914; Stock No. IL 26/118, MA.

29. ILuK Sec. IIc No. 1157.14 to GIdMV, 3 Mar. 1914, Stock No. IL 26/118, MA.

30. KAdL, *Militaerluftfahrt* I, 65–68.

31. *Ibid.*, 266–67.

32. SSdI Delbrueck Reichsdiensttelegram to Valentini (chief of the Civil Cabinet), 15 Apr. 1912, Stock No. IL 2/30, MA.

33. John R. Cuneo, *Winged Mars*, vol. I, *The German Air Service, 1870–1914* (Harrisburg, Pa.: The Military Service Publishing Co., 1942), 99.

34. Supf, *Fluggeschichte* II, 10–11.

35. Philipp, "Flugzeugfuehrer."

36. "Vorschau zur Allgemeinen Luftfahrzeug-Austellung," *Deutsche Luftfahrer Zeitschrift* XVI, No. 7 (3 Apr. 1912), 145–64.

37. Deputy of the Imperial Chancellor No. IA 3453 u. 3519 to Kaiser, 25 Apr. 1912; SSdI No. IA 4614 ev. to SS of the Imperial Post Office, 23 May 1912; RdI No. IA 3335 to all state governments, 17 Apr. 1912; Stock No. IL 2/30, MA; Supf, *Fluggeschichte* II, 454.

38. Reichstag, *Stenographische Berichte* CCLXXXV (62. Sitzung, 14 May 1912), 1998C–2000C; CCLXXXVIII (124. Sitzung, 25 Mar. 1913), 4192A.

39. Booklet on National Aviation Fund, 15 Dec. 1912, Stock No. IL 2/30, MA. KAdL, *Militaerluftfahrt* I, 267–68.

40. KAdL, *Militaerluftfahrt* II, 241 Doc. No. 110.

41. *Ibid.*, 242–43, Doc. No. 111.

42. KMAD Nr. 699/11.12.A7 to the RdI, 28 Nov. 1912, Stock No. IL 26/37, MA.

43. KAdL, *Militaerluftfahrt* I, 267–68. GIdMV Sec. IIc No. 14465.12 to KMAD, 2 Nov. 1912, Stock No. IL 26/37, MA.

44. KAdL, *Militaerluftfahrt* I, 271.

45. Reichstag, *Stenographische Berichte* CCLX (46. Sitzung, 2 Mar. 1910), 1615–1625; CCLXV (49. Sitzung, 16 Mar. 1911), 5501C–5502C; CCLXXXV (66. Sitzung, 20 May 1912), 2127C–2129C. In the intervening two years the Imperial Office of the Interior had commissioned various scientists to write two memoranda on the formation and tasks of, and the need for a research institute. Both memoranda emphasized the necessity for an institute. (KAdL, *Militaerluftfahrt* III, 55.)

46. SSdI No. IA 5529 to VDMI, 1 July 1912; VDMI to RdI (Dr. Albert), 12 Aug. 1912; SSdI No. IA 7369 to VDMI, 10 Sept. 1912; Stock No. IL 2/26, MA.

47. KAdL, *Militaerluftfahrt* III, 99–100.

48. *Ibid.*, I, 269.

49. Euler to RdI (Dr. Albert), 19 Aug. 1912, vol. I, EN, BA.

50. KMAD No. 226/9.13.A7 to GIdMV, 28 Sept. 1913; IdFlieg Sec. IIb No. 12071; ILuK Sec. IIc No. 12430.13; Stock No. IL 26/37, MA. RdI (Dr. Albert) to CDFI, 24 Mar. 1914; RdI (Dr. Trautmann) to Fund business committee, 14 and 27 Nov. 1914; vol. XVa, EN, BA.

51. II No. 3933 to KKM, 30 Apr. 1912, Stock No. M Kr 1379, BKA; SSdI No. IA 3848 to Kaiser, 21 June 1913, Stock No. IL 2/30, MA; KMAD No. 925/4.12.A7 to CDFI, 6 May 1912, Stock No. IL 27/40, MA.

52. DLV memorandum (1919), "Die Foerderung der Luftfahrt vor dem Kriege innerhalb des Rahmens der Betaetigung des Deutschen Luftfahrer Verbandes," Stock No. IL 2/45, MA.

53. SSdI No. IA 3848 to Kaiser, 21 June 1913, Stock No. IL 2/30, MA; II No. 3933 to KKM, 30 Apr. 1912, Stock No. M Kr 1379, BKA.

54. Hptm. a.D. Dr. Alfred Hildebrandt, "Die Notlage der

deutschen Flugzeugindustrie," *Deutsche Luftfahrer Zeitschrift* XVI, No. 13 (26 June 1912), 313–14.

55. DLV memorandum (1919), "Die Foerderung der Luftfahrt vor dem Kriege innerhalb des Rahmens der Betaetigung des Deutschen Luftfahrer Verbandes," Stock No. IL 2/45, MA.

56. Board of Trustees to RdI, 7 Aug. 1913, Stock No. IL 2/30. Oldershausen to GIdMV, 14 Nov. 1913; Flying Battalion No. 4 Sec. I No. 154.14 to IdFlieg, 11 Jan. 1914, and No. 268.14 to IdFlieg; Stock No. IL 26/94, MA. Euler to VDMI, 7 Feb. 1914; VDMI General Secretary to RdI (Dr. Trautmann), 11 Feb. 1914; vol. XVI, EN, BA. Oldershausen to Euler, 9 Dec. 1913 and 12 Dec. 1913, vol. XXXV, EN, BA.

57. "Am Ende des ersten Jahrzehnts," *Deutsche Luftfahrer Zeitschrift* XVII, No. 1 (8 Jan. 1913), 1–4; Euler's answer to newspaper article of 24 Dec. 1912; vol. XXVI, EN, BA.

58. Euler's answer to newspaper article of 24 Dec. 1912; vol. XXVI, EN, BA.

59. This situation is implied in: *Flugsport* V, No. 2 (22 Jan. 1913), 38–39.

60. Euler to VDMI General Secretary, 7 Feb. 1914, vol. XVI, EN, BA. Oldershausen to Euler, 14 Jan. 1913, vol. XXIV, EN, BA.

61. Oldershausen to GIdMV, 27 Oct. 1913 and 14 Nov. 1913, Stock No. IL 26/91, MA.

62. "Sollen wir uns noch flugsportlich betaetigen?" *Flugsport* V, No. 21 (15 Oct. 1913), 779–80.

63. GIdMV Sec. IId No. 3504.14 to KMAD, 25 Mar. 1914, Stock No. IL 27/68, MA.

64. Euler to RdI (Dr. Albert), 2 Dec. 1913, vol. X, EN, BA; Euler to DLV, 19 Jan. 1914, vol. XXVIII, EN, BA; VDMI No. 6095 to GIdMV, 12 Feb. 1914, Stock No. IL 26/93, MA; GIdMV Sec. IId No. 3504.14 to KMAD, 25 Mar. 1914, Stock No. IL 27/68, MA.

65. Euler to Sperling, 7 Feb. 1914; Sperling to RdI (Dr. Trautmann), 11 Feb. 1914, vol. XVI, EN, BA.

66. Oldershausen to Euler, 9 Dec. 1913, 12 Dec. 1913, vol. XXXV, EN, BA. Oldershausen to GIdMV, 14 Nov. 1913, Stock No. IL 26/91, MA.

67. Fl. Bat. No. 4 Sec. I No. 154.14 to IdFlieg, 11 Jan. 1914 and No. 268.14 to IdFlieg, Stock No. IL 26/91, MA.

68. Report of the 3d meeting of DLV, 15 Feb. 1914, Stock No. IL 26/91, MA.

69. Euler to von der Goltz (head of DLV), 14 Feb. and 22 Mar. 1914, Stock No. IL 26/91, MA.

70. Joseph to von der Goltz, Stock No. IL 26/91, MA.

71. DLV memorandum (1919), "Die Foerderung der Luftfahrt vor dem Kriege innerhalb des Rahmens der Betaetiung des Deutschen Luftfahrer Verbandes," Stock No. IL 2/45, MA.

72. Administration of the Prince Henry Flight to CDFI, 26 Mar. 1914, Stock No. IL 26/91, MA; Euler to von der Goltz, 14 Apr. 1914, vol. XVI, EN, BA.

73. Minutes of the board meeting of the DLV, 18 Apr. 1914, vol. XXXIII, EN, BA.

74. *Ibid.*; Oldershausen to GIdMV, 26 Mar. 1914, Stock No. IL 26/91.

75. VDMI to GIdMV, 29 Apr. 1914, Stock No. IL 26/91, MA.

76. KAdL, *Militaerluftfahrt* III, 100, 261 (App. 37).

77. SSdI No. IA 3848 to Kaiser, 21 June 1913, Stock No. IL 2/30, MA. Although Delbrueck mentioned benefits to both the army and the navy, this chapter has discussed only those to the Prussian Army. The German Navy, because of the smallness of its aviation branch, remained very much in the background, even though the Fund did help sponsor naval airplane competitions and construct some naval aircraft bases. The Prussian Army

exercised the controlling influence on the Fund and consequently reaped most of the benefits.

78. Grade to Euler, 14 Feb. 1913, vol. XLVIII, EN, BA.

79. "Wem kommt die Nationalflugspende zu gute?" *Frankfurter Sport-Zeitung*, 28 Jan. 1913, vol. XLVIII, EN, BA.

80. Board of Trustees (Posadowsky Wehner) to RdI, 22 Apr. 1913, Stock No. IL 2/30, MA.

81. The Prussian Army decided against subsidies to aircraft factories in 1911 on the grounds that subsidies to one firm might mean subsidies for all regardless of the necessity for them in terms of increased production facilities. VAdV memorandum, 20 Apr. 1911; ILuK Sec. IIc No. 137.11 to GIdMV, 27 Apr. 1911; GIdMV Sec. IIc No. 3323.11, 6 May 1911; Stock No. IL 27/11.

82. Rumpler to ILuK, 31 Jan. 1912; Richard Goetz to ILuK, 31 Jan. 1912; Stock No. IL 27/11.

83. Buelow, *Luftwaffe*, 14, 18; Neumann, *Luftstreitkraefte*, 20; KAdL, *Militaerluftfahrt* I, 272.

84. The awards for these record flights, for which only civilian pilots were eligible, were awarded by the month and shared by the pilot and the airplane company. Only three factories and their pilots benefited significantly (that is, earned more than 10,000 M.) by the end of the 1913–Albatros with 42,000 M., Aviatik with 110,000 M., and Gotha with 110,000 M.

85. For the budget, see KAdL, *Militaerluftfahrt* I, 263–64; II, Chart No. 106. For airplane orders, see KAdL, *Militaerluftfahrt* III, 316–17 (app.).

86. Gerhard Wissmann, *Geschichte der Luftfahrt von Ikarus bis zur Gegenwart: Eine Darstellung des Fluggedankens und der Luftfahrttechnik* (Berlin: VEB Verlag Technik, 1964), 258–59.

87. Karl Helfferich, *Die Vorgeschichte des Weltkrieges* (Berlin: Ullstein & Co., 1919), 34–36.

88. Arthur Dix, *Wirtschaftskrieg und Kriegswirtschaft: zur Geschichte des deutschen Zusammenbruchs* (Berlin: Mittler und Sohn, 1920), 161.

89. RA, *Kriegsruestung* I, 341–400.

90. Generalmajor Ludwig Wurtzbacher, "Die Versorgung des Heeres mit Waffen und Munition," *Der Weltkampf um Ehre und Recht*, 3 vols., vol. II, pt. 3 (Leipzig: Alleinvertrieb durch Ernst Finking d.F., 1922), 74.

91. Institut fuer Konjunkturforschung, Berlin, *Industrielle Mobilmachung: Statistische Untersuchungen*, Schriften zur kriegswissenschaftlichen Forschung und Schulung, ed. Major Privat-Dozent Dr. Kurt Hesse with the support of official agencies (Hamburg: Hanseatische Verlangsanstalt A.G., 1936), 7.

92. KAdL, *Beitrage zur Entwicklungsgeschichte des Flugzeugwesens und des Flugzeugbaues im Heer und in der Industrie* (No. 30), 2, 57, Stock No. IL 234/32, MA.

93. General von Hoeppner, *Deutschlands Krieg in der Luft* (Leipzig: von Hase und K. F. Koehler Verlag, 1921), 17.

94. Buelow, *Luftwaffe*, 18.

95. Justus Schmidt, *Kriegswichtige Industrie im System der Wirtschaftspolitik* (Berlin: Obelisk Verlags Gesellschaft, 1937).

96. KaDL, *Militaerluftfahrt* II, 152–57, Doc. No. 71.

97. ILuK Sec. IIc No. 12208.13 to GIdMV; German Bristol Works to ILuK, 28 Oct. 1913; IdFlieg Sec. IIb No. 2738.13 to ILuk, 6 Nov. 1913; H. M. F. to GIdMV, 27 June 1914; Stock No. IL 26/68, MA. Because the army ordered Behrens to sever the partnership with the English Bristol company in Feb. 1913 for security reasons, he suffered a net loss of 190,000 M. in his first year of business. In June 1914, Behrens found it impossible to equip the school with up-to-date aircraft and asked the army to buy the H. M. F. and the factory.

98. KAdL, *Militaerluftfahrt* I, 169–70, 179–80.

99. *Ibid.*, II, 166–73, Doc. No. 76.

100. Erich Swoboda, *Igo Etrich und seine 'Taube'* (Vienna: Zweigstelle Vienna, KAdL, 1942); Hackenberger, *Pioniere*, 24; Supf, *Fluggeschichte* I, 244.

101. ILuK Sec. IIc No. 4590.12 to GIdMV, 21 May 1912, Stock No. IL 26/19.

102. KAdL, *Militaerluftfahrt* III, 52.

103. LuVa Sec. III No. 8345.12, 30 Sept. 1912, Stock No. IL 27/37, MA.

104. ILuK Sec. IIc No. 11713.12 to GIdMV, 15 Nov. 1912, Stock No. IL 27/37.

105. GIdMV No. 16716.12 to KMAD, 30 Nov. 1912, Stock No. IL 26/16, MA.

106. ILuK Sec. IIc No. 12385.12, 8 Jan. 1913, Stock No. IL 27/37.

107. Hptm. Krafft No. 141 to II, 10 June 1913, Stock No. M Kr 1382, BKA.

108. GIdMV Sec. IId No. 18569, 10 Oct. 1913, Stock No. IL 26/94, MA.

109. ILuK Sec. IIc No. 7149.13 to GIdMV, 29 May 1913, Stock No. IL 34/26, MA.

110. KAdL, *Militaerluftfahrt* III, 66.

111. *Ibid.*, I, 177–78.

112. Corvette Captain Eckelmann, memorandum on "Das Flug und Luftschiffwesen der Armee nach dem Stande vom 15. Juni 1914" Stock No. 5656, AM, MA; KAdL, *Militaerluftfahrt* III, 95–97.

113. ILuK Sec. Ia No. 1755.14 to GIdMV, 26 Mar. 1914, Stock No. IL 26/118, MA. KAdL, *Militaerluftfahrt* III, 97.

114. Jeannin to GIdMV, 11 Nov. 1913; IdFlieg Sec. IIb No. 1871.13 to ILuK, 15 Nov. 1913; Stock No. IL 26/94, MA. LvG to Fliegertruppe, 5 Sept. 1913, Stock No. IL 27/71, MA.

115. KAdL, *Militaerluftfahrt* III, 75–76.

116. Supf, *Fluggeschichte* II, 115.

117. Kommissions-Verhandlungen, 21 Sept.–20 Oct. 1913, Stock No. IL 26/7, MA; KAdL, *Militaerluftfahrt* III, 76–77.

118. KAdL, *Militaerluftfahrt* III, 78–80, 98–100, 221–34 (apps. 22–24).

119. *Ibid.*, I, 183.

120. *Ibid.*, III, 102–103.

121. Euler to ILuK, 6 Sept. 1913, Stock No. IL 27/71, MA.

122. On Euler's problems with the army, see the following: II No. 4670 to KKM, 20 June 1911, Stock No. M Kr 1377, BKA. Contract between Euler and GIdMV on pilot training, 19 Dec. 1912; IdFlieg commission report on Euler's planes, 11–19 Nov. 1913; agreement between Euler and KM, 23 July 1913; IdFlieg Sec. IIb No. 2206.13 to Euler, 2 Oct. 1913; Euler to IdFlieg, 29 Oct. 1913; Stock No. IL 26/45, MA. Vol. CCXLIII (particularly Euler letter to KM, 25 May 1914), vols. CCXLIV, CCXLVI, CCLII (particularly Euler memorandum on "Das Geschaeftsgebahren der GIdMV unter Generalleutnant v. Haenisch"), CCLX; EN, BA.

123. GIdMV Sec. IId No. 18569.13 to IdFlieg, 10 Oct. 1913; IdFlieg Sec. IIb No. 1506.13, 15 Oct. 1913; GIdMV Sec. II No. 2573.14 to VPK, 14 Feb. 1914; Rumpler to GIdMV, 19 Jan. 1914; Stock No. IL 26/94. Rumpler to KM, 10 June 1914; KMAD No. 596.6.14.A7L to GIdMV, 13 June 1914; Stock No. IL 26/118.

124. VPK Abt. V No. 1264.14V to GIdMV, 17 Mar. 1914.

125. KAdL, *Militaerluftfahrt* III, 239–47 (app. 30).

126. *Ibid.*, 318–20 (app. 71).

127. Fokker and Gould, *Hollaender*, 134–35.

128. Weyl, *Fokker*, 42–64, 353; Stock No. IL 26/83, MA.

129. KAdL, *Militaerluftfahrt* III, 171–72.

130. Landes, *Prometheus*, 306.

131. *Die Rumpler Werke A.G. 1908–1918* (Berlin: Ecksteins Biographischer Verlag, 1919), 55–56, 65, 67.

132. On prices and figures, see KAdL, *Militaerluftfahrt* III, 319 (app. 71). On profits, Seifert, "Geschaeft," *Fdjh*, 26. On plant value of Aviatik, see Kuhne, "Flugzeugbau."

133. Fischer, *Illusionen*, 516–27; Stenkewitz, *Krise*, 149.

134. Rumpler to GIdMV, 19 Jan. 1914, Stock No. IL 26/94, MA.

135. Kommission zur Pruefung von Vertraegen ueber Kriegslieferungen, *Stenographische Berichte, Ergaenzungen zum Vortrag ueber Beschaffungen auf dem Gebiete des Luftfahrwesens*, App. 5, p. 52, Stock No. K 10–4/2540, AM, MA.

136. KAdL, *Militaerluftfahrt* III, 172.

137. *Ibid.*, I, 184 n. 4. Namely, Captain von der Lieth Thomsen.

138. Zu IdFlieg No. Ia 91/14, "Entwurf, Mobilmachungsinstruktion d. GIdMV," 2 Feb. 1914, Stock No. IL 97/17, MA. KAdL, *Militaerluftfahrt* I, 184–85. App. to KKM to 3979, 12 Mar. 1913, Stock No. M Kr 1381; BKA.

139. KAdL, *Militaerluftfahrt* III, 103.

140. Euler to VPK Abt. V, 31 July 1914, vol. CCLX, EN, BA.

141. KAdL, *Militaerluftfahrt* III, 107.

## CHAPTER IV. GERMAN NAVAL AND BAVARIAN AND AUSTRO-HUNGARIAN MILITARY AVIATION, 1909–1914

1. The discussion of naval aviation, unless otherwise footnoted, is based on: KAdL *Militaerluftfahrt* I, 226–50; II, 209–39 (Docs. No. 94–103); III, 118–50.

2. The Ago Aircraft Works was the Johannisthal branch of the Otto Works of Munich, Bavaria.

3. Supf, *Fluggeschichte* II, 139.

4. Ernst Heinkel, *Leben*, 60–65.

5. Geschaeftsstelle Ostseeflug Warnemuende 1914, 20 June 1914 to Admiralstab der Marine (list of competitors), Stock No. 5656, AM, MA.

6. SS d. RMA No. BX305 to Chef des Admiralstabes der Marine, 25 Mar. 1914, Stock No. 5656, AM, MA.

7. Chef des Admiralstabes der Marine A 3157 I/13 to RMA, 23 Feb. 1914, Stock No. 1200, AM, MA.

8. II No. 7182 to KKM, 21 Sept. 1909, Stock No. M Kr 1376, BKA. II to KKM, 7 July 1911; II No. 7450, 6 Oct. 1911; Stock No. M Kr 1377, BKA.

9. Grade to KKM, 22 Sept. 1910; II No. 7490 to KKM, 1 Oct. 1910; App. 20328 KKM, 4 Oct. 1910; Krafft No. 247 to II, 25 Oct. 1910; Stock No. M Kr 1376, BKA.

10. Albatros to KKM, 11 Nov. 1910, App. 23857 KKM; II No. 8684 to KKM, 25 Nov. 1910; Stock No. M Kr 1376, BKA.

11. App. 27483 KKM, 28 Dec. 1910, Stock No. M Kr 1376, BKA.

12. II No. 9770/11, 21 Dec. 1911, Stock No. M Kr 1378, BKA.

13. Otto to KKM, 8 June 1911, and following KKM memorandum on II and Otto Works, Stock No. M Kr 1377, BKA.

14. II No. 570 to KKM, 19 Jan. 1912, Stock No. M Kr 1378, BKA.

15. According to KAdL, *Militaerluftfahrt* II, Chart No. 107, the Bavarian Army Budget for Aviation (airplanes) from 1910 to 1914 was: 1910, 7,500 M.; 1911, 107,100 M.; 1912, 567,900 M.; 1913, 1,863,100 M.; and 1914, 1,109,600 M.

16. On Otto and the contest, see: App. 10706 KKM, 21 May 1912, Stock No. M Kr 1379, BKA. Otto to KM, 15 Feb. 1912; KMAD No. 457/2.12.A7, 1 Mar. 1912; Stock No. IL 26/11, MA. KMAD No. 716.5.12.A7, 25 May 1912, Stock No. IL 27/28, MA.

17. Otto to KM, 16 Aug. 1912, Stock No. IL 27/28, MA. Otto to KKM, 16 July 1912, Stock No. M Kr 1380, BKA.

18. KAdL, *Militaerluftfahrt* III, 213.

19. On Otto and the contest, see: App. 6612 KKM, 2 Mar. 1913,

Stock No. M Kr 1381, BKA. Hptm. Krafft No. 131 to II, 27 May 1913, Stock No. M Kr 1382, BKA.

20. Otto to KM, 2 Oct. 1913; GIdMV Sec. IId No. 18204.13, Stock No. IL 35/4, MA. IdFlieg Sec. IIb No. 1705.13 to ILuK, 31 Oct. 1913, Stock No. IL 26/94, MA.

21. App. 20981 KKM, 18 Sept. 1912, Stock No. M Kr 1380, BKA.

22. Apps. 452 and 949 KKM, 25 Jan. 1913, Stock No. M Kr 1381, BKA.

23. *Ibid.*

24. App. 9789 KKM, 16 May 1913, Stock No. M Kr 1382, BKA.

25. For details on the assignment, see App. 16261 KKM, 3 July 1913, Stock No. M Kr 1382, BKA.

26. App. 18118 KKM, 18 Sept. 1913, Stock No. M Kr 1382, BKA.

27. App. 26313 KKM, 3 Oct. 1913, Stock No. M Kr 1383, BKA.

28. App. 18118 KKM, 18 Sept. 1913, Stock No. M Kr 1382, BKA.

29. KILuK No. 264 to II, 18 Oct. 1913, and No. 842 to II, 20 Nov. 1913, Stock No. M Kr 1382, BKA.

30. KILuK to II, 9 Jan. 1914, Stock No. M Kr 1383, BKA.

31. Brug memorandum, 16 Jan. 1914, Stock No. M Kr 1383, BKA.

32. Brug memorandum, 15 May 1914, Stock No. M Kr 1384, BKA.

33. II No. 5339 to KKM, 25 May 1914, Stock No. M Kr 1384, BKA.

34. KKM Sec. AI4b No. 1354, 22 Jan. 1914, Stock No. M Kr 1383, BKA.

35. App. 16162 KKM, 16 June 1914, Stock No. M Kr 1384, BKA.

36. Otto to KKM, 14 July 1914, Stock No. M Kr 1385, BKA.

37. App. 16582 KKM, 12 June 1914, Stock No. M Kr 1384; II No. 18887 to KKM, 13 Jan. 1915, Stock No. M Kr 1385, BKA.

38. K. Fl. Bat. No. 5814 to KILuK, 14 July 1914; KILuK to II, 20 July 1914; Brug memorandum, 26 July 1914; Stock No. M Kr 1385, BKA.

39. *Die Wegbereiter der Oesterreichisch-Ungarischen Luftfahrt*, 6–8, Fol. No. 50, LA, OK; GSC No. 3702, 21 Oct. 1908, *Oesterreichisch-Ungarische Luftfahrt 1914*, Fol. No. 150, LA, OK.

40. Klaus Peters, "Zur Entwicklung der Oesterreichisch-Ungarischen Militaerluftfahrt von den Anfaengen bis Ende 1915," Ph.D. diss., Univ. of Vienna, 1971, 58.

41. "Auszug aus dem Verwaltungsberichte der KK Stadt Wiener Neustadt in den Jahren 1907–1911," 1, 2, 5–6, Fol. No. 48, LA, OK; VTBK to GSC, Oct. 1908, *Luftfahrt*, Fol. No. 150, LA, OK.

42. MAA to KM, 2 Feb. and 26 May 1909; Wallner to KM, 2 Mar. 1909; Radowitz to KM, 21 Oct. 1909; KM to MAA, 9 Apr. 1909; 1909, KM, OK. Peters, "Entwicklung," 61.

43. *Stand der Luftfahrtindustrie in Oesterreich-Ungarn vor Kriegsbeginn 1914*, 2–3, Fol. No. 36, LA, OK; Richard Lohner, *Ludwig Lohner. Sein Leben und sein Werk*, Fol. No. 163, LA, OK.

44. GSC No. 3346 to KM, 6 Sept. 1909, *Luftfahrt*, Fol. No. 150, LA, OK; *Wegbereiter*, 9, Fol. No. 50, LA, OK; *Luftfahrtindustrie*, 2 Fol. No. 36, LA, OK.

45. *Wegbereiter*, 7, Fol. No. 50, LA, OK.

46. *Luftfahrtindustrie*, 4, Fol. No. 36, LA, OK.

47. VTBK No. 250 to KM, 10 June 1910; 1910, KM, OK.

48. Autoplanwerke to KM, 20 June 1910; 1910 KM, OK.

49. KuK Technisches Militaerkomitee No. 192 to KM, 18 June 1910; 1910, KM, OK.

50. KM No. 5753, 28 July 1910; KM No. 7536, 10 Sept. 1910; 1910, KM, OK.

51. Peters, "Entwicklung," 65, 83–85. *Wegbereiter*, 12, Fol. No. 50, LA, OK.

52. KM No. 8854, 22 Oct. 1910; VTBK to KM, 27 Oct., 1 Nov., and 22 Nov. 1910; Austro-Hungarian Auto-Plane Works to VTBK, 2 Dec. 1910; 1910, KM, OK.

53. VTBK 29/36 to KM, 5 Apr. 1911 and 29/40, 6 May 1911; KM No. 4262, 12 June 1911; KM Nos. 5860, 4961, 4563 of 1911; VTBK No. 29/67, 23 Aug. 1911; 1911, KM, OK.

54. VTBK 20/59 to KM, 7 Nov. 1911; MLG to VTBK, 3 Nov. 1911; VTBK 29/109 to KM, 18 Nov. 1911; 1911, KM, OK.

55. VTBK 20/59 to KM, 7 Nov. 1911, and 29/114 to KM, 17 Nov. 1911; KM No. 8474, 12 Dec. 1911; 1911, KM, OK.

56. Peters, "Entwicklung," 79–80.

57. Ernst Peter, "Die Entwicklung der oesterreichischen Militaerluftfahrt," pt. 2: "Von den ersten Flugparks zu den Luftstreitkraeften 1918," *Oesterreichische Militaer Zeitschrift* VI (1968), 415. Peters, "Entwicklung," 71–72.

58. KM No. 192, 29 Nov. 1912, 1912; *Luftfahrtindustrie*, 9, Fol. No. 36, LA, OK.

59. MLG to VTBK, 29 Feb. 1912, 2 Apr. 1912, 10 Apr. 1912; 1912 KM, OK.

60. KM No. 720, 15 Apr. 1913; KM No. 2475 and App., 30 Oct. 1913; 1913, KM, OK.

61. Oesterreichischer Aero-Club to KM, 18 Apr. 1913; 1913, KM, OK.

62. KM No. 866, 5 June 1913; 1913, KM, OK. From the War Ministry's notes in the margin of the letter, it also refused to consider victorious planes for contracts or to grant 20,000 K. in prizes. Also KM No. 1633, 10 July 1914; 1914, KM, OK.

63. "Wie es in Oesterreich aussieht," *Flugsport* VI, No. 10 (13 May 1914), 409–43.

64. MLG to LSA, 27 Feb. 1913; 1913, KM, OK.

65. LSA No. 459 to MLG, 4 Mar. 1913; LSA 454/MVK to KM, 10 and 14 Mar. 1913; 1913, KM, OK.

66. VTBK 18/14, 11 Mar. 1913; MLG to LSA, 11 Mar. 1913; KM No. 590, 19 Apr. 1913; LSA No. 1033/VA to KM, 19 Oct. 1913; 1913, KM, OK. As the last document explains, Lohner could build biplanes independently, but could only build monoplanes under contract to MLG. Thus only MLG could receive the contract. The War Ministry accepted the recommendation to build the monoplane in the army's factory at the arsenal. KM No. 2628, 12 Nov. 1913; 1913, KM, OK.

67. KM No. 215, 11 Feb. 1913 and App.; 1913, KM, OK.

68. KM No. 259, 2 Apr. 1913 and App.; 1913, KM, OK.

69. KM No. 1633, 10 July 1914; 1914, KM, OK. Oskar Regele, *Feld Marschall Conrad. Auftrag und Erfuellung 1906–1918* (Vienna, Munich: Verlag Herold, 1955), 214–15.

70. KM No. 217, 10 Feb. 1914, and App.; KM No. 2089, 22 July 1914; 1914, KM, OK.

71. KM No. 1633, 10 July 1914; 1914, KM, OK.

72. "Ungunstiger Stand der Militaerluftschiffahrt in Oesterreich-Ungarn," *Neue Freie Presse*, 6 June 1914; "Krise in unserer Militaeraviatik," *Wiener Sonn- und Montagszeitung*, 8 June 1914, in KM No. 1633 App., 1914, KM, OK. See also: "Wie es in Oesterreich aussieht," *Flugsport* VI, No. 10 (13 May 1914), 409–43.

73. Militaerkanzlei No. 4415, 9 June 1914, KM No. 1633 App.; KM No. 1633, 10 July 1914; 1914, KM, OK.

74. GSC No. 2153, App. to KM No. 1633; 1914, KM, OK.

75. KM No. 317, 19 Mar. 1914; KM No. 2170, 30 July 1914, and App.; 1914, KM, OK. *Luftfahrtindustrie*, 11, Fol. No. 36, LA, OK.

76. KM No. 1538, 5 June 1914; KM No. 2089, 22 July 1914; KM No. 2101, 22 July 1914; 1914, KM, OK.

77. KM No. 1108, 7 May 1914; 1914, KM, OK.

78. KM No. 317, App. (memorandum on monopoly system in Austria-Hungary), 19 Mar. 1914; 1914, KM, OK.

79. KM order, 1 Aug. 1914, Supplement III, 1914, *Das Luftfahrwesen*, Fol. No. 19a, LA, OK.

80. Anthony E. Sokol, *The Imperial and Royal Austro-Hungarian Navy* (Annapolis: U. S. Naval Institute, 1968), 74–75.

81. *Die Militaerluftfahrt in Oesterreich-Ungarn bis zum Beginn des Weltkrieges*, p. 40, Fol. No. 37; Lohner, *Lohner*, Fol. No. 163; List of Lohner flying boats (and other aircraft) and dates delivered, Fol. No. 163; LA, OK.

82. *KuK Kriegsmarine. Jahresbericht 1913, Luftfahrt*, Fol. No. 150, LA, OK. KM No. 96, 13 Feb. 1913; KM No. 163, 12 Jan. 1913; 1913, KM, OK. List of Lohner flying boats (and other aircraft) and dates delivered, Fol. No. 163, LA, OK; *Beginn*, p. 44, Fol. No. 37, LA, OK.

## CHAPTER V. CONCLUSION

1. SSdRMA BX 285, 3.2.14, Stock No. 7631, AM, MA. KAdL, *Militaerluftfahrt* II, Chart No. 108.

2. Walter Bartel, *Die Linken in der deutschen Sozialdemokratie im Kampf gegen Militarismus und Krieg* (Berlin: Dietz Verlag, 1958), 92–100.

3. Hans Jaeger, *Unternehmer in der deutschen Politik 1890–1918*, Vol. XXX, Bonner Historische Forschungen (Bonn: Ludwig Roehrscheid Verlag, 1967), 206–209, 212–13. Budgetkommissionsheft fuer 1915, Stock No. 7631, AM, MA.

4. For general details of industrial development, see Landes, *Prometheus*, 293–326.

5. KAdL, *Militaerluftfahrt* III, I.

# BIBLIOGRAPHY

Among the problems encountered in pursuing this research are the destruction in World War II of as much as 70 percent of the documents on Prussian military aviation, and the difficulty of gaining access to sources, specifically documents on the National Aviation Fund from 1912 to 1914 in the Central Archive of the German Democratic Republic in Potsdam. The sources mentioned below have enabled me to relate and evaluate the events in this study with the confidence that, although many documents may be lost forever and the release of new documents may alter some details of the story, the overall picture will remain valid.

The unpublished documents that provided much of the important information on the Prussian Army's relationship with the aircraft industry were those located in the Military Archive's files of the Inspectorates, which handled the daily business of aviation, and of the Imperial Office of the Interior, which played an important role in the National Aviation Fund. The discovery that these remnants of the Prussian documents on aviation contained a more than adequate coverage of prewar military aviation came as a pleasant surprise. The personal collection of August Euler in the Federal Archive in Koblenz was indispensable for its view of an eminent aircraft manufacturer's attitudes toward and dealings with the Prussian Army. German naval documents in the Mili-

tary Archive and Bavarian military documents in the Bavarian War Archive were quite complete in their areas of concentration and informative on Prussian aeronautical matters as well. With regard to Austro-Hungarian military aviation, specific mention should be made of the uncatalogued documents in the Austrian War Archive's aviation section, which contained much on the army's relationship with the aircraft industry.

The three-volume official history *Die Militaerluftfahrt bis zum Beginn des Weltkrieges 1914*, which was written by the Military Science Department of the German Air Force (*Kriegswissenschaftliche Abteilung der Luftwaffe*) in the late 1930s and early 1940s and recently edited by the Military History Research Office (*Militaergeschichtliches Forschungsamt*), provided valuable information, including documents, on the general background of German military aviation, the armed forces, their aircraft, and the aircraft industry. The official history, however, does not discuss the important details of the relationship between the military and industry or of the development of the aircraft industry and civilian interest groups. The *Reichsarchiv's* two-volume study, *Kriegsruestung und Kriegswirtschaft*, is a standard and essential work on Germany's overall preparations for war. *Memoirs.* The memoirs of Anthony Fokker and Ernst

Heinkel were most useful, as would be expected, since both were important manufacturers. Clemens von Delbrueck and Karl Helfferich, as key government figures of the prewar era, provided general background information; General von Hoeppner, the commander of the German air forces in the latter part of World War I, made generalizations, though sometimes of debatable value, on prewar aviation; and Georg von Tschudi, director of the major airfield at Johannisthal, gave insight into the operation of the field.

Of the secondary works, the following deserve mention for their information on the industry: two biographies of Anthony Fokker, one favorable by Henri Hegener, the other extremely critical by A. R. Weyl; *Die Rumpler Werke A. G. 1908–1918* for its details on a major firm of the period; K. D. Seifert's informative though ideologically skewed book and article on the development of German aviation (an East German, he apparently had access to documents unavailable to others). On the military aspects of aviation, the work of Hilmer von Buelow, John Cuneo, Hans Ritter, Klaus Peters, and the Military History Research Office was especially useful. Peter Supf's two volumes contained many anecdotes and details on German aviation in general during the period, while Erich Swoboda's book on the Etrich Taube examined in depth the development of a particularly important plane by the military and industry. Finally, the *Deutsche Luftfahrer Zeitschrift* and *Flugsport*, the aviation periodicals of the period, were informative on aviation in general, as well as on the industry and the military.

UNPUBLISHED DOCUMENTS

Bundesarchiv Militaerarchiv Freiburg (MA).
  Reichsamt des Innern (RdI). Reichsverkehrs-ministerium. Ab-
  teilungen fuer Wasserstrassen, Luft- und Kraftfahrwesen. Stock Nos. IL 2/26, 2/30, 2/35, 2/38, 2/45.
Grosser Generalstab (GG). Stock Nos. IL 11-2/12, 11-2/19.
Inspektion der Verkehrstruppen (IdV). Stock Nos. IL 25/32, 25/35, 25/36.
General-Inspektion des Militaer-Verkehrswesens (GIdMV). Stock Nos. IL 26/2, 26/6, 26/7, 26/9, 26/11, 26/12, 26/16, 26/19, 26/24, 26/28, 26/29, 26/33, 26/37, 26/45, 26/50, 26/58, 26/65, 26/68, 26/82, 26/83, 26/85, 26/91, 26/93, 26/94, 26/118.
Inspektion des Militaer-Luft- und Kraftfahrwesens (ILuK). Stock Nos. IL 27/2, 27/11, 27/17, 27/28, 27/37, 27/40, 27/57, 27/68, 27/71, 27/98.
Versuchs-Abteilung der Verkehrstruppen (VAdV). Stock Nos. IL 34/15, 34/26, 34/31, 35/4.
Reichsarchiv (RA). Sammlung Luftstreitkraefte. Stock No. IL 76/11, 91/3, 93/6, 97/17, 97/20.
Sammlung Luftwesen vor 1918. Stock No. L 05-1/1.
Reichsluftfahrtministerium. Kriegswissenschaftliche Abteilung der Luftwaffe (KAdL). Stock Nos. IL 234/1, 234/32.
Archiv der Marine (AM). Stock Nos. 5656, 7631, K 10-4/2532, K 10-4/2540, 1200.
Bayerisches Hauptstaatsarchiv. Abteilung IV. Kriegsarchiv (BKA).
  Koeniglich Bayerisches Kriegsministerium (KKM). Stock Nos. M Kr 1360, 1361, 1370, 1376–1385.
Bundesarchiv Koblenz (BA).
  Nachlass August Euler (EN). Vols. 1, 10, 13, 15a, 28, 45, 48, 50, 59, 238–40, 242–47, 252, 253, 260, 267.
  Deutsches Museum Munich (DM).
  Nachlass Hermann Dorner (DN).
  Oesterreichisches Kriegsarchiv Vienna (OK).
  Luftfahrtarchiv (LA). Kriegswissenschaftliche Abteilung der Luftwaffe. Zweigstelle Wien. Folio Vols. 10, 19a, 32, 36, 37,

48, 50, 51, 55, 150, 153, 163. Also eight cartons of un-catalogued documents.

KuK Kriegsministerium (KM). Docs. for the years 1909–1914.

## OFFICIAL PUBLICATIONS AND PUBLISHED DOCUMENTS

Hoesslin, Rittmeister a.D. Hubert von. *Die Organisation der K. B. Fliegertruppe 1912–1919.* Ed. Bayerisches Kriegsarchiv. Munich: Verlag des Bayerischen Kriegsarchivs, 1924.

Kriegswissenschaftliche Abteilung der Luftwaffe, ed. *Mobilmachung, Aufmarsch und erster Einsatz der deutschen Luftstreitkraefte im August 1914.* (Dritte Einzelschrift der Kriegsgeschichtlichen Enzelschriften der Luftwaffe). Berlin: Mittler und Sohn, 1939.

———. *Die Militaerluftfahrt bis zum Beginn des Weltkrieges 1914.* 3 vols. 2d ed. rev. and ed. Militaergeschichtliches Forschungsamt. Frankfort on the Main: Verlag Mittler und Sohn GmbH, 1965, 1966.

Kriegswissenschaftliche Abteilung (zugleich Forschungsamt) der Marine, ed. *Atlas deutscher und auslaendischer Seeflugzeuge.* 2 vols. Vol. I: *Warnemuende 1917. Seeflugzeug-Versuchs-Kommando.* Vol. II: *Warnemuende 1918.*

Ludendorff, Erich, ed. *Urkunden der Obersten Heeresleitung ueber ihre Taetigkeit 1916–18.* Berlin: Mittler und Sohn, 1920.

Oesterreichisches Bundesministerium fuer Heereswesen und Kriegsarchiv. *Oesterreich-Ungarns Letzter Krieg 1914–1918.* 7 vols. Vienna: Verlag der Militaerwissenschaftlichen Mitteilungen, 1931–1938.

*Rangliste der Kaiserlich Deutschen Marine.* 1913, 1914. Berlin: Mittler und Sohn.

*Rangliste der Koeniglich Preussischen Armee.* 1911–1914. Berlin: Mittler und Sohn.

Reichsarchiv. *Kriegsruestung und Kriegswirtschaft.* 2 vols. Berlin: Mittler und Sohn, 1930.

Reichstag. *Stenographische Berichte.* Vols. CCLXI–CCCV.

## MEMOIRS

Delbrueck, Clemens von. *Die wirtschaftliche Mobilmachung in Deutschland 1914.* Ed. Joachim von Delbrueck. Munich: Verlag fuer Kulturpolitik, 1924.

Fokker, A. H. G., and Gould, Bruce. *Der fliegende Hollaender. Das Leben des Fliegers und Flugzeugkonstrukteurs A. H. G. Fokker.* Trans. Dr. Carl Hans Pollog. Leipzig, Stuttgart, and Zurich: Rascher, 1933.

Heinkel, Ernst. *Stuermisches Leben.* Ed. Juergen Thorwald. Stuttgart: Mundus-Verlag, 1953.

Helfferich, Karl. *Die Vorgeschichte des Weltkrieges.* Berlin: Verlag Ullstein, 1919.

Hirth, Hellmuth. *20,000 Kilometer in Luftmeer.* Berlin: Verlag Gustav Braunbeck GmbH, 1913.

Hoeppner, General von. *Deutschlands Krieg in der Luft: Ein Rueckblick auf die Entwicklung und die Leistungen unserer Heeres-Luftstreitkraefte im Weltkrieg.* Leipzig: von Hase und Koehler Verlag, 1921.

Tschudi, Georg von. *Aus 34 Jahren Luftfahrt. Persoenliche Erinnerungen.* Berlin: Verlag von Reimar Hobbing, 1928.

Wrisberg, Generalmajor a.D. Ernst von. *Heer und Heimat 1914–1918: Erinnerungen an die Kriegsjahre in Koeniglich Preussischen Kriegsministerium.* Vol. II. 3 vols. Leipzig: Verlag von Koehler, 1921.

BOOKS, ARTICLES, AND DISSERTATIONS

Arndt, Archivrat Major a.D. Hans. "Die Fliegerwaffe," *Der Stellungkrieg 1914–1918*, Sec. VI, pt. 6, 310–69. Berlin: Mittler und Sohn, 1926.

———. "Der Luftkrieg," *Der Weltkampf um Ehre und Recht.* IV, 529–651. Ed. Generalleutnant Max Schwarte. 4 vols. Leipzig: Alleinvertrieb durch Ernst Finking d.F., 1922.

Bartel, Walter. *Die Linken in der deutschen Sozialdemokratie im Kampf gegen Militarismus und Krieg.* Berlin: Dietz Verlag, 1958.

Benedikt, Heinrich. *Die Wirtschaftliche Entwicklung in der Franz-Joseph-Zeit.* Vienna, Munich: Verlag Herold, 1958.

Bley, Wulf. *Sie waren die Ersten . . . Erstleistungen bei der Eroberung des Luftraumes.* Biberach on the Riss: Koehlers Verlagsgesellschaft, 1953.

Blunck, Richard. *Hugo Junkers: Ein Leben fuer Technik und Luftfahrt.* Duesseldorf: Econ-Verlag, 1951.

Born, Karl Erich, ed. *Moderne deutsche Wirtschaftsgeschichte* (Neue Wissenschaftliche Bibliothek). Cologne and Berlin: Kiepenheuer & Witsch, 1966.

Brembach, Hellmuth, ed. *Adler ueber See: 50 Jahre deutsche Marineflieger.* Oldenburg/Hamburg: Gerhard Stalling Verlag, 1962.

Buelow, Major a.D. Hilmer Freiherr von. *Geschichte der Luftwaffe: Eine kurze Darstellung der Entwicklung der fuenften Waffe.* Frankfort on the Main: Verlag Moritz Diensterweg, 1934.

Cuneo, John R. *Winged Mars.* 2 vols. Vol. I: *The German Air Weapon, 1870–1914.* Vol. II: *The Air Weapon, 1914–1916.* Harrisburg, Pa.: Military Service Publishing Company, 1942, 1947.

Demeter, Karl. *The German Officer Corps in Society and State.* Rev. ed. Trans. Angus Malcolm. London: Weidenfeld & Nicolson, 1965.

Dix, Arthur. *Wirtschaftskrieg und Kriegswirtschaft: zur Geschichte des deutschen Zusammenbruchs.* Berlin: Mittler und Sohn, 1920.

Eberhard, Generalleutnant Walter von, ed. *Unsere Luftstreitkraefte 1914–1918: Ein Denkmal deutschen Heldentums.* Berlin: Vaterlaendischer Verlag Weller, 1930.

Faber, Kapitaenleutnant. "Entwicklung und Ende des deutschen Seeflug- und Luftschiffwesens," *Marine Rundschau.* XVIII (Oct. 1921), 410–17.

Fischer, Fritz. *Germany's Aims in the First World War.* New York: Norton, 1967.

———. *Krieg der Illusionen: Die deutsche Politik von 1911 bis 1914.* Duesseldorf: Droste Verlag, 1969.

Franke, Generalmajor z.V. Hermann Franke, ed. "Die Luftwaffe," *Handbuch der neuzeitlichen Wehrwissenschaften,* vol. III, pt. 2. Berlin: Mittler und Sohn, 1937.

Goerlitz, Walter. *History of the German General Staff, 1657–1945.* Trans. Brian Battershaw. New York: Praeger, 1953.

Goodspeed, D. J. *Ludendorff. Genius of World War I.* Boston: Houghton, 1966.

Gordon, Arthur. *Die Fliegerei.* Trans. and eds. Georg Hensel and Guenter Lohrengel. Guetersloh: Bertelsmann Verlag, 1964.

Guenter, Adolf. *Vom Gleitflieger Lilienthals zu den Luftflotten Goerings.* Stuttgart: Alemannen Verlag Albert Jauss, 1941.

Hackenberger, Willi. *Die Alten Adler: Pioniere der deutschen Luftfahrt.* Munich: Lehmanns Verlag, 1960.

———. *Deutschlands Eroberung der Luft. Die Entwicklung deutschen Flugwesens.* Berlin: Verlag Hermann Montanus, 1915.

Haddow, G. M., and Grosz, Peter M. *The German Giants: The Story of the R-planes, 1914–1919*. London: Putnam, 1962.

Hallgarten, G. W. F. *Imperialismus vor 1914*. 2 vols. Munich: Beck'sche Verlagsbuchhandlung, 1951.

Hartung, Fritz. *Deutsche Geschichte 1871–1919*. 6th ed. rev. Stuttgart: Koehler Verlag, 1952.

Hegener, Henri. *Fokker—The Man and the Aircraft*. Letchworth, England: Harleyford, 1961.

Herzfeld, Hans. *Die deutsche Ruestungspolitik vor dem Weltkriege*. Bonn, Leipzig: Kurt Schroeder Verlag, 1923.

Higham, Robin. *Air Power. A Concise History*. New York: St. Martin's, 1972.

Hillmann, Dipl.-Ing. Wilhelm. *Der Flugzeugbau Schuette-Lanz*. Berlin: Deutsche Verlagswerke Strauss, Vetter & Co., 1919.

Institut fuer Konjunkturforschung, Berlin. *Industrielle Mobilmachung: Statistische Untersuchungen*. (Schriften zur kriegswissenschaftlichen Forschung und Schulung). Ed. Major Privat-Dozent Dr. Kurt Hesse with the support of official agencies. Hamburg: Hanseatische Verlagsanstalt A. G., 1936.

Italiaander, Rolf. *Spiel und Lebensziel. Der Lebensweg des ersten deutschen Motorfliegers Hans Grade*. Berlin: Gustav Weise Verlag, 1939.

Jaeger, Hans. *Unternehmer in der deutschen Politik (1890–1918)*. (Vol. XXX, Bonner Historische Forschungen). Bonn: Ludwig Roehrscheid Verlag, 1967.

Joachimczyk, Dipl.-Ing. Alfred Marcel. *Moderne Flugmaschinen*. Berlin: Verlag Klasing & Co. GmbH, 1914.

Jost, Oberstleutnant Walter, and Felger, Friedrich. *Was wir vom Weltkrieg nicht wissen*. 2d ed. Leipzig: Fikentscher Verlag, 1938.

Kaelble, Hartmut. *Industrielle Interessenpolitik in der Wilhelminischen Gesellschaft: Centralverband deutscher Industrieller, 1895–1914*. (Veroeffentlichungen der Historischen Kommission zu Berlin beim Friedrich-Meinecke-Institut der Freien Ueniversitaet Berlin, Bd. 27). Berlin: de Gruyter, 1967.

Kann, Robert A. *The Habsburg Empire. A Study in Integration and Disintegration*. New York: Praeger, 1957.

Kessler, Harry Graf. *Walther Rathenau. Sein Leben und sein Werk*. Wiesbaden: Rheinische Verlags-Anstalt, 1963.

Killen, John. *The Luftwaffe: A History*. London: Muller, 1967.

Landes, David S. *The Unbound Prometheus: Technological Change and Industrial Development in Western Europe from 1750 to the Present*. Cambridge: Cambridge Univ. Press, 1969.

Lemmen, Kapitaenleutnant a.D., and Nedden, Oberleutnant zur See a.D. "Das Marineflugwesen," *Unsere Marine im Weltkriege 1914–1918*, 401–24. Ed. Vizeadmiral a.D. Dr. ess. Eberhard von Mantey. Berlin: Vaterlaendischer Verlag Weller, 1927.

*"Luft-Fahrzeug" GmbH*. Berlin: n.p., 1913.

*Der Luftschiffbau Zeppelin und seine Tochtergesellschaften*. Berlin-Halensee: Verlag Schroeder, ca. 1925.

May, Arthur J. *The Habsburg Monarchy 1867–1914*. New York: Norton, 1951, 1968.

Meyer, Willy. *Von Wright bis Junkers: Das erste Vierteljahrhundert Menschenflug 1903–1928*. Berlin: Deutsche Verlagsgesellschaft fuer Politik und Geschichte m.b.H., 1928.

Moll, Hermann. "Das deutsche Marine- und Seeflugzeug von 1909 bis 1918," *Marine Rundschau* LV (1958), 168–80.

Militaergeschichtliches Forschungsamt, ed. "Organisationsgeschichte der Luftwaffe von den Anfaengen bis 1918," *Handbuch zur deutschen Militaergeschichte, 1648–1939*, Part V. 3d ed. Frankfort on the Main: Bernard und Graefe Verlag fuer Wehrwesen, 1968.

Muellenbach, Herbert. *Eroberung der Luft. Vom "Fliegenden*

Menschen" zum "Grossen Dessauer." Munich: Zentral-Verlag der NSDAP, Frz. Eher Nachf., ca. 1941.

Neumann, Georg Paul. *Die deutschen Luftstreitkraefte im Weltkriege.* Berlin: Mittler und Sohn, 1920.

———. *Flugzeuge.* Bielefeld, Leipzig: Verlag von Velhagen & Klasing, 1912/13.

Nimfuehr, Dr. Raimund. *Die Luftfahrt: Ihre wissenschaftlichen Grundlagen und technische Entwicklung.* Leipzig: Verlag von Teubner, 1913.

Norman, Aaron. *The Great Air War.* New York: Macmillan, 1968.

Nowarra, Heinz J. "Die Alten Adler. Aus den Anfangstagen der deutschen Flieger," *Jahrbuch der Luftwaffe,* IV (1967), 108–14.

———. *50 Jahre deutsche Luftwaffe 1910–1960.* Vol. I: *1910–1915.* Berlin: Eigenverlag des Verfassers, 1961. Vol. II: *1916–1917.* Vol. III: *1918.* Genoa: Interconair System Italia, 1964, 1967.

Peter, Ernst. "Die Entwicklung der Oesterreichischen Militaerluftfahrt. 1. Teil. Die KuK Luftschiffertruppe bis 1911," *Oesterreichische Militaer Zeitschrift.* Sonderheft 1965/1, 47–56.

———. "Die Entwicklung der Oesterreichischen Militaerluftfahrt. 2. Teil. Von den Ersten Flugparks zu den Luftstreitkraeften 1918," *Oesterreichische Militaer Zeitschrift,* VI (1968), 415–23.

Peters, Klaus. "Zur Entwicklung der Oesterreichisch-Ungarischen Militaerluftfahrt von den Anfaengen bis 1915." Ph.D. diss., Univ. of Vienna, 1971.

Poturzyn, Hauptmann a.D. Fischer von, ed. *Junkers und die Weltluftfahrt. Ein Beitrag zur Entstehungsgeschichte deutscher Luftgeltung 1909–1934.* Munich: Richard Pflaum Verlag, 1935.

Regele, Oskar. *Feldmarschall Conrad. Auftrag und Erfullung 1906–1918.* Vienna, Munich: Verlag Herold, 1955.

Reynolds, Quentin. *They Fought for the Sky.* New York: Holt, 1957.

Ritter, Gerhard. *Staatskunst und Kriegshandwerk: Das Problem des "Militarismus" in Deutschland.* 4 vols. Vol. II; *Die Hauptmaechte Europas und das wilhelminische Reich (1890–1914).* Munich: Verlag Oldenbourg, 1960.

(Ritter, Hans). *Kritik des Weltkrieges: Das Erbe Moltkes und Schlieffens im grossen Kriege.* Leipzig: Verlag von Koehler, 1920.

Ritter, Hans (Hauptmann im Generalstab a.D.). *Der Luftkrieg.* Berlin, Leipzig: Verlag von Koehler, 1926.

Robinson, Douglas H. *Giants in the Sky. A History of the Rigid Airship.* Seattle: Univ. of Washington Press, 1973.

———. *The Zeppelin in Combat. A History of the German Naval Airship Division, 1912–1918.* London: Foulis, 1962.

Rotth, August. *Wilhelm von Siemens: Ein Lebensbild.* Berlin, Leipzig: Vereinigung wissenschaftlicher Verleger–Walter de Gruyter & Co., 1922.

*Die Rumpler-Werke A. G. 1908–1918.* Berlin: Ecksteins Biographischer Verlag, 1919.

Schiller, Kapitaen Hans von. *Zeppelin: Wegbereiter des Weltluftverkehrs.* Bad Godesberg: Kirschbaum Verlag, 1966.

Schmidt, Justus. *Kriegswichtige Industrie im System der Wirtschaftspolitik.* Berlin: Obelisk Verlags Gesellschaft m.b.H., 1937.

Schwerin von Krosigk, Lutz Graf. *Die grosse Zeit des Feuers. Der Weg der deutschen Industrie.* 3 vols. Vols. II, III. Tuebingen: Rainer Wunderlich Verlag Hermann Leins, 1958, 1959.

Seifert, Karl Dieter. *Geschaeft mit dem Flugzeug: Vom Weg der deutschen Luftfahrt.* Berlin: VEB Verlag fuer Verkehrswesen, 1960.

———. "Das grosse Geschaeft. Anfang und Weg der imperialistischen deutschen Flugzeugindustrie," *Fluegel der Heimat* VII, No. 11 (Nov. 1958), 24–26.

Silberstein, Gerard E. *The Troubled Alliance: German-Austrian Relations 1914–1917*. Lexington, Ky.: Univ. Press of Kentucky, 1970.

Solff, Oberleutnant a.D. R. *Motorluftschiffe und Flugmachinen.* Berlin: Hermann Hillger Verlag, ca. 1910.

Stenkewitz, Kurt. *Gegen Bajonett und Dividende: Die politische Krise in Deutschland am Vorabend des ersten Weltkrieges.* Schriftenreihe des Instituts fuer deutsche Geschichte an der Karl-Marx-Ueniversitaet Leipzig. Berlin: Ruetten und Loening, 1960.

Supf, Peter. *Das Buch der deutschen Fluggeschichte.* 2d ed. 2 vols. Vol. I: *Vorzeit. Wendezeit. Werdezeit.* Vol. II: *Vorkriegszeit. Kriegszeit. Nachkriegszeit.* Stuttgart: Drei Brunnen Verlag, 1956, 1958.

Swoboda, Erich. *Igo Etrich und seine "Taube."* Vienna: Zweigstelle Wien der Kriegswissenschaftlichen Abteilung der Luftwaffe, 1942.

Thomsen, Hermann. "Die Luftwaffe vor und im Weltkriege," *Die deutsche Wehrmacht 1914–1939*, 487–527. Berlin: Mittler und Sohn, 1939.

Vogelsang, C. Walther. *Die deutschen Flugzeuge im Wort und Bild*, Pt. 2. 2d ed. Berlin-Charlottenburg: C. J. E. Volckmann Nachf. GmbH, 1914.

Wehler, Hans-Ulrich (ed.). *Moderne deutsche Sozialgeschichte.* 2d ed. (Neue Wissenschaftliche Bibliothek). Cologne, Berlin: Kiepenheuer & Witsch, 1968.

Wentscher, Bruno, ed. *Deutsche Luftfahrt.* Berlin: Verlag Deutsche Wille, 1925.

Weyl, A. R. *Fokker: The Creative Years.* Ed. J. M. Bruce. London: Putnam, 1965.

Wilamowitz-Moellendorff, Hauptmann a.D. "Die Luftwaffe," *Das deutsche Wehrwesen in Vergangenheit und Gegenwart*, 415–72. Stuttgart, Berlin: Konradin-Verlag, 1936.

Wissmann, Gerhard. *Geschichte der Luftfahrt von Ikarus bis zur Gegenwart: Eine Darstellung der Entwicklung des Fluggedankens und der Luftfahrttechnik.* Berlin: VEB Verlag Technik, 1964.

Zeman, Z. A. B. *Twilight of the Habsburgs, The Collapse of the Austro-Hungarian Empire.* New York: American Heritage, 1971.

Zuerl, Walter. *Deutsche Flugzeugkonstrukteure: Werdegang und Erfolge unserer Flugzeug- und Flugmotorenbauer.* 3rd ed. Munich: Curt Pechstein Verlag, 1942.

PERIODICALS

*Deutsche Luftfahrer Zeitschrift.* Vols. XIII–XIX (1909–1915).

*Die Luftflotte.* Vols. I–VIII (1909–1916).

*Deutsche Luftwacht, Ausgabe Luftwelt.* Vols. III–VI (1936–1939).

*Flugsport.* Vols. I–VII (1909–1915).

*Illustrierte Flug-Welt.* Vols. I, II (1919, 1920).

*Jahrbuch des Deutschen Luftschifferverbandes, 1911.*

*Jahrbuch der Luft-Fahrzeug-Gesellschaft.* (formerly *der Motor Luftschiff-Studiengesellschaft.*). Vol. VI, 1913.

# INDEX

Ago aircraft company, 91–93, 95–96
Airship Battalion, Prussian, 14–15, 17
Albatros Works, 27, 29, 33, 35–36, 41, 45, 55, 65, 75–76, 79, 83–86, 91–94, 96–97, 103, 112–113
Albert, Heinrich, 58–59, 62
*Allgemeine Elektrizitaets Gesellschaft* (AEG), 5, 26, 43, 53, 75, 83–84, 86, 93, 96
*Allgemeine Flug Gesellschaft* (AFG), 91–92
Anatra airplane company, 55
Army League, 9
Association of German Motor Vehicle Industrialists, 36. *See also* Convention of German Aircraft Industrialists
Auffenberg-Komarow, General Moritz von, 108
Austrian Aero Club, 109
Austrian Air Fleet Fund, 108, 117, 119
Austrian Automobile Club, Aero Section, 103
Austro-American Rubber Company, 104
Austro-Daimler Motor Company, 104
Austro-Hungarian Auto-plane Works, 105
Austro-Hungarian military aviation, viii, 103–17, 119–21
Austro-Hungarian military establishment, 11, 13
*Automobil und Aviatik* (Aviatik), 26, 29, 35–36, 39, 41, 55–56, 65, 73, 76, 83–86, 91, 93, 96–97, 111–13
Aviation Unit, Austro-Hungarian, 108–109, 111

Baltic Sea Flight 1914, 92
Bartel, Walter, 120

Bassermann, Ernst, 19
Bavarian military aviation, viii, 88, 93–103, 115, 117, 119
Bavarian Military Flying School, 95
Beese, Melli, 49
Behrens, Hermann, 75
Benz, Carl, 3
Benz motor company, 30
Berlin Flying Week, 30
Berlin Society for Aviation, 19, 67
Bier, Adolf, 112
Blériot, Louis, 15, 21, 29
Boehm, Richard, 86
Borsig company, 26
Brosien, Richard, 19
Brug, General Karl von, 63, 93–97, 99–101. *See also* Inspectorate of Engineers, Bavarian
Brunnhuber, Simon, 29
Buelow, Major Hilmer von, 6, 17, 30, 47, 72

Castiglioni, Camilio, 92, 104, 108
Catholic Center Party, 61
Central Association of German Industrialists, 9
Chatel, Georges, 39
Circuit of Germany Flight, 35, 41, 44
Cologne Commission, 31, 44, 116
Convention of German Aircraft Industrialists, 36–37, 39–40, 48–49, 53, 59, 62, 65–66, 87
Coulman, naval master builder, 89
Craig, Gordon, 6
Curtiss, Glenn, 91, 114

Daimler motor company, 30, 86

Daimler, Gottlieb, 3
Delagrange, Léon, 15, 25
Delbrueck, Clemons von, 9, 11, 57–58, 61, 63, 69, 70–72
de le Roi, Captain Wolfram, 14, 17, 21, 27, 31, 116
*Deutsche Bank*, 5
*Deutsche Flugzeugwerke* (DFW), 35, 41, 45, 55, 76–77, 83, 86, 91, 96, 111–13
*Deutscher Luftfahrer Zeitschrift*, 49
Dewall, Captain Job von, 80
Dix, Arthur, 71–72
Dorner Aircraft Company, 26, 36, 39, 41, 44, 89
Dorner, Hermann, 21
*Dresdener Bank*, 5

Eckenbrecher, Lieutenant Helmuth von, 79
Eichhorn, General von, 25
Eighteenth Army Corps, 25–26
Elsner, Lieutenant, 112
English aviation, 87, 93
Ernst Guenther, Duke of Schleswig-Holstein, 59
Esnault-Peltérie, Robert, 16
Etrich, Igo, 41, 75–76, 103, 105. *See also* Taube
Euler, August, 25–27, 29, 37, 43, 58, 59, 62, 65–67, 69–71, 80–81, 87, 94
Euler Works, 25, 36, 41, 76–77, 83–84, 96

Farman, Henri, 15, 17, 25, 30
Fischer, Fritz, 6, 84
Fitzgerald, A. Ernest, *The High Priests of Waste*, viii
Flight Technology Association, 103

*Flugsport*, 66
*Flugzeugbau Friedrichshafen* (FF), 91–93
Flying Machine Association, 103
Flying Troops, Prussian, 49, 51, 63
Fokker Aircraft Construction Company, 75–76, 83, 96
Fokker, Anthony, 43, 51, 81, 122
Frankfort Flying Week, 30
*Frankfurter Sportzeitung*, 69
Franz Ferdinand, Archduke of Austria-Hungary, 104–12
Franz Joseph, Emperor of Austria-Hungary, 11
French military aviation, 31, 47, 87
Fritsch, Lieutenant, 89

Geerdtz, Lieutenant Franz, 51, 83
General Inspectorate of Military Transportation, Prussian, 31, 33, 35–36, 40–41, 47–49, 51–52, 55, 66–67, 69, 73, 75–77, 79–81, 95–96, 122
General Staff, Austro-Hungarian, 103, 106–107
General Staff, German, 5–6, 14, 30, 85–86. *See also* Ludendorff, Lieutenant Colonel Erich; Moltke, General Helmuth von
German Air Fleet League, 19, 21, 23, 45, 91
German Airship Association. *See* German Aviators Association
German Army, 8, 13
German Aviators Association, 19, 23, 37, 45, 59, 62–63, 65–67, 69, 89, 92, 117
German Bristol Works, 41, 76
German Empire, 3
German Flight Association of Weimar, 61
German Naval League, 9
German Research Institute for Aviation, 61–62, 79, 87
Germany (Bavarian aircraft company), 99
Goerlitz, Walter, 5–6
Goetze, Richard, 39

*Gothaer Waggonfabrik* (Gotha), 52, 75, 83–84, 86, 93, 101
Grade, Hans, 21, 36, 69
Gross, Major Hans, 15, 21
Gruetzner, Captain Karl, 31, 84

Haenisch, General Karl Heinrich von, 53, 66–67, 80–81
Halberstadt Military Flying School, 75
*Hansa Brandenburgische Flugzeugwerke* (Hansa Brandenburg), 92–93
Harlan aircraft company, 36, 41
Hasse, Major Ernst, 48
Heeringen, General Josias von, 7, 11, 21, 44, 49, 58
Heinkel, Ernst, 122
Heinrich, Prince of Prussia, 58, 67, 117
Helfferich, Karl, 71
Hering, Lieutenant Max, 89
Hinterstoisser, Captain, 104
Hoeppner, General Ernst Wilhelm von, 72
Hoetzendorff, General Franz Conrad von, 13, 103, 105–107, 111–12, 117
Hoffmann project, 21–23
Hoffmann, W.S., 21
Hohenborn, General Adolf Wild von, 53
Hungarian Airship and Flying Machine Company, 108, 113
Hungarian Lloyd Aircraft and Motor Factory, 113
Huth, Walter, 27, 29

Illner, Karl, 105, 113
Imperial Aero-Club, 21, 67
Imperial Archive (*Reichsarchiv*), *Kriegsruestung und Kriegswirtschaft*, 72
Imperial Automobile Club, 19
Imperial German Navy, 7–8, 88–89, 91–93, 103
Imperial Naval Office, 59, 89, 91–93

Imperial Office of the Interior, 37, 58–59, 79, 92, 117
Inspectorate of Engineers, Bavarian, 85, 93–95
Inspectorate of Flying Troops, Prussian, 96
Inspectorate of Military Aviation and Motor Vehicles, Bavarian, 95, 99–100
Inspectorate of Military Aviation and Motor Vehicles, Prussian, 33, 35–36, 41, 53, 55, 57, 62. *See also* Messing, General Wilhelm
Inspectorate of Transport Troops, Prussian, 15, 31
Instruction and Research Institute for Military Aviation, Prussian, 40, 76

Jeannin Aircraft Company, Emil, 75, 77, 83
Johannisthal Airfield Company, 26, 30, 37, 61
Johannisthal Flying Week, 30
Joseph, Ludwig, 67, 69–70

Kapp, Wolfgang, 79
Kehler, Richard von, 37, 39
Keim, Major General August, 11
Kiel Week, 41
Kober, Friedrich, 91
Koeberle, Colonel, 95, 99
Krupp Works, Friedrich, vii, 3, 5, 26, 55, 120, 122

Langfeld, Walter, 89
Lanz, Karl, 17, 19, 21
League of Industrialists, 9
Lewald, Theodor, 58–59
Lieben, Robert von, 104
Lieth Thomsen, Captain Hermann von der, 14–15, 43, 87
Lilienthal, Otto, 3
Loewe armaments firm, Ludwig, 14, 26
Loew, Karl, 89
Lohner company, Jakob, 104, 106–109, 112, 114–15

Lohner, Ludwig, 104
Lokomotivfabrik Krauss, 97
Ludendorff, Lieutenant Colonel Erich, 6–7, 11, 15, 31, 44. *See also* General Staff, German
*Luftfahrzeuggesellschaft* (LFG), 45, 83–84
*Luftverkehrsgesellschaft* (LVG), 35, 39–41, 43, 45, 65, 77, 83–84, 91, 100, 112–13
Luitpold, Prince Regent of Bavaria, 59
Lyncker, Lieutenant General Alfred von, 19, 21, 33, 35–36, 43, 58, 76

Maschke, Georg, 113
Meister, Lieutenant Colonel Paul, 48–49
Mendelsohn, Franz von, 58–59
Messing, General Wilhelm, 31, 33, 35, 37, 44–45, 48–49, 53, 55, 57–59, 61, 76–77, 80
Military Aeronautical Institute, Austro-Hungarian, 104
Military Science Department of the German Air Force, 72, 122
Military Technical Committee, Austro-Hungarian, 105
Ministry of Commerce, Hungarian, 111
Ministry of Justice, Hungarian, 113
Moltke, General Helmuth von, 7, 27, 30, 44, 48. *See also* General Staff, German
Motor Airship Study Company, 14, 17, 26, 45
*Motorluftfahrzeuggesellschaft* (MLG), 92–93, 104, 106–109, 113–14
Mueller, Arthur, 26, 35, 37

National Aviation Fund, 57–71, 117
*Neue Automobil Gesellschaft* (NAG), 30
Neumann, Major Georg, 45
Nieber, Lieutenant General Stephan von, 19, 21, 26
Noske, Gustav, 53

Oberursel Motor Company, 80, 86

Oelerich, Heinrich, 86
Oertz Aircraft Company, 92–93
Oldershausen, Baron von, 66
Opel, Adam, 3
Oschmann, Major Albert, 49, 51
Otto Works, 94–97, 99–101, 103

Parseval, August von, 17
Peugeot automobile company, 35
Pfalz Aircraft Works, 101
Pohl, Admiral Hugo von, 93
Posadowsky Wehner, Count Arthur von, 58–59, 70
Prince Heinrich Flight, 66, 96–97, 99
Prussia, 3
Prussian Army, vii, 3; and technological modernization, 5–8; aviation agencies, 16, 33–34; and aircraft procurement policies, 41–43; and the National Aviation Fund, 57–71; mobilizes the aircraft industry, 1912–1914, 71–87; and Bavarian aviation, 96, 100–101; and aviation, overall conclusions on, 115–17, 119–20

Radowitz, Count Clemens Maria von, 104
Rasch, F., 65
Rathenau, Walter, 9, 26, 43
Reims Air Week, 29
Research Unit, Prussian, 14–15, 29, 122
Ritter, Captain Hans, 6
Rumpler Aircraft Construction Company, Edmund, 26–27, 35–36, 39, 41, 43, 45, 52, 65, 75–76, 79, 83–84, 86, 91, 93, 97, 99, 103
Rumpler, Edmund, 37, 81, 89, 122

Santos-Dumont, Albert, 3, 14
Saxon Flight, 41
Schelies, Richard, 21
Schendel, Georg, 44
Schleyer, Major General von, 104

Schmidt, Justus, *Kriegswichtige Industrie im System der Wirtschaftspolitik*, 73
Schmiedecke, Lieutenant Colonel Hugo, 21, 31, 35–36, 48–49, 58, 95. *See also* War Department, Prussian; War Ministry, Prussian
Schneider, Franz, 43
Schoenaisch, General Franz von, 105–106, 108
Scientific Society for Flight Technology, 79, 87
Seifert, K.D., 44
Siegert, Major Wilhelm, 67, 79, 81, 86–87, 116
Signal Corps, U.S. Army, 5
Silberer, Victor, 104
Skoda Works, 119
Social Democrats, 9, 59, 119
Southwest German Overland Flight, 37
Sperling, Curt, 39, 53, 67, 69
sport aviation, in imperial Germany, 62–69, 123; in Weimar and Nazi Germany, 122
Stenkewitz, Kurt, 84
Stinnes company, 26
Stoeffler, Viktor, 86

Taube, 41, 75–77, 79, 97, 99, 106, 108–109, 117
Tirpitz, Admiral Alfred von, 8, 9, 11, 58, 89
Transportation Technology Test Commission, Prussian, 77, 79–80
Transport Troops Brigade Command, Austro-Hungarian, 104–109, 122
Tschudi, Major Georg von, 26

Universal Aviation Exhibition, 58
Upper Rhine Flight, 41
Uzelac, Colonel Emil, 108, 116

*Vierteljahrsheft fuer Truppenfuehrung und Heereskunde*, 72
Voigts-Rhetz, Colonel Werner, 31
*Vossischer Zeitung*, 49

*Waggonfabrik Jos. Rathgeber AG*, 97
Wallner, Carl, 104
Wandel, General Franz von, 7, 36, 49, 51
War Department, Prussian, 36, 41, 80
War Ministry, Austro-Hungarian, 104–109, 111–114
War Ministry, Bavarian, 93–94
War Ministry, Prussian, 6, 14–15, 19, 22–23, 25, 27, 29–31, 33, 35–36, 47–48, 52, 71–87, 95, 115–16, 121. *See also* Schmiedecke, Lieutenant Colonel Hugo; War Department, Prussian
Wels, Franz, 103
Weyl, A.R., 26, 83
Wiener, Otto, 35–36, 43
Wildt, Lieutenant, 93–94
Wilhelm II, Emperor of Germany, 9, 15, 21, 26, 59, 117
Winterfeldt, Major Detloff von, 29
Wissmann, Gerhard, 71
Wright brothers, 3, 5, 14
Wright Flying Machine Company, 26–27, 29, 36, 39, 44–45, 55
Wrisberg, Major Ernst von, 48
Zeman, Z.A.B., 13
Zeppelin, County Ferdinand von, 15
Zeppelin Fund 1908, 15, 57